ENVIRONMENTALISM AND CULTURAL THEORY

The last decade has seen a dramatic increase in the attention paid by social scientists to environmental issues, and a gradual acknowledgement in the wider community, of the role of social science in the public debate on sustainability. At the same time, the concept of 'culture', once the property of anthropologists, has gained wide currency among social scientists. This book shows how an understanding of culture can throw light on the way environmental issues are perceived and interpreted, both by local communities and within the contemporary global arena.

Taking an anthropological approach the book examines the relationship between human culture and human ecology, and considers how a cultural approach to the study of environmental issues differs from other established approaches in social science. This book adds significantly to our understanding of environmentalism as a contemporary phenomenon, by demonstrating the distinctive contribution of social and cultural anthropology to the environmental debate. It will be of particular interest to students and researchers in the fields of social science and the environment.

Kay Milton is Lecturer in Social Anthropology at the Queen's University, Belfast.

ENVIRONMENT AND SOCIETY
Edited by Steven Yearley

Environmental Sociology
John Hannigan

Citizen Science
Alan Irwin

Environmentalism and Cultural Theory
Kay Milton

ENVIRONMENTALISM AND CULTURAL THEORY

Exploring the role of anthropology in environmental discourse

Kay Milton

London and New York

First published 1996
by Routledge
11 New Fetter Lane, London EC4P 4EE

Reprinted 1999

Transferred to Digital Printing 2003

Simultaneously published in the USA and Canada
by Routledge
29 West 35th Street, New York, NY 10001

Routledge is an imprint of the Taylor & Francis Group

Phototypeset in Garamond by Intype London Limited

British Library Cataloguing in Publication Data
A catalogue record for this book is available from the British Library

Library of Congress Cataloguing in Publication Data
Milton, Kay
Environmentalism and cultural theory: exploring the role of
anthropology in environmental discourse / Kay Milton.
p. cm. – (Environment and society)
Includes bibliographical references and index.
1. Environmentalism – Social aspects. 2. Culture. 3. Ethnology.
I. Title. II. Series.
GE195.M55 1996
303.2 – dc20–95–26822

ISBN 0–415–11529–9 (hbk)
ISBN 0–415–11530–2 (pbk)

Printed and bound by Antony Rowe Ltd, Eastbourne

To Morse,
who arrived at the beginning
and left at the end

CONTENTS

CONTENTS

ACKNOWLEDGEMENTS

Many people have contributed to this project in various ways. In particular, I should like to thank Michael Redclift for his encouraging comments during the early preparation of the book; Tim Ingold, Roy Ellen and Hastings Donnan, who kindly supplied me with pre-publication material; Laura Rival, Peter Rawcliffe and participants in the Oxford Centre for the Environment, Ethics and Society Seminar at Mansfield College, for their helpful comments on various parts of the manuscript; Anne Gee for her patience as I overran several deadlines; Steven Yearley for his constructive criticism of earlier drafts and his editorial encouragement throughout; my colleagues at Queen's University, particularly Elizabeth Tonkin, for giving me the time and space needed to complete the project. The extract from the *Rubáiyát of Omar Khayyám* (Fitzgerald 1947) is included by kind permission of HarperCollins Publishers Limited. I am especially grateful to John Stewart for his comments on various drafts, his constant support and endurance of many bouts of bad temper. A final word of thanks is due to the many students whose enthusiastic exchanges and awkward but insightful questions have helped me to develop the ideas expressed in this book.

INTRODUCTION
Social science and environmental discourse

More than perhaps any other issue, the 'environment' calls
upon the social sciences to develop internationally comparative and interdisciplinary approaches.

(Jamison *et al.* 1990: vii)

... the interpretation of the environment in the social
sciences assumes territoriality of its own.

(Benton and Redclift 1994: 13)

Anthropologists are in the habit of storing up their favourite
anecdotes from fieldwork for appropriate occasions. Here is one
of mine. One afternoon during the short dry season of 1979, I
was engaged in 'participant observation' in the Kasigau village of
Rukanga, weeding the maize crop under the baking African sun
with a group of neighbours. One of my companions paused in his
work, spat the dust from his mouth and surveyed the shimmering
landscape. After some thought, he said, 'We heard a few years ago
that some Americans were going to the moon. Is this true? Did
they really go?' I assured him that it was true, that I had read
about it in the newspapers and seen it on television. He laughed,
and those around us joined in the laughter: 'What was the matter
with them?' he asked, 'Didn't they have anything to do here on
Earth?'

At the time, I treated this open and light-hearted derision of
something my own society considered to be a pinnacle of human
achievement as a source of insight into the pragmatic character of
the culture I was engaged in studying. Fifteen years later, I am
more inclined to acknowledge his insight into the follies of my
own culture. Today, it seems, we all have a great deal to do on

1

Earth. According to one widely respected British environmentalist, our task involves,

> nothing less than permanently arresting the deterioration in the functioning of the biosphere as a viable life support system for the earth. The time limit must permit the biosphere to recover its equilibrium, and to renew its vigour sufficiently to enable human, animal and plant life to continue to flourish into the indefinite future.
>
> (Nicholson 1987: 193)

I experience mixed responses to this challenge. The environmentalist in me wants to get on with the work, to plant trees, lobby politicians, stop pollution, save the whales and the woodlands, halt the destruction wrought by the blind pursuit of profit and 'progress'. The trained anthropologist, irritatingly, wants to stop and ask questions. Why do we believe what the scientists tell us? Why do we consider whales and woodlands important? What kinds of assumptions underlie the claim that the Earth is in danger? How does this particular way of understanding the world differ from those proffered by other cultures, and why are they different?

These conflicting responses express one of the central dilemmas of social science: how to study that of which we are a part and still remain part of it. How can we, at the same time, be full, committed participants in society and detached observers of it?[1] In the past, anthropologists have responded to this dilemma in diverse ways. Some have felt that involvement in moral issues, particularly where the rights of indigenous people are concerned (see Paine 1986), is a natural entailment of their role as students of society (Berreman 1968: 391). Others have preferred to remain detached observers, and have seen any involvement in the course of social change as incompatible with serious analysis. This divergence of views has, at times, seriously threatened the peace of the discipline (Schensul and Schensul 1978: 124–5) and created an image of 'applied' anthropology as a poor relation to mainstream, academic anthropology.[2] This view has changed as an increasing proportion of anthropologists has found employment in practical spheres outside academia.

My own answer to the dilemma is to suggest that anthropology neither obliges its practitioners to adopt a moral stance on anything, nor precludes them from doing so. I shall argue in Chapter 1 that involvement in advocacy is entirely consistent with the principles of anthropological theory; that there is nothing entailed in our role as analysts of human culture that requires us to remain detached from moral issues. Equally, there is nothing that requires us to take up a particular moral stance. Indeed, we should be highly suspicious of any argument that seeks to identify anthropology with a particular position on anything, for the one thing that *is* entailed in an anthropological approach is that we should apply 'systematic doubt' (Morgan 1991: 224) to all views, including our own.[3] Anthropology's tool for doing this is cultural theory.

In this book I try to show how anthropologists, through their use of cultural theory, can make a distinctive contribution to environmental discourse. Some of the arguments are not fully formed, some have evolved during the process of writing. There are, I have no doubt, some contradictions and inconsistencies, but I comfort myself with the thought that if all arguments were perfectly composed there would be little to say about them. The book is not intended as a definitive statement, but as an exploration of the potential of cultural theory to throw light on environmental issues, and on the nature and content of environmentalism itself, as a way of understanding the world. It will be clear from the argument presented above that I am not trying to tie anthropology to an environmentalist position; the insights generated by cultural theory might just as easily be used in opposing environmentalist arguments as in supporting them. But it may be worth declaring that I have written this book because, from an anthropological viewpoint, the intellectual foundations of environmentalism look a little shaky, and I consider it important that they be strengthened. In this sense, the analysis in the following chapters is not value free.

Anyone who has just a casual acquaintance with anthropology may be surprised to learn that it can contribute to environmental discourse. Its popular image, fostered by television documentaries, is of a subject concerned with esoteric rituals and exotic forms of marriage, or with the reconstruction of unrecorded histories. Anthropology, it appears, looks back or sideways, but not forwards. What could such a discipline have to say about the future of life on Earth? Others may dismiss anthropology's claim to relevance as just another arrival on the environmental bandwagon. Everyone, it seems, has something to say on the environment, so why not anthropologists? Either response would be mistaken, for anthropology's popular image is misleading, and the bandwagon model of environmental concern, while it may have some basis, obscures an important trend.

There are sound reasons why an increasing range of specialists has been drawn into environmental discourse. Our perception and understanding of environmental problems and their possible solutions have shifted over the years. What began (in so far as a beginning can be identified) as problems of nature, have progressively been reshaped as problems of technology, of resource management, of health, of economics, of international politics and of ideology. 'Natural' scientists still have the role of examining the interactions of organisms and substances, to explain the physical consequences of pollution and predict the ecological impact of environmental change. But technologists are also involved, to try to make industry and other economic activity conform to environmental constraints; so are legal experts, to adjust national and international law to the requirements of environmental protection; economists, to bring environmental costs and benefits into the sphere of economic planning; sociologists and political scientists, to examine the patterns of social interaction which promote or mitigate damaging practices; philosophers and theologians to examine conventional values and beliefs for the foundations of an environmental ethic. Environmental problems are seen as penetrating all spheres of human activity, so the search for solutions has recruited an enormous diversity of expertise.

The contribution of social science has been slow to gain recognition among policy makers and environmental activists. The development of both capitalist and socialist economies was driven by the view that 'nature' is to be exploited for human benefit, and by an unquestioned confidence in the ability of human ingenuity to overcome difficulties. The firm conviction that environmental problems can be solved by technology was a logical consequence of this underlying ethos, and decision makers assumed that the physical and biological sciences would identify problems and appropriate responses (Benton and Redclift 1994: 13–14). In recent years, the social sciences have gained recognition, initially as tools for identifying the impacts of environmental changes and devising appropriate policies (Benton and Redclift 1994: 14), but eventually as components in the overall understanding of environmental problems. National and international funding bodies now regularly support social scientific research on environmental issues, and programmes which span the boundary between the natural and the social sciences have become commonplace (Redclift 1992: 343).

From the viewpoint of the social sciences, the most significant shifts in the perception of environmental issues (those which have defined and enhanced their role) have taken place since the early 1980s. Gradually, the impact of non-technological (particularly economic and political) factors on the environment has been recognized, if not fully understood. Some of the financial policies of national governments and international funding agencies came to be recognized as environmentally damaging. In particular, the devastation caused by major dam projects and by new roads through the rainforests was widely publicized. Through these revelations, the rights of indigenous peoples have been linked to environmental issues (see Cowell 1990, Cummings 1990), adding a new dimension to the efforts to conserve wildlife habitat and biodiversity. In Britain, the government's fiscal policies were blamed for the loss of important habitat to commercial forestry in northern Scotland, and throughout the European Community (EC, now the European Union) the severe environmental impacts of the Common Agricultural Policy were becoming clear. Environmental activists throughout the world turned their attention to matters of policy and financial accounting.

At the same time, consumer choice emerged as a powerful tool in environmental campaigning. For instance, the European campaign to ban the import of baby seal products from Canada, backed by a consumer boycott of Canadian fish products, led to a significant reduction in seal hunting, and unintentionally damaged the economies of Arctic communities (Wright 1984, Wenzel 1991). More recently, demands for 'dolphin-friendly tuna' have had an impact on fishing methods. The general rise in 'green consumerism' has changed the ways in which manufacturers market their products. Environmental claims and messages are now commonplace in advertising campaigns (see Yearley 1992a: 98ff.).

The combined effect of all these trends has been that environmental activists and policy makers have come to recognize the importance of understanding all aspects of human thought and action. It is not simply technology that determines the human impact on the environment, but a combination of technology with economic values, ethical standards, political ideologies, religious conventions, practical knowledge, the assumptions on which all these things are based and the activities that are generated by them. Through this recognition, the role of the social sciences in environmental discourse has become firmly established.

However, until very recently, and with a few notable exceptions,[4] the voice of anthropology in this arena has been almost silent, despite the fact that anthropologists have sometimes become involved in environmental issues, particularly where they have implications for human rights (see, for instance, Cowell 1990: 169). The relative absence of anthropology from environmental discourse should be a cause for concern, given that a great deal of the knowledge generated by anthropological research, particularly on the ways in which people understand and interact with their environments, could be of value in the search for solutions to environmental problems.

As well as attracting a very wide range of specialists, environmental discourse is characterized by demands for 'interdisciplinary' approaches. This implies more than a bandwagon-load of diverse specialisms. It suggests that the quest for a viable future should be a combined and collaborative effort, in which specialists pool their expertise and generate new analytical models. I find it difficult to imagine just what an interdisciplinary social-scientific approach might look like, and I shall have more to say on this in the final chapter. For the moment, it is important to start from a point of mutual understanding. One of the main reasons for writing this book was to explore, for anthropologists and other social scientists alike, what anthropology, in its guise as cultural theory, has to offer.

The argument that cultural theory can contribute to an understanding of environmental issues depends on the idea that culture plays a role in human–environment relations. The first two chapters develop this idea, first by explaining what anthropologists mean by culture and cultural theory (in Chapter 1), and then by considering how anthropologists have related the concept of culture to human ecology (in Chapter 2). As will be seen, anthropologists are by no means agreed on what 'culture' means, nor on its role in ecological relations. So developing the case for cultural theory is not just a matter of describing what anthropology is about; it involves distilling an argument out of a number of diverse and sometimes contradictory perspectives. The first two chapters also establish a working definition of 'environmentalism' and discuss its status as a 'cultural' phenomenon.

In arguing that anthropology can offer a distinctive contribution to environmental discourse, it is important to demonstrate that a cultural analysis is different from the approaches offered by the other social sciences. Chapter 3 presents an analysis of existing social-scientific studies on environmentalism and compares them with an approach from cultural theory. The argument is that anthropology broadens the enquiry by employing concepts which are more widely applicable than those used by other disciplines, enabling comparisons to be made across the full human cultural repertoire. Chapter 4 puts this into practice by comparing perspectives on the environment from a range of cultural contexts, including both industrial and non-industrial societies,[5] and considering how far they can be seen as environmentalist in character. The comparison is centred on a popular environmentalist 'myth', the assertion that non-industrial societies possess a degree of ecological wisdom which has been lost in the process of industrial development. Chapter 4 also considers the value of cultural diversity itself as a condition important for the fulfilment of environmentalist objectives.

Chapters 5 and 6 move the discussion into the global arena. It is important to do this, because anthropology is often seen as being trapped within the local context, incapable of saying anything significant about large-scale processes, and because 'the environment' is now widely understood in global terms. Chapter 5 discusses the ways in which social scientists have tried to understand 'globalization', and identifies an approach that is consistent with cultural theory. In Chapter 6, this approach is applied in an account of the cultural content of global environmental discourse. Chapter 7 presents a selective summary of what has been learned from this exploratory journey.

1

ANTHROPOLOGY, CULTURE AND ENVIRONMENTALISM

> While anthropologists perform archaistic studies of odds and ends of humanity, municipal authorities struggle with the chemical, geological, economic and political problems of toxic wastes – with little help from social scientists.
>
> (Bennett 1990: 435)

Boundaries in social science are not permanent fixtures; they come and go according to context. Sometimes they appear in the arena of academic politics, as the practitioners of each discipline stake out their territories in the contest for student allegiance and financial resources. Sometimes they acquire significance in scientific debate, as specialists in one discipline strain to grasp the subtleties of another's jargon. Illusions of similarity are created by the tendency to use the same terms (structure, function, culture) for different things, and illusions of diversity are created by the opposite tendency to call the same thing by different names. If social science is to meet the challenge of providing interdisciplinary approaches to the environment, we need to know first what each discipline has to offer. Since my main purpose in this book is to explore what anthropology has to offer to environmental discourse, it is important to begin by establishing what is distinctive about anthropology, what makes it different from the other social sciences.

HOW IS ANTHROPOLOGY DIFFERENT?

The most obvious and well-known distinguishing feature is anthropology's interest in non-industrial indigenous and 'traditional' societies,[1] the study of which was initially fostered by colonial expansion. It is this heritage that has given anthropology

8

its exotic public image. This image is not unfounded, but it is misleading because it conceals the fact that an increasing number of anthropologists are studying various aspects and consequences of industrialism,[2] writing about major issues of public concern,[3] and commenting on the implications of contemporary technological change.[4] It also masks anthropology's deep concern with what is general in the human condition, as well as with what is particular to specific societies. 'Other' societies have always been held up as mirrors to our own (however 'we' might be defined), and the wealth of human diversity has been treated as a source from which to draw insights into the nature of social processes. The minute analysis of ritual, for instance, exemplified in the work of Turner (1967, 1968), is conducted in the context of a broader understanding of what ritual is, how it operates and why people engage in it, built up through knowledge of the diversity and similarity exhibited in a range of human societies. The theories that emerge from such studies are often about humanity in general and, as Turner himself demonstrated (1969, 1974), are just as enlightening on the processes at work among political revolutionaries or crowds at a football match as on the traditional motivations and concerns of a central African community. Thus, anthropologists often share the concerns of sociologists and political scientists but have come to them through a different route. Anthropology's traditional interest in the full range of human societies is important in shaping its contribution to environmental discourse, as future chapters will demonstrate.

Equally important, but less accessible to public gaze, is the distinctiveness of anthropological theory, where the most enduring and consistent presence has been the concept of culture. This is not to say that culture has been the exclusive territory of anthropologists, far from it, especially in recent decades as 'cultural studies' has acquired an identity as a discipline.[5] But there is no doubt that culture has had a more central position in anthropological thought than in any other social science, at least until the emergence of cultural studies, and that anthropologists have accorded it a great deal of analytical significance. Indeed, in contrast with what anthropologists have written over the years, the manner in which other social scientists view culture sometimes seems rudimentary. As recently as 1992, Featherstone observed,

The last decade has seen a marked increase in interest in

culture in the social sciences. For many social scientists, culture has been seen as something on the periphery of the field as, for example, we find in conceptualizations which wish to restrict it to the study of the arts. Even when this view became extended to incorporate the study of popular culture and everyday life, culture was still regarded by many as esoteric and epiphenomenal.

(1992: vii)

It is distressing and frustrating for an anthropologist to read these words, for it is as if the last hundred years or so of anthropological theory had never happened. What many social scientists have become aware of only during the last decade or so (if Featherstone's observation is accurate), that a concept of culture, appropriately defined, can offer fundamental insights into the human condition and can 'challenge the viability of our existing modes of conceptualization' (Featherstone 1992: vii), has been understood and taken for granted by anthropologists for many years (cf. Robertson 1992: 32).

The shifting centre

It is one thing to state that the use of culture as a central analytical concept distinguishes anthropology from other social sciences. It is quite another to state what that concept is or how it is used in anthropology, for the level of inconsistency, disagreement and debate that has surrounded it is as great as for any key concept in social science. Wallerstein's comment is pertinent, even though he probably was not thinking of anthropology when he made it: 'Culture is probably the broadest concept of all those used in the historical social sciences. It embraces a very large range of connotations, and thereby it is the cause perhaps of the most difficulty' (1990a: 31). At least part of the 'difficulty' with culture in anthropology stems from a dilemma over whether culture is itself an object of analysis, or whether it is part of a broad framework for the analysis of something else, usually something that is seen as a part of culture and therefore as 'cultural' in nature. In other words, do anthropologists consider the question of 'how culture is constituted, how we should theorize culture' (Featherstone 1992: vii), or do they study the functions and meanings of more specific phenomena which fall within the broad category of culture? This dilemma was neatly expressed by Bohannan:

> Culture is a black box for most anthropologists. We define culture by whatever purpose we ascribe to it in our theorizing, and are hence allowed to continue on our way without examining it. Anyone who needs a black box named culture in order to carry out his activities should have it. But one man's black box is another man's field of investigation.
>
> (1973: 358)

Anthropological theory has tended to shift between the two enterprises. For much of the time, anthropologists have studied cultural things, rather than culture itself. The nature of the black box has been glimpsed from time to time, as the theoretical spotlight has focused on its contents: kinship, symbolism, systems of exchange, religious beliefs. Periodically, however, the spotlight has been turned on culture itself, and the shape and dimensions of the black box have been redrawn. This has tended to happen, not surprisingly, during important fundamental shifts in social science theory, in which anthropology has participated. It happened, for instance, during the 1960s and 1970s. At this time, anthropology, like the other social sciences, was shedding the cloak of positivism which it had worn conspicuously throughout its domination by various forms of structuralist theory, and moving towards a more interpretative approach. Pronouncements about the nature of culture (Geertz 1966, Goodenough 1957, 1981 [1971]) were followed by publications which assessed the contemporary state of thinking on culture (Bohannan 1973, Keesing 1974).

There are signs that social science theory is currently experiencing another fundamental shift, the nature of which is not entirely clear as yet, but which appears to be characterized by three prominent trends. First, there is dissatisfaction with the cultural relativist perspective which has characterized anthropology in the post-structuralist era, but which, it is felt by some, has largely outlived its usefulness (see Descola 1992: 108). Second, there is a widespread reaction, both within and outside anthropology, against the 'Cartesian' dualisms of mind–body, thought–action, nature–culture, which are seen as obstructing progress in anthropological theory. In particular, the conceptual opposition between nature and culture, which was the mainstay of some forms of structural anthropology (most famously in the work of Lévi-Strauss) and remained

11

firm through the post-structuralist phase, is under serious attack
as a framework for understanding the human condition (see Croll
and Parkin 1992: 3, 13; Ingold 1996). This development echoes
fundamental questions that are continually raised in environmentalist discourse about the role of humankind within the natural
order (Grove-White 1993: 24), and is therefore likely to be highly
significant for anthropology's contribution to environmental discourse.

Third, and perhaps most important, social scientists are paying
increasing attention to 'globalization', which is characterized by
the spread and exchange of ideas, practices and technologies on a
world-wide scale. Some degree of exchange among societies has
always been a part of human history, but the ability of contemporary communications to transcend the barriers of time and space
has led social scientists to ask whether it is appropriate to speak
of a 'global culture'. The focus on world systems is far from new
in social science (see, for instance, Wallerstein 1979, Nash 1981,
Chirot and Hall 1982). What *is* relatively new is the conceptualization of such systems in terms of culture. Anthropology is in
danger of being confined to the margins of this discourse, despite
its long history of cultural theory, for the images of culture being
imported into social-scientific thinking on globalization are drawn,
not from anthropology, but from the disciplines which, as
Featherstone observed (1992: vii), used to define it as 'esoteric and
epiphenomenal'. The spectre of a global culture would seem to
offer a direct challenge to anthropological tradition, whose
central analytical practice, cross-cultural comparison, would be
difficult to sustain in the absence of boundaries between cultures.
The nature of this challenge will be examined more closely in
Chapter 5.

Environmental discourse appears to be characterized by a high
degree of globalization. This is expressed, for instance, in the
tendency for environmentalists in industrial society to 'borrow'
philosophies and practices from non-industrial peoples, in the
creation of international arenas for negotiating agreements and
setting environmental standards (most notably, through the United
Nations, the European Union and other such alliances), and in the
imposition, through these mechanisms, of 'western' concepts of
science, value and nature in countries where such concepts are
not indigenous. More than any other important contemporary
discourse, the debate on the environment has adopted the concept

of the global as both 'motive and motif'.[6] Environmental problems
are represented as global in their extent and consequences, and
this image is used as a spur both for local effort (through such
slogans as 'think globally, act locally') and for international negotiation. The global motif thus might be said to fuel the globalization of environmentalist ideas. However, globalization is an
ambiguous and contested concept in social science and its relevance
to an understanding of environmental issues needs to be explored
rather than assumed. The question of whether a concept of globalization provides a useful framework for developing an anthropological perspective on environmental discourse will be discussed
in Chapter 5.

THE CONCEPT OF CULTURE IN ANTHROPOLOGY

The argument of this book will shift, as anthropological thought
itself has done, between a focus on culture itself, as an analytical
concept, and a focus on cultural things. I shall argue that anthropology's contribution to environmental discourse depends on
environmental issues being seen as cultural in character. This
requires some attention to what it means, in anthropology, to label
something as 'cultural'.

Any attempt to describe anthropologists' shared understanding
of culture very quickly runs into difficulties. Probably most would
agree that culture is something that all human beings have, that it
enables them to live in social groupings and that it is acquired
through association with others. Beyond this, however, one is in
dangerous territory. Even the apparently innocent declaration that
culture is shared (Nanda 1987: 68; Peoples and Bailey 1988: 19;
Ferraro 1992: 19) raises awkward questions about the manner of
the sharing, and conjures up images of group mind and common
consciousness, which many anthropologists find difficult to live
with (see Goodenough 1981 [1971]: 51ff.). If it is impossible to
state precisely what anthropologists mean by culture (since there
is no universal agreement on this), it is at least possible, and useful,
to explore the concept by focusing on some of its ambiguities and
shifts in meaning.

Culture is general, culture is specific

Culture, however it is defined, is used in two main senses in anthropology, a general sense and a specific one. In its general sense, culture is a phenomenon that is part of all human experience. In its specific sense, *a* culture is an entity associated with a particular society or category of people. In the first sense, we refer simply to 'culture'; in the second sense, we refer to 'Japanese culture', 'Irish-American culture' or 'youth culture'. Anthropologists have not always acknowledged the distinction between the two, as the following definitions indicate: '*Culture* . . . is the patterned way of life shared by a group of people' (Nanda 1987: 68, emphasis added); '*Culture* is the socially transmitted knowledge shared by some group of people' (Peoples and Bailey 1988: 18, emphasis given). Howard appears to avoid the confusion: 'Culture itself is the manner in which human groups learn to organize their behaviour and thought in relation to their environment' (1986: 5). But in doing so he has deprived culture of its substance and turned it into a manner in which something is done (in this case, in which certain skills are learned). In this form, it is no longer a category, and is of little use as a black box.

Culture operates as a black box in anthropological analysis in both its general and its specific senses. It is in terms of a general understanding of culture that we identify phenomena (such as marriage, ritual, classifications of plants and animals) as cultural and proceed to examine their detailed characteristics. The more specific understanding of culture provides countless black boxes for the purpose of ethnographic description and analysis. 'Irish culture', for instance, becomes the framework within which, say, Irish traditions of hospitality are described and their relations with other Irish cultural items examined.

As long as we stay within the box, we do not need to worry about its dimensions. In the more general sense, and as Bohannan implied (1973: 358), as long as we are concerned only with things cultural, we do not need to worry about what it is that makes them cultural. We can treat culture as the category that encompasses religious beliefs, political systems and kinship obligations, and discuss the relationships among these things, even drawing examples for comparison from different societies, without worrying about what culture itself is. Similarly, in the more specific sense, as long as we are writing about Irish culture, we do not need to be concerned about whether the things we describe are exclusively Irish, or whether some things are 'shared' with other cultures. We might, for instance, analyse the relationship between religion and political ideology in Irish culture without concerning ourselves with parallels that might be drawn with, say, British or American culture. In many contexts, anthropologists can get away with failing to indicate whether they are referring to culture in its general or its specific sense, either because it is obvious which is intended or because it does not matter. In some contexts, however, it is important to bear the distinction in mind, as will become clear in the discussion on culture and globalization (in Chapter 5).

The more specific understanding of culture, apart from providing black boxes for ethnographers, has had fundamental implications for the development of anthropology. Cross-cultural comparison, which is present, either explicitly or implicitly, in most anthropological writing, depends on cultures being seen as boxes of some kind; comparing cultures means comparing the contents of different boxes. There have also been many analyses of how specific items move between cultures, through processes such as 'cultural integration' and 'acculturation'. However, although the study of cultural change, and of cultural exchange, have formed a significant field within anthropology, the discipline has suffered from a notorious inability, or reluctance, to produce models for the analysis of 'macro-processes'. Anthropology has become famous for analysing the minutiae of cultural change, but equally famous for ignoring the big picture, for failing to cope with large-scale social movements and worldwide communications systems. Not surprisingly, this failing has meant that, with a few exceptions, anthropologists have played little part in the debate over globalization. The failure to develop models of large-scale cultural change can be attributed in part to two prevailing features of anthropological thought: the assumption that cultures are systems, and the 'spectre' (Holy and Stuchlik 1981: 28) of cultural relativism.

Cultures as systems

One of the most pervasive anthropological assumptions about cultures (in the specific sense) is that they are systems. This image persists, regardless of how the contents of cultures are defined. Keesing, for instance, represented cultures in turn as 'adaptive systems', 'cognitive systems', 'structural systems', 'symbolic systems' and 'ideational systems' (1974: 74–83). The important questions about cultures have been taken to be whether they are adaptive, cognitive, structural and so on; that they are *systems* has been taken for granted. There is considerable variation in what social scientists mean by the term 'system'. Wuthnow pointed out that, in its strictest sense, it 'implies only relationships' (1983: 61). It is unlikely that any anthropologist would disagree with the characterization of cultures as systems in this minimal sense. But many would assume that system implies more than relationships, and would take it to indicate a significant degree of order and boundedness.[7]

Thus to represent a culture as a system is, for many analysts, to see it as something more than a mere box with contents. It implies that the contents are organized, that the relationships among them are structured. This, in turn, gives cultures a degree of boundedness which mere boxes with contents do not have. If a culture is nothing more than a box with contents, then it is a relatively easy matter to remove or copy something from it and put it in another box. Cultural exchange and integration appear relatively straightforward processes. This is not the case if a culture is a system. Any cultural item cannot be easily removed without disrupting the set of relationships into which it is locked. And it cannot be imported into another culture without bringing with it some of the trappings of those former relationships and disturbing its new surroundings. One of the most apt illustrations of this kind of complication is the 'borrowing' of marriage systems among neighbouring Australian aboriginal peoples (see Keesing 1975: 83). When a society adopts the marriage rules of its neighbours, the new rules do not always fit the extant pattern of relationships, with the result that some existing marriages are rendered illegal!

Because many analysts treat it as an assumption, there has been little attempt to justify the view that cultures are structured systems. Any attempts that have been made tend to take a rather dogmatic, 'it must be so' form. It is argued that social life would not make sense if cultures were not structured systems. Leach asserted that logical relations between the parts of a culture *must* exist, 'at some deeply abstract level' (1976: 11). It is important to recognize the contribution that this model of culture has made to anthropology; the intricate ethnographic analysis that has characterized much anthropological writing has made good use of it. But it is important also to understand the limitations of this view. The assumption that cultures are structured systems has led anthropologists to exaggerate the problematic nature of cultural change. This does not mean that they have shied away from analysing it, but it has meant that their analyses have tended to focus on the minutiae; they have been more inclined to use the microscope than the wide-angle lens. While communication across cultural boundaries has been happening in the world around us, anthropologists have continued to puzzle over how such a thing is possible.

Culture is broad, culture is narrow

Cultural relativism, the second feature which, I have suggested, has prevented anthropologists from developing models of large-scale cultural change, has been a part of anthropological thinking for many decades, but it acquired a new dominance following the theoretical shift away from structuralist perspectives in the 1960s and 1970s. Before exploring the concept, it will be helpful to outline the course of this shift, particularly as it forms a basis for the concept of culture developed in Chapter 2 as the most useful in considering anthropology's contribution to environmental discourse.

Early definitions of culture, in its general sense, saw it as all-inclusive. It was 'that complex whole' (Tylor 1871), and was often described as consisting of three kinds of phenomena: actions, ideas and material objects. Introductory texts in anthropology sometimes still define culture in this way. Ferraro, for instance, defined culture as, 'everything that people have, think and do as members of a society' (1992: 18; cf. Hicks and Gwynne 1994: 46), and Howard stated that 'culture has three different aspects: *behavioural, perceptual* and *material*' (Howard 1986: 5, emphasis given). This broad concept of culture was appropriate when anthropologists were mainly concerned with describing and understanding whole ways of life, whole 'systems'. Once this approach to anthropology began to be questioned and replaced by something different, the concept of culture needed to be adjusted.[8]

From the late 1950s, anthropologists began to split the material they studied into two different kinds of phenomena: things which, it was assumed, can be observed more or less directly (consisting mainly of what people do and say and discernible patterns of

17

activity),[9] and things assumed to exist in people's minds, which therefore can only be inferred from what they do and say (material objects were often left out of the picture altogether). The terms used to label these two types of data are often confusing. In the work of American anthropologists, the 'observable' category was often glossed as 'social structure', a misleading term given that, for some anthropologists, the distinction was made as part of a move away from structuralism. Other labels for this category of data include 'actions', 'interactions', 'social processes' and 'social organization'. But none of these is entirely satisfactory since each excludes a part of what is intended to be included. The terms 'actions' and 'interactions' cannot be applied with ease to the sustained trends and patterns (in, for example, marriage or residence choices, or religious observance) which can be observed as prevalent over time or throughout a population. But the terms 'social processes' and 'social organization', which readily describe the more prevalent or sustained patterns, do not apply easily to individual actions. One widely accepted solution is to use the term 'society' to refer to the category of observable data, but this is also confusing since 'society' is more often used to refer to a group of people who share the same 'culture'.

The term 'culture' came to be reserved for the category of phenomena assumed to exist in people's minds (Kroeber and Parsons 1958, Goodenough 1961, Kay 1965). Again, there is a confusing range of terms used to gloss this category of phenomena, including 'ideas', 'knowledge' (Holy 1976) and 'folk models' (Holy and Stuchlik 1981). Again, none of these is entirely appropriate, since the category is intended to include everything that exists in people's consciousness: the sum total of perceptions, assumptions, values, norms, theories and any other mechanisms through which they understand their experiences.

The value of distinguishing between what people do and what they think, feel and know was that it opened up the possibility of studying the relationship between them. This relationship was seen as 'characteristically dialectical' (Keesing 1971: 126). Whatever people hold in their minds forms a basis for their actions, which, through being observed and interpreted, feed back into their consciousness, reinforcing and modifying their understanding of the world. By using the term 'culture' to refer only to what people hold in their consciousness, anthropologists were narrowing it down in order to give it more analytical power (Geertz 1973: 4).

Instead of assuming a one-to-one relationship between what people do and what they think, feel and know, or focusing entirely on one level while ignoring the other (both of these having been characteristic of various types of structuralist analysis), anthropologists were now asking how the observable patterns of social organization were generated (Barth 1966, Keesing 1971), and how people's actions changed their understanding of their own society (Stuchlik 1977) and generated new norms (Holy 1986).

Cultural relativism and its consequences

It was the narrowing down of 'culture' (in both its general and its specific senses) to the things people hold in their minds that gave prominence to the principle of cultural relativism, which has appeared to dominate anthropological thought during the past two decades. Instead of being different ways of life, cultures became different ways of knowing, different ways of perceiving and understanding the world. Locked away in people's minds, cultures could no longer be 'seen', and ethnographers could no longer feel confident that their accounts were accurate descriptions of the cultures of those they studied. Although it is not always clear what anthropologists understand by cultural relativism, it is often taken to mean that cultures can only be properly understood 'in their own terms' (Holy and Stuchlik 1981: 29). This claim has in turn been taken to imply that cross-cultural comparison is impossible, and that a society's culture can only be satisfactorily interpreted by its own native members (a suggestion which, if widely accepted, might threaten to kill off anthropology altogether!). If this were so, it would be difficult to conceive of the transmission of knowledge across cultural boundaries. Most anthropologists would not wish to take the argument this far, but the implications of cultural relativism have led them to exaggerate the problems of cross-cultural communication, and this, like the assumption that cultures are structured systems, has restricted our ability to understand large-scale cultural change, and particularly to develop frameworks for analysing the emergence of worldwide communications. Once again, it appears to have been going on around us while we have been asking ourselves how such a thing can happen.

Cultural relativism carries other implications: that all cultures are equally worthy of respect (see Herskovits 1949: 76), and that all cultures are equally valid interpretations of reality. These ideas have had considerable influence both within anthropology and in the wider world, and have helped to shape anthropologists' views on how their own specialist knowledge should be applied (Schensul and Schensul 1978: 128). It is important to address this issue, albeit briefly, since the central tenet of this book, that anthropology can make a valuable contribution to environmental discourse, rests on the assumption that it is appropriate to use anthropological knowledge to influence the direction of cultural change, and that anthropologists can do this without violating any of the discipline's theoretical principles.

Both the idea that all cultures are equally worthy of respect and the idea that all cultures are equally valid interpretations of reality, have been important weapons against ethnocentrism and discrimination, and have made many anthropologists advocates for cultural pluralism and the rights of minorities (Schensul and Schensul 1978, Paine 1986). Paradoxically, they have also had the opposite effect of lending support to the view that anthropologists should not be advocates for anything (see Smith, quoted in Schensul and Schensul 1978: 128), and that active involvement in cultural reform is not a proper activity for anthropologists. Involvement in reform means making judgements, and the view that all cultures are equally worthy of respect and equally valid interpretations of reality has made some anthropologists reluctant to make judgements, where this means favouring one cultural perspective over another. This view depends on a sharp separation between anthropological analysis and involvement in social life. It implies that the practice of social science can be detached from the practice of social activity, or at least from social (or cultural) reform (Berger 1963). Although this view was once widespread amongst anthropologists, it has been undermined by the changes in the way culture is understood.

The dialectical relationship between culture (meaning what people hold in their minds) and what people do, which has been a main focus of post-structuralist anthropological analysis, consists of two complementary processes: that whereby culture generates actions, and that whereby culture is sustained, reinforced or modified through actions. The first process has probably received more analytical attention. Patterns of action, discernible, for instance, in recruitment to social groups, have been understood in terms of the knowledge which guides the individual actions contributing to the overall pattern (see, for instance, Leach 1961, Keesing 1971, Stuchlik 1976, Riches 1977). Less attention has been paid to the

20

ANTHROPOLOGY, CULTURE AND ENVIRONMENTALISM

ways in which culture is sustained or changed through the actions people perform (see Stuchlik 1977, Riches 1979, Holy 1986). Nevertheless, the way in which this process has been conceptualized by anthropologists has far-reaching implications for their own involvement in cultural change.

Culture is sustained and modified through social interaction, in which individuals act on the basis of their own knowledge, their own cultural understandings. In other words, by engaging in social activity, people are bringing their knowledge to bear on a situation and participating in the generation of new knowledge or the reinforcement of existing knowledge.[10] Social activity cannot help but contribute to this process, which encapsulates cultural reform. It has been argued that the involvement of anthropologists in advocacy is a logical consequence of this way of conceptualizing the relationship between culture and social interaction (see Harries-Jones 1986). Social interaction becomes an arena in which the participants each assert their particular way of knowing the world, in which they try to make their knowledge count (Harries-Jones 1991) in the process through which culture is continually recreated.

Anthropologists have used the knowledge gained through their study of cultural diversity in many different ways. Some have used it in defence of cultural pluralism and human rights, some have used it primarily to further their own academic careers, others have probably been content to assume that they are contributing to the sum of human knowledge. Those who have argued that anthropologists should not participate in social reform have, through their very arguments, helped to perpetuate an image of value-free social science and to give scientific considerations precedence over moral ones (see Milton 1993: 13). This is as much a case of involvement in cultural change as is anything done by a missionary or a prophet. The only way of opting out of cultural change is to keep our knowledge to ourselves, in which case it counts for nothing. The choice to participate in environmental discourse or any other public discourse must always remain with the individual analyst, but it must be understood that, far from violating the discipline's fundamental principles, such a choice is entirely consistent with the way in which many anthropologists define their central theoretical concerns.

21

Culture as process

The current stirrings in social science theory, characterized by the disenchantment with cultural relativism and with 'Cartesian' oppositions between thought and action, mind and body, culture and nature, are engendering yet another shift in the way culture is conceptualized by anthropologists. The distinction between culture, as something held in the mind, and people's activities, which was central to the development of post-structuralist anthropology, is now regarded as unsatisfactory by some scholars, who see it as reproducing and reinforcing the opposition between mind and body. In an attempt to eliminate the dualism, the term 'culture' is being used less to refer to what people know and think, and more to refer to the process by which that knowledge and those thoughts are generated and sustained. In other words, the whole dialectical process outlined above is becoming synonymous with culture itself.

Harries-Jones (1986: 238) refers to a model of culture in an 'active' sense. Culture and action are no longer distinct; instead, action and knowledge are part of the single process that is culture. This image of culture is very close to some understandings of the concept of discourse, as a process in which knowledge is generated through communicative action. It is also reflected in recent developments in ethnographic writing, in which the distinction between subject and object is dissolved, and the production of ethnographic knowledge is seen as the joint enterprise of the ethnographer and the members of the society they are studying (Clifford 1986: 13ff.). For reasons to be discussed in Chapter 2, I do not consider this processual concept of culture particularly helpful in developing anthropology's role in environmental discourse. The concept of discourse itself will be discussed more fully in Chapter 5.

ANTHROPOLOGY AND ENVIRONMENTAL DISCOURSE

Having considered in detail the central concept of anthropological thought and its most significant variations in meaning, I am now in a position to suggest, in a preliminary way, what anthropology's contribution to environmental discourse might look like. Such a contribution might take two main forms. First, the knowledge generated by anthropologists about the diversity of human culture

22

might be important in addressing environmental problems. This means treating anthropology as the study of human ecology, and applying its findings in much the same way as the work of other ecologists is applied. Second, anthropologists might use their distinctive approach to study environmentalism itself as a cultural phenomenon and contribute to the development of environmentalist thought. The theoretical bases of these two suggestions are explored in Chapters 2 and 3 respectively; here, it is important simply to clarify what is meant by them.

Anthropology as the study of human ecology

One important way in which anthropologists have understood the concept of culture has deliberately been omitted from the discussion so far, the view of culture as an ecological mechanism. This idea exists in two main forms. First, many anthropologists have assumed that culture is *the* medium through which people interact with their environment; that culture is essential to their survival because, without it, they would not be able to obtain from their environment whatever they need to sustain their physical and social well-being. This view is not universally accepted (see Ingold 1992a), but has nevertheless been a pervasive and persistent idea in anthropological thought. Second, some anthropologists have assumed that culture is the medium through which people *adapt to*, rather than merely *interact with*, their environment (Burnham 1973: 93; Ingold 1992a: 39). The difference between these views lies in the degree of power attributed to the environment in the development of human society. While the first treats the environment simply as the source of human sustenance, the second implies that it has shaped human society by setting the conditions for its development. Some anthropologists have seen the environment as the 'prime mover' in human cultural evolution.

Neither of these ideas is incompatible with the various ways of conceptualizing culture discussed above. A culture may be seen as a whole way of life, as a way of thinking about and understanding the world, or as the process through which that understanding is generated, and still be a mechanism through which the people whose culture it is, interact with or adapt to their environment. The possibility of treating culture, for analytical purposes, as an ecological mechanism is therefore not affected by the theoretical shifts outlined in the previous sections. Nevertheless, those shifts

have influenced the extent to which anthropologists have incorporated culture into ecological studies, as the discussion in the next
chapter will demonstrate.

Ecological anthropology, in which the relationship between
human beings and their environments has been an explicit and
central focus, has a long history, which has to some extent run
parallel to, but somewhat detached from, the major theoretical
shifts outlined above. In this field, the concept of culture has
played varying roles, which will be examined in detail in Chapter
2. The important point to be made here is that, if culture is to be
seen as a mechanism through which people interact with their
environment, then there is a sense in which the study of culture
itself (and of cultures) – the whole of cultural anthropology, in fact
– becomes the study of human ecology. This makes anthropology's
potential contribution to environmental discourse somewhat
clearer. For environmental problems are generally defined as ecological, as involving the way in which organisms interact with their
environments. Human activity is also generally seen as the most
important agent of environmental change. A discipline which can
claim to be the study of human ecology should also be able
to claim a central place in the way environmental problems are
examined and addressed.

Anthropologists as theorists of environmentalism

The second way in which anthropology might contribute to
environmental discourse is through the analysis of environmentalism itself. In many societies environmentalists are advocates of
cultural and social change. They want people to change the ways
they understand, value and use their environments. Their success
depends on the extent to which they can persuade others that
their interpretation of reality is correct, and that the changes they
advocate are important and necessary. Cultural revolutions inevitably acquire theorists who analyse their ideas, examine their
underlying assumptions, expose contradictions and inconsistencies.
Such scrutiny may not necessarily benefit a cause, and may effectively destroy it if, as a result, its ideology is seen to be fundamentally unsound. But causes which are destined to exert long-term
political influence need strong intellectual foundations, and these
can develop only through the continual analysis and refinement of
their ideas. This has always been an important role for social

scientists, and causes such as liberalism, socialism and feminism have progressed through constructive analysis.

Environmentalism has also acquired its theorists and benefited from their scrutiny. They have tended to come from political science (Dobson 1990, Goodin 1992a), sociology (Cotgrove 1982, Yearley 1992a), or from a background of active involvement in environmental discourse (Spretnak and Capra 1985, Grove-White 1993). With a few exceptions (Douglas 1972, Ellen 1986, Redclift 1987) and until very recently,[11] anthropologists have had little to say about environmentalist thought. In Chapter 3 I shall argue that, by treating it as a cultural phenomenon, anthropology can offer distinctive insights into environmentalism, which complement those provided by the other social sciences.

It will immediately be obvious, following the discussion in this chapter, that when an anthropologist calls something 'cultural' this does not establish very clearly what kind of a thing it is. We need to know in what sense culture itself is understood. This will be discussed further in the following sections, but I wish to avoid putting the finishing touches to this particular black box until the end of Chapter 2, after the concept of culture has been examined in the context of human–environment relations. It is important, for that discussion, that the reader does not have in mind the impression that a particular definition of culture is being advocated.

However, there are some definitions which cannot be left aside. I have suggested that environmentalism is both a project to which anthropologists might contribute and an object which they might analyse. This means that we need to be able to identify it empirically, and this in turn requires some criteria for doing so; in other words, a definition. There is widespread misunderstanding about what definitions are for in social science, and particularly in anthropology, and it would be wise to clarify this issue before proceeding.

Definitions in anthropology

Social scientists often get into deep trouble over definitions. The reasons for this are easy to understand but difficult to overcome. In order to analyse something, we need to have some way of recognizing it; we need to know, in some sense, what it is. And yet the nature of the thing we are studying is revealed in the analysis itself, and our conclusions may lead us to revise our initial impressions. This continual modification of understanding is a normal part of scientific enquiry and is not, in itself, worrying, but it does pose the problem of where to start, how to establish some initial criteria for identifying what we are studying. Bohannan's apparently helpful suggestion, that defining an object of analysis 'should never amount to more than being specific about what one excludes' (1973: 357), turns out, on close inspection, not to be helpful at all. Since most definitions are intended to exclude more than they include, being specific about it can amount to rather a lot! Not surprisingly, most social scientists persist in narrowing down their objects of study by stating what they are, rather than what they are not.

Definitions have been especially problematic in anthropology because they have been required to span cultural boundaries. This was a lot to ask, even before cultural relativism became dominant as a guiding principle. Attempts to formulate 'universal' definitions of cultural phenomena such as marriage (Leach 1955, Gough 1959) and religion (Goody 1961, Horton 1960, Spiro 1966,) invariably led to unwanted exclusions and inclusions.[12] Cultural relativism deepened the dilemma by casting doubt on the whole enterprise of cross-cultural comparison. The principle that all cultures are equally valid interpretations of the world, that they are all equally 'true', appears to deny the existence of an independent reality (Keat and Urry 1982: 5), and therefore to deprive us of any overarching criteria for comparing across cultural boundaries. These kinds of arguments have been made and countered many times over (for instance, Holy and Stuchlik 1981: 29), and their persistence indicates a deep-seated unease which, while seeming to constrain the potential of anthropology, has also been a driving force in its development.

My response to the dilemma is as follows. First, there is no need to pretend that the definitions employed in anthropology are somehow culturally 'neutral'. It is undeniably the case that anthropology requires phenomena generated in one cultural context to be interpreted in terms of ideas generated in a different cultural context. This also happens continuously in everyday life, and increasingly so in a world of global communications (see Chapter 5). The challenge for anthropology has always been to devise guidelines for cross-cultural interpretation that enable it to teach us something useful and interesting about the human condition.

Second, definitions are only problematic if we insist that they describe the true essences of things. Since social scientists study *social* reality – that is, reality as it is understood by people, and not essential truths – this demand is both unreasonable and inappropriate (cf. Holy and Stuchlik 1981: 30).[13] In proposing cross-cultural definitions, anthropologists are simply setting up analytical frameworks which may or may not collapse when put to the test, which may or may not prove useful for interpreting a range of cultural responses. If we treat definitions as conceptual tools for interpreting reality, and avoid confusing them with reality itself, their failure to grasp essential truths is not a difficulty. We can use a definition for as long as it remains useful, and change it when it outlives its usefulness.

EXPLORING ENVIRONMENTALISM

Thus far, I have referred to 'environmentalism' assuming that readers will have their own broadly similar interpretations of the term. I also trust that nothing I have written so far will have seriously stretched or contradicted the vast majority of such interpretations. But developing an anthropological perspective on environmentalism, and presenting it for analysis as a cultural phenomenon, will require some modification of popular conceptions. This is the task to which I now turn.

In its everyday use, the term 'environmentalism' typically refers to a concern that the environment should be protected, particularly from the harmful effects of human activities. Environmentalism is expressed in many ways: through public support for organizations dedicated to environmental protection, through government policies aimed at decreasing pollution or conserving wildlife, through 'green' political parties, through demands for changes in land use, through the purchase of goods whose producers claim to be sensitive to environmental needs. For individuals, it may be a deep commitment which informs every aspect of their lifestyle or it may be a marginal concern which has little effect on everyday life. It appears to have grown, over the past thirty years, out of a long-standing but relatively low-key minority interest, to become a significant, but far from dominant political influence at national and international level. Described thus, environmentalism is a feature of what I have chosen to call 'industrial' society. Within this context, because it is seen as a relatively new and growing phenomenon, it is often described by analysts as a social move-ment. And because it has become an important and distinctive component of political discourse, it is often characterized as an ideology. The ways in which social scientists have interpreted it in these terms will be examined in detail in Chapter 3.

Environmentalism beyond industrial society

There is a widespread awareness, expressed mainly through tele-vision documentaries and news reports, that something akin to environmentalism is being expressed in specific locations outside industrial society and at the interface between the industrial and non-industrial worlds. Public attention has been drawn to the plight of indigenous peoples such as the Amazonian Indians and the Penan of Malaysia, who have opposed the destruction of their rainforest environments by commercial interests. Chico Mendes gained international recognition as the leader of Amazonia's rubber-tappers against the environmentally destructive forces of large-scale cattle ranching (Cowell 1990, Revkin 1990). Sunderlal Bahuguna gained similar recognition as spokesman for the Chipko (tree-hugging) movement in India, which also opposed the destruc-tive commercial exploitation of the forests (Weber 1988, Guha 1993). These events are seen as similar to environmentalism in industrial societies in two senses: first, in the fundamental sense that they express a concern that the environment should be pro-tected from the effects of human activities; and second, in the sense that they are protests against a dominant commercial ethos, and therefore tend to exhibit the characteristics of social movements.

However, there is another sense in which something akin to environmentalism has been said to exist in non-industrial societies. Environmentalists frequently point to some non-industrial societies as models for a 'sustainable' or 'conserver' society (Paehlke 1989: 137–41). The extractive economies of rainforest peoples, who gather most of their food from the forest, who cut branches for firewood rather than felling whole trees and who restrict their commercial activities to those which have little impact on the forest ecosystem (such as the harvesting of rubber and Brazil nuts), are contrasted with the destructive and exploitative activities of commercial loggers, who clear large areas of forest just to remove a few commercially valuable trees. The reverence and respect with which hunters in non-industrial societies are seen as treating their quarry species is contrasted with the apparently wasteful practices of commercial fishing and whaling, which can decimate whole populations and bring species to the brink of extinction. The spiritual ties between some non-industrial peoples and their land are contrasted with the way in which industrial society turns land into a commercial good, whose value is assessed in terms of what it can produce. These kinds of contrast have contributed to an impression, widespread among environmentalists in industrial societies, that non-industrial peoples live in harmony with nature (see Ellen 1986, Rayner 1989) whereas industrial processes work against natural ones. This impression is expressed in the contention that it is industrialism that is the root cause of environmental problems (see Dobson 1990: 29).

Ecosystem people and biosphere people

The opposition between industrial and non-industrial relationships with the environment is neatly encapsulated in Dasmann's distinction between ecosystem people and biosphere people (1976: 304). Ecosystem people are those who live within a single ecosystem, or at most within two or three adjacent ecosystems (such as people who live at the coast and use the resources of both land and sea). Dasmann included within this category traditional, non-industrial societies, and people who have opted, or been pushed, out of 'technological' society. Biosphere people are those whose way of life is tied in with the 'global technological system'. They use the resources of the whole biosphere: they may receive grain from America, beef from Argentina, coffee from Brazil, tea from India, electrical goods from Japan, oil from Saudi Arabia, cars from France, and so on.

Expressed in these terms, the opposition between ecosystem people and biosphere people generates certain expectations concerning environmental responsibility. Ecosystem people depend on their immediate ecosystem for their survival and, if they understand the ecological consequences of their actions, might be expected to take care not to destroy it. In other words, an ecosystem economy might be expected to engender a sense of responsibility towards the environment. Biosphere people do not experience the same constraints. They draw on a wide range of ecosystems to meet their needs, and if supplies from one source are exhausted or destroyed, they turn to another. Biosphere people therefore might be less likely to feel the need to protect any one ecosystem; a biosphere economy is more likely to engender a cavalier exploitative attitude than a sense of environmental responsibility. One of the central arguments of environmentalist thought in industrial societies is that the consequences of this attitude are now coming home to roost and the whole biosphere is endangered as a result of biosphere people's thoughtless exploitation of its resources.

The distinction between ecosystem people and biosphere people is misleadingly simple (as, indeed, is the distinction between non-industrial and industrial societies). It cannot begin to represent adequately the range of different ways in which human economies impact on the environment. But it does provide an attractive idiom in which to discuss the relationship between environmental sensitivity and environmental exploitation. The history of colonial expansion and industrial progress can be seen as a process in which ecosystem peoples have been transformed into biosphere peoples, often unwillingly, often forcibly, but often (and perhaps increasingly in recent decades) with their enthusiastic co-operation. After all, the biosphere economy offers previously undreamed-of material rewards and it is safer, in principle, to spread dependence over the whole biosphere than to rely on one ecosystem. But the impact of the biosphere economy has been, effectively, to turn the whole planet into a single ecosystem and, according to some environmentalists, threaten its ability to sustain life. In accordance with this interpretation, some environmentalists aim to transform biosphere people into ecosystem people. By advocating and, in some cases, practising greater degrees of self-sufficiency, some environmentalists are aiming to create (or recreate) a higher level of dependency on the immediate environment, and thus to generate a greater level of responsibility towards it. This effort is based on the assumption that if a community is producing most of its own food, then the quality of its land becomes more important than if it is producing food that will be eaten elsewhere. And if a community is more dependent on its immediate ecosystem, it is less dependent on other people's immediate ecosystems, allowing them more opportunity to become self-sufficient.

Primitive ecological wisdom?

This discussion raises questions which are of central importance both to environmental discourse and to anthropology's participation in that discourse. To what extent is the impression that non-industrial peoples live in harmony with the environment an accurate one? Are the expectations that ecosystem peoples have a greater sense of responsibility towards their environments fulfilled in reality? Do they really possess a kind of 'primitive ecological wisdom'?[14] The image of non-industrial communities living in harmony with the environment is well established in environmentalist thought and widely accepted in global environmental discourse, not least by non-industrial peoples themselves. Indeed, I think it reasonable to suggest that this image has the status of a 'myth', by which I mean, not that it is necessarily untrue, nor that it has some special, 'symbolic' truth, but that its truth is treated as a dogma (Robinson 1968, Milton 1977), in no need of proof and not easily amenable to refutation. Environmentalists cling to the image of non-industrial peoples as paragons of ecological virtue because it forms a basis for some of their most cherished arguments, particularly for the environmentalist critique of industrialism. One of the ways in which anthropologists can help to improve our understanding of environmentalism is by examining the role of this myth in environmentalist discourse (cf. Ellen 1986: 12). I shall return to this point in Chapter 6.

However, it is also important to study the myth in another way, by examining its basis in reality. Anthropologists do not normally concern themselves with whether or not particular myths are true, but in this case the myth in question is about the very subject matter of anthropology, the character of specific cultures and kinds of culture. The myth states that non-industrial peoples understand and interact with their environments in harmonious, non-destructive ways. It could be extremely important for the future of the planet, and particularly of human life, to know whether or not this myth has any sound basis. If, as many environmentalists argue, the industrial economy (and with it industrial culture) is fundamentally and inevitably destructive towards the environment, then the future will rest with alternative ways of living. It will obviously be important to select alternatives that are genuinely benign towards the environment and not just held dogmatically to be so. As Ellen (1986) has demonstrated, the kind of knowledge required to test the accuracy of the myth is precisely that which anthropologists habitually acquire in the practice of their discipline (see also Keesing 1981: 506). These points will be discussed more fully in Chapters 2 and 4.

Diverse environments

Thus far, I have also referred to 'the environment' unproblematically as something that people interact with and depend upon by using its resources for their survival and well-being. But it would be misleading to suggest that people, even within the same society, all share the same understanding of the environment. Ecologists, for example, trained in the same broad tradition of western science, have been found to conceptualize 'nature' in different ways, as robust, fragile, capricious or robust within limits (see Douglas 1992: 262). These diverse 'myths' of nature give rise to different understandings of the risks involved in our use of the environment, and the character and degree of our responsibilities towards it (see Chapter 3). A much greater diversity is found between different cultural traditions. For some, the environment may be passive and amenable to management by people, for others it may be personified as an all-powerful being who controls human destiny, or it may be inhabited by agents which interact with people in a reciprocal manner.

The question of whether something like environmentalism exists in any given society will depend on how the environment itself is defined. A concern that the environment be protected is incompatible with an image of the environment as infinite and invincible. And personal responsibilities to protect the environment are unlikely to be felt by people who, for generations, have seen themselves as living under *its* protection or at its mercy (Richards 1992a). On the other hand, an environment that is seen as consisting of impersonal objects and substances in limited supply, particularly if it has been seriously depleted by human use, may well be thought of as in need (and deserving) of human protection and amenable to human management. Several ways in which the environment is defined, and their implications for human interaction with it, will be examined in Chapter 4.

Environmentalism as part of culture

In its everyday usage, the term 'environmentalism' typically signi-
fies a perspective that has evolved to oppose the harmful impacts of
the biosphere economy. The myth of primitive ecological wisdom,
however misleading it may be, is useful in drawing attention to
the fact that a concern to protect the environment from the effects
of human activity need not be part of an oppositional ideology. It
may be part of the cultural *status quo*, part of the way in which
the members of a particular society have always understood their
place in the world. I want to suggest that, for analytical purposes,
environmentalism be identified as a concern to protect the environment, wherever and in whatever form it exists. In some contexts
it will stand in opposition to an exploitative and damaging perspective and, when it does so, may indeed drive a social movement. In
other contexts it will have a place in the set of assumptions and
values that shape a society's habitual way of doing things. I should
also stress that I see it as a concern *to protect* the environment
through human effort and responsibility, rather than simply a
concern that the environment be protected. Given the various ways
in which the environment itself is culturally defined, it is possible
to envisage a society in which a concern for the environment is
strongly held, but in which agents other than human beings are
seen as responsible for its protection: ancestral spirits, for instance,
or an all-powerful divine being.

Defined in these terms, environmentalism is unambiguously part
of culture in the narrower sense of that term identified above. In
other words, it is a part of the way in which people understand
the world and their place within it. It belongs to the sphere that
includes people's feelings, thoughts, interpretations, knowledge,
ideology, values and so on. It is, I suggest, a type of 'cultural
perspective' (taking 'culture' in its narrower sense),[15] a particular
way of understanding the world. As such, while not itself located
in people's actions and patterns of action, environmentalism has
implications for, and is expressed in, the things people do.

The reason for distinguishing, analytically, between environmentalism as a part of culture and the actions through which people
express and implement their perceived responsibilities towards the
environment is that it enables the relationship between them to be
treated as problematic (just as, in general terms, anthropologists
began distinguishing between what people are assumed to hold in

their minds and what they are observed to do, in order to examine the relationship between them). Without this distinction, it might be assumed that an environmentalist perspective will always generate the same kinds of action. In fact, a concern to protect the environment through human effort might be expressed in many different ways, depending on how the environment itself and the forces that impact upon it are defined. Even where the protection of the environment is seen as being in the hands of a divine being or spirits, these agents may require human obedience and respect in return for their protection. In these circumstances, responsibility for the environment is in human hands, but may be implemented through actions which, from the viewpoint of industrial society, would not easily be recognized as environmentalist: acts of worship, for instance, or the daily maintenance of certain standards of behaviour (fulfilment of kinship obligations, avoidance of incest or adultery). On the other hand, in an atheistic culture, or one in which the responsibilities of the divine are assumed to exclude the environment, or one in which the divine is seen to have delegated responsibility to people, a concern to protect the environment has different implications for human action.

The relationship between an environmentalist perspective and the actions that might be based upon it is problematic in another sense. Very often, with the best of intentions, people get things wrong. Actions that are intended to protect the environment turn out not to have the desired effect. For instance, when the tanker *Torrey Canyon* was wrecked off the south-west coast of England in 1967, detergents used to disperse the oil added to the biological damage (McCormick 1989: 57). In these kinds of circumstances, the knowledge on which the actions are based is thrown into question, and people may ultimately revise their understanding of the world.

I have suggested that the analytical concept of environmentalism proposed here might be seen as incorporating a wider range of phenomena than is implied in the everyday usage of the term, in that it covers any concern to protect the environment which implies a human responsibility, whether it exists as part of a 'traditional' cultural perspective or as the basis of an oppositional movement. There is also a sense in which the concept proposed here might be seen as including less than is normally understood by environmentalism, both in everyday contexts and in social-scientific analysis. People who refer to themselves (and are referred to by others) as environmentalists often intend to imply more by this label than a concern to protect the environment. They see it as implying a range of values and principles which inform their political allegiances, their behaviour as consumers and the way they allocate their personal time and resources. In many instances it could reasonably be argued that all these things hinge on a concern to protect the environment, and are expressions of this guiding principle. But some would certainly argue that the term 'environment' is itself too narrow to represent adequately the object of so-called 'environmentalist' concerns. Quite often, environmentalism implies a respect for life itself, and a concern for the quality of life of human beings and other species. Both in everyday contexts and in the work of social scientists (see Chapter 3), it may designate a comprehensive political ideology which includes views on how human society should be organized, as well as on how environmental issues should be addressed.

I have no quarrel with the term 'environmentalism' being used in this broad sense, and the proposed definition does not contradict this usage in any way. Just as definitions in social science are not required to grasp essential truths, so they should not be expected to specify the full range of things that might be suggested by a concept, a range which, in any case, will vary from one cultural context to another. The test of an analytical definition is not its completeness, but its usefulness in identifying phenomena that might be analysed and compared.

The proposed concept of environmentalism, as a concern to protect the environment which implies human responsibility, has two purposes in the context of this study. First, it identifies environmentalism as an enterprise to which anthropology might contribute. The knowledge generated by anthropologists in their study of human cultures, indeed, in their study of human ecology, might be useful in trying to fulfil our responsibilities to protect the environment, in understanding environmental problems and seeking solutions. Second, it identifies environmentalism as an object which anthropologists might analyse. A concern to protect the environment is present in a range of different cultural contexts. Through analysis and comparison, anthropologists can study the ways in which this concern, and the responsibilities generated by it, are defined and expressed. These two projects combine in anthropology's potential contribution to the worldwide discourse on environmental problems and responsibilities. An understanding of environmentalism in its diverse cultural forms might help to refine environmentalist thought and generate a more informed understanding of our environmental responsibilities and how they might be fulfilled. In the latter part of this book, the two projects will be discussed as one, but for the moment it is important to keep them apart in order to examine the potential of each. The next chapter examines anthropology's contribution as the study of human ecology and considers in detail the role of culture in human–environment relations.

2

CULTURE AND ECOLOGY

Human ecology *is* human behaviour.
(Bennett 1990: 436)

... human ecology *is* human society.
(Croll and Parkin 1992: 13)

Ecologists study the relationships between organisms and their environments. Environmentalists seek (among other things) to use the knowledge generated by ecologists to modify the relationships between organisms and their environments, in such a way as to minimize environmental damage. One of the reasons why an environmental discourse has emerged as a public, political phenomenon, rather than remaining an esoteric interest of ecologists, is that human activities have increasingly been identified as major sources of environmental damage. The understanding that, if environmental damage is to be curtailed or reduced, human activities must be changed, has turned ecology into a social commitment and led environmental activists to seek alternative models for the organization of human society. This much is clear, but is worth stating since it forms the starting point for the argument that cultural theory can help us to understand environmental issues. This argument also hinges on the assumption that culture has something to do with the relationship between human beings and their environment.

Human–environment relations are the central focus of what is generally known as 'ecological anthropology'. So it is essential, in exploring anthropology's contribution to environmental discourse, to consider the work of ecological anthropologists; this is the first task for this chapter. But it would not be appropriate to give a comprehensive overview of ecological anthropology. Not only

37

would this be too large an undertaking for a single chapter, it would also go beyond the main purpose of this book, which is to argue that cultural theory, an approach that is central to, but not coterminous with, the whole of anthropology, can make a valuable contribution to environmental discourse. The following sections therefore focus specifically on how the concept of culture has been treated in ecological anthropology.[1] The second task in this chapter is to draw on the discussion (in Chapter 1) on the meaning of culture in anthropology, and the discussion (in this chapter) of its status in ecological anthropology, to develop an understanding of culture that is appropriate for interpreting the way people interact with their environment.

At one time, the assumption that culture has something to do with the relationship between human beings and their environment would have been uncontroversial within anthropology, but during the past three decades, the relevance of culture to an understanding of human ecology has become uncertain and has even been denied. The uncertainty is reflected in the two quotations at the beginning of this chapter, neither of which mentions culture. Both refer to phenomena, 'society' and 'behaviour', which, until about thirty years ago, would have been accepted by almost all anthropologists as part of culture, but which, following the developments outlined in Chapter 1, are now often excluded from a concept of culture which has come to refer to people's feelings, thoughts and knowledge about the world. Thus the marginalization of culture in ecological anthropology has had as much to do with the shifts in how culture has been conceptualized, as with the way in which ecology has been understood by anthropologists. My argument in this chapter will be that culture needs to be firmly established at the centre of ecological anthropology. There is nothing new about this argument, though my reasons for proposing it are different from those that many anthropologists would use, in that I am as much concerned with the value of cultural theory as a tool for helping to address environmental issues, as with any academic purpose. In order to argue that culture should be central to ecological anthropology it is useful to establish how and why it has become marginalized. The following sections present an analysis of the part played by a concept of culture in ecological anthropology.

CULTURE AS MEDIATOR

There is a widespread assumption, both within and outside anthropology, that human beings without culture would be more or less incapable of keeping themselves alive. 'Culture ... is something which man interposes between himself and his environment in order to ensure his security and survival' (Carneiro 1968: 551–3). This assumption is present in the assertion that human beings enter the world with their programmes for living incomplete (Berger and Luckmann 1966: 65ff.). The mind of a new-born child is a relatively clean slate, on which society writes its portrayal of reality and its script for living. It is implied in the many contrasts which anthropologists draw between human activities and those of non-human animals, the most famous of which is probably the case of dam building by beavers and by humans. Beavers, we are told, enter the world with their dam-building programmes intact, contained within their genes. For human beings to build a dam, they need a concept, a design, a set of instructions to follow, a culture (cf. Geertz 1966: 7).

The image of the infant human mind as a void waiting to be filled is perhaps most vividly portrayed in the observations of children brought up among non-human animals. Armen's wild child, discovered living with a herd of gazelles in Mauritania, had acquired many of the gazelles' behavioural characteristics. He had learned to climb, run, eat, mark territory, groom, communicate and use his senses, all, as far as his physique would allow, in the manner of the gazelles. Armen listed the attributes acquired by the boy as a result of his 'gazelle acculturation', alongside those he was assumed to have acquired during the first few months of his life, before losing his human family (1976: 96–7).

The impression that culture mediates between human beings and their environment is equally strong whether culture itself is perceived as consisting primarily of characteristics assumed to be observable, such as actions, techniques and institutionalized modes of behaviour (see Hawley 1944: 404; Steward 1955: 44), or whether, as in more recent anthropological thought, it is restricted to what people know, think and feel. Goodenough's portrayal of culture as consisting of standards for deciding what is, what can be, what one feels about it and what to do about it (Goodenough 1961: 522) carries the clear implication that without culture human beings could not even define their environment; they would have no means of knowing what is or what can be. Forde's description of the ecological role of culture was remarkably ahead of its time in suggesting that culture is distinct from, but related to, human activity: 'Between the physical environment and human activity there is always a middle term, a collection of specific objectives and values, a body of knowledge and belief: in other words, a cultural pattern' (1949: 463).

While the assumption that human–environment relations are mediated by culture has been fundamental to ecological anthropology (Ingold 1992a: 39), the nature of those relations and of culture's mediating role has been the principal area of debate. There have been three broad ways of conceptualizing the relationship between human beings and their environments: first, human beings adapt to and are therefore shaped by their environments; second, human beings adapt their environments to suit their own needs, and therefore determine or shape those environments; third, human beings interact with their environments in such a way that they shape each other. In the first two models, the mediating role of culture remained largely unquestioned. Indeed, the concept of a relationship between human beings and their environment mediated by culture tended to be conflated into a relationship between culture and the environment. Since anthropologists were interested primarily in the reasons for and causes of cultural diversity, questions tended to be phrased in terms of the relationship of culture to the environment, and gave rise to two broad perspectives: environmental determinism (in which culture is seen as being shaped by the environment) and cultural determinism (in which the environment is seen as being defined by culture). It is in the third model, in which human beings and their environment are seen as shaping each other, that culture has been marginalized.

ENVIRONMENTAL DETERMINISM

Until the 1960s, ecological anthropology was dominated by the view that environments shape cultures; that is, not only that environmental factors *determine* cultural characteristics, but also that environments act on *cultures*, as distinct from other units such as human societies or populations. Environmental determinism, in its various forms, addressed the questions of how cultures and cultural features originate, change, adapt and function. Given that biological processes were the inspiration for this approach, it was inevitable that much of the discussion would centre on the appropriateness of the biological analogy. Debate centred on the questions of whether cultures evolve in the same way that species evolve, whether cultures adapt to their environments in the same way that organisms do, and whether there are cultural equivalents to the processes of natural selection and mutation (see Burnham 1973, Diener *et al.* 1980).

Anthropogeography and possibilism

It is easy to appreciate the simple appeal of the idea that environments shape cultures. It opened up the possibility of explaining all cultural features, thereby accounting for cultural diversity, through reference to environmental influences. Understanding the environment of a region would lead to an understanding of the cultures occupying that region. Accordingly, early analyses sought correlations between areas distinguished by their natural features and types of culture, classified in terms of their technologies (for instance, Mason 1896). Huntington (1924) saw climate as the principal influence in the advancement of civilizations, not only in their more technological aspects, but also in matters such as religious belief and ritual. This mechanistic linking of culture to environment was often referred to, somewhat confusingly in the current context, as 'environmentalism' (Ellen 1982: 1) or 'anthropogeography' (Geertz 1963: 1–2; Ellen 1982: 2), and is represented, for instance, in the work of Ratzel (1896) in Europe and Fewkes (1896) and Holmes (1919) in America.

It became clear at an early stage that the anthropogeographic approach could not account for observed realities. Cultures were grouped together on the grounds that they occupied the same type of habitat and shared a few seemingly significant features. And yet some of the cultural characteristics which most occupied anthropologists' minds, such as kinship terminologies, marriage rules and political systems, varied quite markedly within geographical areas. It appeared that, whatever the effects of the environment on such institutions, they were not directly causal. In Britain, following the influence of Durkheim (1964 [1895]), Radcliffe-Brown and Malinowski, anthropologists responded by turning their attention to the social, rather than the ecological, functions of cultural institutions. In America, through the work of Boas, Wissler (1926) and Kroeber (1939), the emphasis on environmental factors remained, but shifted. Rather than having a dynamic or creative influence, the environment was seen as limiting the development of cultural characteristics. For instance, maize growing in aboriginal America was limited to areas where climatic conditions permitted a growing season of at least four months (Kroeber 1939, cited in Hardesty 1977), and cattle herding in Africa was limited by the occurrence of the tsetse fly (Stenning 1957).

This way of conceptualizing the relationship between environment and culture, often referred to as 'possibilism', appeared to offer an acceptable alternative to the view that the environment directly causes cultural features.[2] It proved to be a pervasive influence in ecological anthropology (Meggers 1954, Hardesty 1977: 3), perhaps because, as Geertz argued (1963: 2), it cannot easily be refuted. The limiting influence of the environment is self-evident; agricultural activities *are* restricted by climate; technology *is* limited by whatever materials the environment provides. But possibilism suffers from the same disadvantage as the anthropogeographic model, in that it lacks the potential to account for cultural diversity in any but the most superficial sense. Once the environmental limitations on the development of a culture have been established, there is still a great deal to be explained. For instance, Strehlow (1965) argued that the relatively productive environment of the Aranda peoples of Central Australia enabled them to develop more elaborate traditions of art, ritual and mythology than their neighbours to the west who lived in a harsher environment. The implication is that when a society is 'affluent', in the sense that their material needs are easily met (Sahlins 1968), they have greater opportunity for cultural elaboration. But this observation can explain nothing about the detail of Aranda culture, the content of their myths and rituals, the nature of their religious knowledge.

Thus environmental determinism, in both its positive (anthropogeography) and negative (possibilism) forms, suffers from a lack of analytical potential. It can, as Geertz argued, 'ask only the grossest of questions: "How far is culture influenced by environment?" ... And can give only the grossest of answers: "To a degree, but not completely" ' (1963: 3). It can establish general principles 'applicable to any cultural-environmental situation', but can say nothing about 'the origins of particular cultural features and patterns which characterize different areas' (Steward 1955: 36). The search for a more precise understanding of the relationship between cultures and their environments, and a concern to explain the origins of specific cultural institutions, led Steward to develop the methodology which he called 'cultural ecology' (1955: 30–42).

Cultural ecology

Cultural ecology was based on the assumption that cultures have evolved within their local environments, and that a close analysis of the relationships between specific cultural institutions and their local environmental features will reveal how and why those institutions both originated and persisted. Steward did not accord the same ecological status to all cultural institutions. He identified a 'cultural core' of those features 'most closely related to subsistence activities and economic arrangements', that is, to people's utilization of their environment, which he saw as being more directly linked to environmental factors than others (Steward 1955: 37). Precisely which features would constitute the cultural core could not be prejudged, but had to be established through empirical analysis. The methodology of cultural ecology consisted of three phases. First, the relationship between the environment and the technology employed in its utilization should be examined; second, the behaviour patterns involved in the use of that technology should be analysed; and third, the extent to which other cultural features are affected by those behaviour patterns should be ascertained (1955: 40–1).

Just as some cultural features are more closely tied to a society's use of the environment than others, so are some environmental features more relevant than others to subsistence activities, and therefore more influential in shaping cultural development. For instance, the organization of hunting activities will vary according to the characteristics of the quarry animals: whether they are small or large, sedentary or migratory, gregarious or solitary. In one of Steward's most famous applications of his model, in which he considered the evolution of the patrilineal band, he argued that similar forms of social organization have developed in societies living in very different environmental conditions, as a result of the fact that they hunt similar types of game (1955: 122–42).

It was suggested that cultural ecology represented a significant innovation in the way the relationship between culture and the environment is conceptualized. Geertz argued that the earlier

43

perspectives – anthropogeography and possibilism – shared a 'serious conceptual defect', in that they treated culture and environment as separate independent wholes which affect each other externally (Geertz 1963: 2–3). By leading the analyst to identify a core of cultural traits and a corresponding set of relevant environmental features, cultural ecology created the concept of an integrated system, effectively an 'ecosystem', within which cultural and environmental features interact: 'The sharpness of the division between analyses from the side of "man" and analyses from the side of "nature" therefore disappears, for the two approaches are essentially alternative and interchangeable conceptualizations of the same systemic process' (1963: 8). This seems to suggest that the old mechanistic determinism, in which environment was always assumed to influence culture, was being replaced by a less directional model which would enable the analyst to establish how local ecosystems work.

However, this promise is not borne out by Steward's own presentation and application of his model. On the contrary, he favoured a strongly deterministic approach and criticized analyses conducted in the possibilist tradition for assigning the environment too passive a role in cultural evolution (Steward 1955: 35). He wished to reinstate the theory that the environment has a dynamic, creative role in shaping culture. His complaint about the old anthropogeographic model was that it was too general, that it offered no scope for understanding how specific cultures related to their local environments. Geertz was right to point out that cultural ecology departs from the image of cultures and environments as independent wholes, but the resulting explanations were no less deterministic or directional than previous ones had been. Steward merely reproduced environmental determinism at a more precise level. Instead of whole environments shaping whole cultures, he suggested that specific environmental features shape specific cultural features – for example, that the type of game shapes band organization.

It would be misleading to suggest that Steward saw the environment as the sole influence in cultural change. He acknowledged that some cultural traits 'are determined to a greater extent by purely cultural-historical factors – by random innovations or by diffusion' (Steward 1955: 37), but these are relegated to the status of 'secondary features', being less closely connected to the environmentally determined core. This distinction between the cultural core and secondary features was one of the most problematic elements of the cultural ecology model for several reasons. Steward's methodological guidelines gave no criteria for deciding where the cultural core ended and the secondary cultural features began. Given that anthropologists tend to see cultures as integrated systems whose features are all interlinked in some way, there was always the danger of the core dissolving into the whole (Ellen 1982: 61), with the inevitable conclusion (which Steward had sought to avoid) that the lines of environmental determinism run through whole cultures.

This raises the question of how environmental influences might be distinguished from other kinds. Only the first of Steward's three methodological steps entails an analysis of the direct connections between the environment and cultural features (the technology employed in utilizing the environment). The second two steps require the analyst to examine how cultural features (technology and patterns of behaviour) are linked to other cultural features. One might ask in what sense these intracultural connections are different from those 'cultural-historical' factors which Steward would wish to omit from the analysis because they only influence 'secondary' features. As Ellen pointed out, 'history itself is only the product of numerous determining forces, with their proximate origins in both material and social relations, and of accumulated innovations which embody environmental responses' (1982: 62). In short, and contrary to the claims made for it at the time, cultural ecology provides no clear model for explaining how cultural features originate and persist, nor for determining the extent of environmental influence in the evolution of specific cultures.

The problem of adaptation

Despite difficulties with their application, the principles established by Steward formed the basis of a range of studies which set out to demonstrate the adaptive nature of cultural institutions. Harris, in particular, although critical of Steward in some respects, adopted the method of tracing connections from environmental factors through technology to other cultural features such as group organization, ritual practices and belief systems (1968: 4), in order to reveal an underlying materialist rationality. The main objection to this approach was that it tended to assume that all cultural features are adaptive, and implicitly, if not explicitly, denied the

45

possibility that some might be maladaptive. It has been argued many times that this assumption is untenable, that cultures do not necessarily hold their populations in balance with their environments and may even endanger their own survival.

For instance, there is no doubt that many societies with restricted space and resources have practised infanticide as a means of controlling their population size. If practices of this kind were truly adaptive to environmental conditions, they could be expected to change if and when conditions change. In other words, if the level of resources increased, or if the population fell to dangerously low levels, population control measures would be modified accordingly. The inhabitants of San Cristobal, in the Solomon Islands, traditionally killed their first-born children. It is not known whether this practice originally developed as a population control measure. In the late nineteenth and early twentieth centuries, around 80 per cent of the population was wiped out by introduced diseases. If culture were adaptive to environmental conditions, one would expect the practice of infanticide to stop in order that the population might recover. But the San Cristobal inhabitants continued to kill their first-born, 'because their custom required it' (Keesing 1981: 163). A better-known example of failure to adapt is provided by the population of Easter Island, in the south-east Pacific, whose disappearance was once regarded as a mystery. A current, widely accepted theory suggests that their use of timber in erecting their large stone statues so depleted the island's forests that they no longer had enough wood to build their homes or construct canoes, and the quality of the soil declined once the tree cover was removed. Instead of adapting their practices once they became aware of these dangers, the Easter Islanders apparently intensified their statue building and hastened their demise (see Ponting 1991: 1–7).

Environmental determinism and environmentalism

The question of whether specific cultural practices are adaptive or maladaptive is important in the context of the need to understand and solve environmental problems. It would clearly be helpful to be able to distinguish those cultural features which help to promote survival in a given environment from those that endanger it. But environmental determinism is not an appropriate framework for this project because it does not leave questions of cultural adaptability open to investigation. Instead it assumes that environments shape cultures, and that cultures therefore adapt to environmental conditions. This assumption has to be abandoned in order to ask *whether* specific cultural features are adaptive. The two examples given above indicate two ways in which cultural features might be maladaptive. They might prevent a population from adapting to changing environmental conditions (as on San Cristobal) or they might actively change the environment on which people depend in a detrimental way (as on Easter Island). Asking questions about cultural adaptability therefore requires us to examine how cultural features impact on the environment, as well as on the population itself. Again, this is incompatible with the assumption that environments shape cultures.

Probably none of the analysts who sought environmental explanations for cultural phenomena would have denied that culture also influences environmental change. To have done so would have appeared absurd, given that the ethnographic literature abounds with descriptions of the ways human societies modify their environments to meet their needs: the burning of bushland by hunting communities to encourage the new growth which attracts and sustains game; the manipulation of water flows through irrigation schemes; the clearing of forests for cultivation; and so on. But environmental determinism, by definition, addresses only the influence of the environment on culture, and ignores the complementary process. Once it is assumed, for analytical purposes, that environments shape cultures, then the possibility of asking how cultures shape environments is effectively precluded.

There is a further reason why environmental determinism is incompatible with the environmentalist concern to protect the environment through human effort. The assumption that human activities are somehow caused by environmental factors, that the environment is the 'prime mover' in human affairs, implies that human beings are helpless in the face of natural forces, in much the same way that some religious doctrines imply that we are helpless in the face of supernatural forces. In other words it induces a 'rationality of fatalism', in which planning is redundant and in which 'outcomes, good or bad, are simply to be enjoyed or endured, but never achieved' (James *et al.* 1987: 9). While a fatalist perspective might accord closely with many people's experience of the world, it has limited potential as a basis for action.

The approaches described above were prominent at a time when the prevailing concept of culture employed by anthropologists embraced actions and the material products of action as well as what people hold in their minds – thoughts, feelings, ideas, knowledge. Many of the anthropologists engaged in ecological studies focused primarily, or even exclusively, on these more readily observable components of culture. Hawley, for instance, discussed culture in terms of the 'techniques' and 'habits' involved in ensuring survival (Hawley 1944: 404; 1950: 68), while Steward defined culture as 'learned modes of behaviour that are socially transmitted' (1955: 44). When, from the late 1950s, anthropologists increasingly restricted the term 'culture' to what cannot be directly observed, the components in which ecological anthropologists had shown the most interest were more or less excluded from the concept. This marked a parting of the ways in ecological anthropology. Those analysts who retained a prime interest in the workings of ecological relations found that they could get by quite well without the modified concept of culture. Those who wished to explore the analytical potential of the new, narrower concept of culture, shifted their emphasis from ecology to 'ethnoecology' (Fowler 1977), and redefined the relationship between culture and environment as one of cultural determinism.

CULTURAL DETERMINISM

The shift in the meaning of culture had been engendered by dissatisfaction with the failure of structuralist and functionalist models, not only to interpret actions and explain social change, but also to provide adequate analyses of people's interpretations of the world, to understand 'the native's point of view' (Geertz 1976). This gave rise to two significant trends in anthropology. First, there was a flourishing of ethnographic descriptions of people's world views or 'folk models' (Holy and Stuchlik 1981: vi). Heralded as a 'new departure' in ethnography (Tyler 1969: 1–3), this trend sought to fill the gap in the structuralist and functionalist literature by providing detailed analyses of the ways different societies define the world. Second, the thesis that people construct their view of reality through social interaction (Berger and Luckmann 1966) came to dominate anthropological thought. These trends both fuelled, and were fuelled by, a growing appreciation of the importance of classification, as a thought process, for gener-

48

ating symbolic and ritual action (Douglas 1966, Turner 1967, Tambiah 1969).

Ethnoecology

'Ethnoecology' emerged as that branch of the new ethnography which describes people's conceptual models of their environment. It is distinguished primarily by its subject matter, which includes classifications of plants (Berlin *et al.* 1974, Friedberg 1979), animals (Bulmer 1957, 1967, Kesby 1979), land forms (Conklin 1967), and so on, and shares its methods and underlying premises with the broader field of 'cognitive anthropology' (Tyler 1969) to which it belongs. The prefix 'ethno-' is used to denote a field of knowledge defined from the viewpoint of the people being studied (Fowler 1977: 216) and is similar in meaning to the term 'folk' (as in 'folk knowledge', 'folk model', 'folk medicine'). Thus, ethnoecology is a branch of 'ethnoscience' (Frake 1962), which also includes 'ethnomedicine', 'ethnobiology' and so on. The use of the prefix 'ethno-' is essentially 'ethnocentric'; it implies that those bodies of knowledge not labelled 'ethno-', usually those generated by academic study in the 'western' tradition, are somehow privileged: 'Scientific knowledge, as we conceive it, has cross-cultural validity; ethnoscience, on the other hand, refers to knowledge that is indigenous to a particular language and culture' (Glick 1964: 273).[3]

Through its early development, cognitive anthropology was dominated by formal methods of data collection. It was understood that, in the course of everyday life, people's knowledge of the world is exposed in piecemeal fashion and that, however long an anthropologist might spend engaged in participant observation, they would never learn everything that was known on a particular subject (Milton 1981: 138). Formal methods were designed to elicit large amounts of knowledge quickly. Informants were asked, among other things, to compile exhaustive lists of terms, to sort written statements into piles according to their similarity (Cancian 1975), or to complete sentences by supplying missing words (D'Andrade 1976). Some formal methods involved systematic questioning of the kind anthropologists had developed for recording genealogies (Black 1969).

All such techniques require the analyst to exercise a considerable degree of control over the way in which knowledge is revealed. The everyday purposes and contexts in which people use

CULTURE AND ECOLOGY

knowledge were ignored in favour of what Ellen called 'naive mechanical exercises in elicitation' (1982: 233). As anthropologists became more aware of the importance of context in understanding people's knowledge, they turned to the more informal methods which anthropologists most often employ: interviews (Agar and Hobbs 1985), direct observation and participation. These methods enabled them to study knowledge in use (Dougherty and Keller 1985, Hunn 1985), and to participate in its learning and invocation (Gatewood 1985). It would probably be fair to say that, in this transition, cognitive anthropology largely lost its distinctive character. The description of people's cultural perspectives on the world has simply become a part, perhaps the main part, of what ethnographers do, and whether or not such descriptions include a society's 'ethnoecology' depends on whether ecology itself is a particular interest of the analyst. At the same time, the theoretical concern with how knowledge is elicited and described evolved into a broader interest in the process whereby knowledge, including ethnographic knowledge, is produced (Crick 1982). This interest is reflected in debates on ethnographic writing (Clifford 1986), and in the recent emergence of a processual concept of culture, described in Chapter 1.

The social construction of reality

The flourishing of ethnographic interest in people's world views helped to establish a new orthodoxy in cultural theory. Studies of folk knowledge demonstrated that a very wide range of phenomena, even apparently basic perceptual categories like colours (Conklin 1955), are subject to cultural variation. Assuming that there is just one real world in which all societies live, it seemed impossible that the diversity of cultural perspectives could be given in the reality itself. World views therefore had to be derived, at least in part, from something else. The answer provided by post-structuralist thinking in both sociology and anthropology was that they are 'constructed' through people's social experience.

The constructivist model comes in both extreme and moderate forms. In its extreme form, it is best exemplified by Sapir's contention that 'the worlds in which different societies live are distinct worlds, not merely the same world with different labels attached' (1961: 69). This statement appears to deny the existence of any common reality, particularly when combined with one of the tenets of cultural relativism, that all cultures are equally true. However, we can assume that neither Sapir, nor those who have taken his contention seriously (for instance, Bright and Bright 1965) intended to deny the existence of a common reality, for if societies really did live in distinct worlds, cultural diversity would not be problematic. World views would be different simply because the worlds they depict are different. A more reasonable reading of the extreme form of constructivism is that societies construct distinct worlds, composed of different truths, out of the same raw material. The more moderate form of constructivism is the more familiar, in that it forms the basis of much that has been written in the name of symbolic or semantic anthropology. It holds that diverse world views are different interpretations of a common reality. Rather than being composed of diverse truths, cultures are composed of diverse meanings.

The distinction between these versions of the constructivist model is significant in that, while only a few anthropologists would claim to espouse the more extreme view, very many feel at ease with the more moderate form. The image of human beings enveloped in worlds of meaning which they create through their own activities is widely accepted and vividly portrayed in the literature (see, for instance, Geertz 1973). And yet the difference between the two views is illusory. In the more extreme form, reality is unknowable, since even its truths are constructed; in the more moderate form, reality without cultural interpretation is devoid of meaning (cf. Ingold 1991: 13; 1992a: 40). As a basis for action, a meaningless reality is no better than an unknowable one; truths and meanings become, to all intents and purposes, indistinguishable.

The implications of this observation for ecological anthropology have been discussed by Ingold (1992a), and will be addressed below. For the moment, I wish only to consider its importance for ethnoecology, the branch of ecological anthropology which embraced the modified concept of culture as consisting of what people hold in their minds. In both the extreme and the moderate versions of the constructivist model, culture is seen as determining the environment by defining it, by imbuing it with truth or meaning. This raises the question of what constitutes the raw material for the cognitive construction. If the environment in the absence of human thought is devoid of truth or meaning, can there be anything of substance out of which to construct the cultural image

51

(Ingold 1992a: 39; 1996)? Descriptions of culture based on the constructivist model make no reference to anything outside themselves and their process of construction. They cannot draw in material from outside, since that material would not be recognizable as anything until it had been constructed through the cognitive process.

This might not matter if the aim of the analysis is merely to describe people's knowledge of the world, as studies in ethnoecology set out to do. However, the broader and explicit aims of ecological anthropology are to explain the external relations of human societies, to address the relationship between culture and the reality which culture supposedly models or constructs. This becomes impossible if, as the constructivist model implies, that reality consists of nothing, or at least nothing that is knowable or meaningful. Thus, in the face of a constructivist concept of culture, the whole enterprise of ecological anthropology collapses. Not surprisingly, many ecological anthropologists, until quite recently, did not even attempt to incorporate ethnoecological accounts into their analyses. Although it represented a highly significant development in the field of cognitive anthropology, ethnoecology became, for a time, something of a cul-de-sac in ecological anthropology, treated as a 'special topic' (Hardesty 1977), out of the mainstream and leading nowhere.

Cultural determinism and environmentalism

In some ways, ethnoecological accounts provide precisely the kind of insights that might be useful in understanding and seeking solutions to environmental problems. If the source of environmental damage is human activity, then an understanding of the rationale on which damaging activity is based is important as a starting point for instigating constructive change. For instance, specific agricultural practices may be damaging because they cause soil erosion, destroy wildlife habitat or use polluting chemicals. In seeking to replace such practices with more benign alternatives it could be important to know what kind of attachment people have to their established but harmful ways of doing things. Are they motivated by practical or economic considerations, or do the existing practices have religious connotations, or advantages for solidarity among kin, which might be difficult to relinquish? It is equally important to understand the rationale that underlies environmentally benign practices. Why, for instance, do some societies gather firewood by taking only a few branches from each tree, while others kill whole trees for the same purpose? It could be for economic reasons (because trees provide some other resource as well as firewood), for aesthetic reasons (because people like to see trees in their landscape), for personal comfort (trees provide shade and shelter) or for religious reasons (to avoid divine retribution). It might be important to understand what kinds of cultural interpretations of the world predispose people towards environmentally benign practices, if such practices are to be successfully adopted and encouraged.

It is undoubtedly the case that many, perhaps most, of the changes that have been introduced in the name of environmental conservation have been insensitive to local cultures, particularly those which have disrupted people's traditional ways of using their environment. The exclusion of the Ik people from their traditional hunting grounds, following the designation of the Kidepo Valley National Park in northern Uganda, apparently resulted in the more or less total collapse of their society (Turnbull 1972).[4] In their plans to designate the Matopo National Park in Zimbabwe, successive governments sought to override the Ndebele people's attachment to the area as part of their heritage (see Ranger 1989). If an understanding of local cultures is built into the formulation of environmental policies, there is less risk of alienating the local population, on whose co-operation the success of the policies may depend. If it were ever decided to mount a campaign in the New Guinea Highlands to conserve the cassowary, it might be crucial to know that, for the Karam people, cassowaries are not birds but metaphorical kin, with whom they share a special relationship (Bulmer 1967). It might also happen that cassowaries are found to thrive more successfully in Karam territory than elsewhere, precisely because of the people's cultural understanding of them. There are many instances in which the knowledge anthropologists have gained of people's understandings of their environments would support the view (widely held among environmentalists) that the best way of protecting those environments is to enable local, traditional cultures to survive. This point, and the broader but related issue of the value of cultural diversity, will be taken up later in this chapter and in Chapters 4 and 6.

It should also be said that some environmental organizations have been sensitive to cultural differences. From 1986, the World

Wide Fund for Nature (WWF) ran a campaign to promote environmental awareness through diverse religious doctrines. Leaders of five world religions, Buddhism, Christianity, Hinduism, Islam and Judaism, met in Assisi to declare their commitment to conservation (WWF 1986, Beyer 1994: 209). Within two years, Baha'i and Sikh leaders had also joined the initiative (WWF 1988). On a more local level, the Royal Society for the Protection of Birds (RSPB) has initiated several conservation programmes in West Africa, working with local communities in Nigeria to protect wetlands (Stowe and Coulthard 1990), and in Ghana to replace the traditional trapping of terns for sport (and, to a lesser extent, food) with less destructive ways of appreciating birds (see Everett et al. 1987). In Sierra Leone, they initiated a scheme to protect the bird life of the Gola Forest, and selected the endangered species *Picathartes gymnocephalus* as its central focus. This proved an important step in winning the support of the local populations, for whom this bird has a special symbolic significance (Richards 1992a: 151).

The application of ethnoecological knowledge for environmental benefit is thus already a reality and is likely to become more widespread, but it needs to be dissociated from the constructivist model of culture, which its analysis by anthropologists has helped to foster. The recognition that different cultural models of the environment exist, and that an understanding of them is useful in securing environmental protection, does not depend on the assumption that the environment is culturally determined through cognitive construction. If the environment were nothing more than a cognitive construct, we could change it by constructing different truths, different meanings; we could will environmental dangers out of existence through thought alone. Thus, the constructivist model is incompatible with environmental activism, which depends on the recognition of an independent reality that can be modified by human actions. Constructivism implies that we can mend the 'hole' in the ozone layer by thinking it out of existence. Activism depends on the assumption that it exists independently of our thoughts and therefore presents a real threat to the physical state of the Earth and its inhabitants.

Thus, neither the view that environments determine cultures, nor the view that cultures determine environments, offers a sound basis for arguing that cultural theory is a valuable resource for the environmentalist cause. On the other hand, the recognition that

CULTURE AND ECOLOGY

environmental knowledge varies among cultures, and the description and analysis of this diversity, are important resources in the quest for environmental protection and improvement. Does this mean that anthropology's contribution to environmental discourse is destined to be one of fact rather than theory; one of providing the ethnographic knowledge to enable environmental planners and activists to operate effectively in a range of cultures? Or is a theory of culture's role in human–environment relations still possible? This question can only be answered by addressing directly the logical difficulties posed by the constructivist model, and an appropriate way of doing this is to examine approaches which, either intentionally or by default, leave culture out of the human–environment relationship.

LEAVING CULTURE OUT

Probably no anthropologist writing today would describe the relationship between human beings and their environments as deterministic, in either direction. Instead of either shaping or being shaped by environmental factors, human beings are understood to interact with their environments in mutually constitutive ways. Within this broad approach, two models in particular have important implications for cultural theory: first, the ecosystem model, which has been prominent in ecological anthropology since the late 1960s, and second, the concept of direct perception, which has entered anthropological thought from psychology only during the past five years or so.

The ecosystem approach

The interactive nature of the relationship between human beings and their environment is often expressed through the idea of an 'ecosystem' (Geertz 1963, Rappaport 1967, 1971) or 'ecological system' (Hardesty 1977, Burnham and Ellen 1979). The concept was introduced into biology in the 1930s and 1940s through the work of Tansley, and further established through the work of Odum (1953) and others.[5] Various definitions of 'ecosystem' have been proposed. Some of these stress their bounded nature: 'the total of living organisms and non-living substances bound together in material exchanges within some demarcated portion of the biosphere' (Rappaport 1971: 238). Others focus on the nature of the exchanges among components: 'a dynamic set of relationships between living and non-living things through which energy flows and materials cycle' (Hardesty 1977: 14). Studies of ecosystems have tended to focus on their internal operation, and in particular on the process of 'homeostasis', the maintenance of stability through the exchange of matter and energy among the participating organisms and their physical environment (see Ellen 1982: 74).

Probably the most important contribution of the ecosystem model, both in biology and in anthropology, was the promotion of an holistic approach to the study of organisms in their environments. Instead of seeking single environmental causes for specific physical and behavioural traits, analysts shifted their attention to the total complex of relationships in which organisms engage. The model is, to some extent, incompatible with the study of a single species, since its emphasis is explicitly non-specific; its role in analysis is to elucidate the nature of relationships among a complex of organisms and other factors. A focus on one species runs the risk of losing the holistic perspective which the ecosystem model provides.

Nevertheless, anthropologists adapted the model to their own needs by conceptualizing human populations as participants in ecosystems, and by describing the ecosystemic relationships in which those populations engage. 'A generation of anthropologists, trained in ecology and systems theory, went to the field to measure the flow of energy through the trophic levels of the ecosystems of which humans were but a part' (Moran 1990: 13). The techniques employed in this kind of study enabled anthropologists to measure, in quite precise terms, the material consequences of economic activities (see, for instance, Lee 1969), generating much more accurate assessments than had previously been possible, of the efficiency of various subsistence systems (Ellen 1990: 191). Discussion of the ecosystem approach within anthropology has focused on several issues, including the problems of delineating the boundaries of ecosystems (Ellen 1990: 192–6), the dangers of assuming that ecosystems are in balance (Vayda and McCay 1975) and – the issue of concern here – the role of culture in the ecosystems model.

The ecosystem approach helped to marginalize the concept of culture in several ways. As Ellen (1982: 76) and Moran (1990: 3) remarked, the adoption of the ecosystem model was part of a reaction, within anthropology, against what were seen as the problematic aspects of the concept of culture. The inability of cultural determinism to address ecological relations was becoming clear, and the image of cultures as closed systems was everywhere denied by evidence of trading networks and other forms of exchange which spanned the boundaries between cultures. The ecosystem model provided a way of reclaiming the external relations of human societies as a respectable field of study, and maintained an emphasis on ecology, as distinct from ethnoecology.

Until the adoption of the ecosystem approach, cultures and cultural features had been the principal units of analysis and objects of explanation in ecological anthropology. The study of ecosystems required anthropologists to focus on the units that participate in ecosystems. As Rappaport and others have pointed out, cultures do not engage in ecological relations: 'Cultures may induce people to polish their fingernails, but food supplies do not limit them, disease does not debilitate them, nor do predators feed on them' (Rappaport 1969: 185). These things happen to populations, which in turn prey upon and affect the survival opportunities of other populations. Thus human populations, occupying ecological niches, became the principal units of analysis, and cultural ecology gave way to a broader human ecology.

That a concept of culture should be marginal to the study of ecosystems is to be expected, given that the model was developed and refined by biologists, through the study of organisms which, it was generally assumed, did not possess culture. When the model was adopted into anthropology, it arrived without a cultural component, and with no obvious niche into which culture might fit. Insofar as the ecosystem model was considered adequate for understanding human ecology, it appeared to suggest that culture was redundant to such an understanding. This needs to be qualified, however, for although the study of ecosystems might logically appear to squeeze culture out of the reckoning, this has been vigorously denied by some anthropologists. Their arguments hinge on the questions of what culture is understood to mean, and what constitutes an adequate or appropriate understanding of human ecology.

First there is the argument that culture is present in the ecosystem model in any case, as part of the human contribution to the operation of the system. All organisms have 'distinctive means by which they maintain a common set of material relations within the ecosystem in which they participate' (Rappaport 1971: 238). Culture constitutes part of the distinctive means employed by human beings. The mechanisms identified by anthropologists as constituting human participation in ecosystems usually take the form of activities or patterns of activity, such as household organization and land tenure (Netting 1969), seasonal patterns of subsistence and consumption (Lee 1969) and inter-group trading relations (Ellen 1990). Within the ecosystem model, human activities are seen as equivalent to the behaviour of non-human animals:

> The slaughter and consumption of a deer by a lion ... and by hunters armed with bows and arrows or shotguns ... are, ecologically speaking, transactions of the same general type. It does not, from the ecosystemic point of view, matter that the behaviour of the men is cultural and the behaviour of the lion is not.
>
> (Rappaport 1971: 242)

Before the 1960s, few anthropologists would have disputed that activities are cultural phenomena, but when the concept of culture was narrowed down in order to give it greater analytical power, actions and patterns of action were excluded. Anthropologists who studied ecosystems were able to claim that they incorporated culture into their models because they continued to use a broad concept of culture, while many of their colleagues were confining the term to what people hold in their minds. What was marginalized in the ecosystem approach was this modified concept of culture, consisting of the knowledge, thoughts and feelings through which people understand their world and which guide their actions.

This is not the full story, however, for it has also been argued that the ecosystem approach can and should incorporate people's understanding of the environment (Rappaport 1969: 186; 1971). Ellen pointed out that some formulations of 'ecosystem' include information as an essential component, alongside matter and energy (Ellen 1982: 74). Organisms acquire information, from their environment and from each other, which determines or guides their ecological activities. Culture consists of information acquired by human beings through their experience of their environment and through their communication with each other, and forms 'a significant part of the complex mechanism producing the actual physical behaviour by which ecological relations are directly manipulated' (Ellen 1982: 206; cf. Vayda and Rappaport 1968). The ecological function of culture is thus similar to that of other forms of information, such as sensory information to which organisms respond through reflex behaviour, and genetic information transmitted chemically. In this formulation, the dam-building programme of the beaver and the dam-building instructions drawn up by an engineer are ecologically equivalent.

But to establish that culture is part of the mechanism that produces human ecological activities is not, in itself, sufficient justification for incorporating it into the study of ecosystems. The study of non-human animals again provides an appropriate analogy. Ecologists may assume that the beavers' dam-building programmes are contained in their genes, but they do not feel compelled to incorporate genetics into their understanding of beaver ecology; genetics and ecology remain separate fields of study. The question is, why should human ecology require an understanding of the mechanisms that produce ecological behaviour, while ecology in general does not? Ellen's answer was that if we confine our observations to physical behaviour, and fail to include information on people's knowledge and decision-making processes, then we can produce only mechanistic explanations which prevent us from understanding 'what is distinctively human about human ecology' (Ellen 1982: 233–4). Culture, presumably, is what Ellen saw as distinctively human; by taking culture into account, we prevent human ecology from dissolving into a general ecology. For this very reason, the inclusion of culture represents a deviation from a strict ecosystem model.

There is no doubt that the ecosystem approach developed by ecologists in the 1940s and 1950s, and adopted into anthropology in the 1960s, held no place for an understanding of culture in its narrower sense – people's thoughts, feelings and knowledge about the world. But what emerged, after an initial burst of enthusiasm for studies of energy flows and homeostatic processes, was a human ecology which incorporates both people's ecological activities and their understanding of the world, and which seeks to understand the relationship between these two spheres. There are sound practical reasons why this approach offers a potentially valuable contribution to environmental discourse. I shall return to this point after discussing the second approach, which leaves culture out of an understanding of human ecology.

Direct perception

As indicated in the discussion of ethnoecology (above), the study of diverse ways of understanding the world has been informed by the constructivist model of culture, the view that people define or impose meaning on the world through cognitive processes. What makes this model unsuitable for human ecology is that it reduces the environment to a cultural construct; it implies that the real, unconstructed world is unknowable or at least has no inherent meaning (Ingold 1992a: 39). Human ecology is concerned with the ways human populations interact with their environments, but the constructivist model of culture implies that there is nothing recognizable or meaningful for people to interact with, and leaves us with what Steward called 'the fruitless assumption that culture comes from culture' (Steward 1955: 36). It has been suggested that the root of this difficulty is a confusion between perception and interpretation. Most anthropologists refer to perceptions and interpretations of the environment as if they are phenomena of the same kind, both 'constructed'. Ingold argued that this creates a disjunction, 'an absolute barrier' between the environment itself and people's perceptions of it (Ingold 1992a: 52); there is no route through which information can flow from the real world to the perceived world.

Drawing on the work of Gibson (1979, 1982), Ingold has suggested that perception should be seen as a different kind of phenomenon from interpretation. People do not need to construct reality in order to perceive it; rather, we perceive it directly, through our active involvement in it. Similarly, we do not need to know the world in order to act in it; rather, we come to know it through our actions, by making use of what our environment offers us, its 'affordances' (Ingold 1992a: 42 ff.). Perception is the creation of knowledge through action; the world we perceive comes into being as we act in it (Ingold 1991: 16). This is a persuasive argument, not only because it appears to eliminate the fundamental difficulty of the constructivist approach – that it renders the real world meaningless – but also because it is intuitively satisfying. It accords well with everyday life, which for most of us, I suggest, is more a 'continuous flow of lived-through experience' (Giddens 1976: 74), than a design-and-build exercise. But where does this leave the role of culture in human ecology? For Ingold, 'Culture is a framework not for perceiving the world, but for *interpreting* it to oneself and others' (1992a: 53, emphasis given). The process of interacting with the environment entails perception, but it does not entail interpretation. Culture can therefore be left out of the ecological equation; it does not mediate between human beings and their environment, and therefore need not be taken account of in an analysis of that relationship.

It is important to understand the implications of what Ingold is suggesting, not only for human ecology, but also for cultural theory. He is not only defining ecological relations in such a way that they exclude culture, he is also defining culture in such a way that it excludes much of what anthropologists have hitherto taken to be cultural. In Ingold's formulation, culture does not consist of 'whatever it is one has to know or believe' (Goodenough 1957: 167), but of means for making knowledge explicit, both to oneself and to others (Ingold 1992a: 52). Anthropologists might raise many objections to this. I shall confine my comments to one of the more obvious.

It may be acceptable to posit a distinction in theory between perception and interpretation, to suggest that they are different mental processes; indeed, social scientists and psychologists routinely use these terms to identify broad areas of mental activity. But it is a different matter to suggest that such a distinction might form the basis of key analytical concepts such as culture. This would require us to distinguish empirically between perception and interpretation, to differentiate between knowledge which is derived from people's perceptions of their environment and that which is derived from their (or others') interpretations of it. I suspect that this is impossible, using the research methods available to social scientists,[6] in which case it would also become impossible to use culture as an analytical concept.

BRINGING CULTURE BACK IN

The purpose of the preceding discussion is to work towards a theory of culture's role in human–environment relations, which both avoids the difficulties anthropologists have experienced in the past, and establishes the nature of anthropology's potential contribution to environmental discourse. In Chapter 1, I deliberately avoided giving a preferred definition of culture in order not to prejudge the discussion in this chapter. It is now appropriate to consider how culture and its ecological role might usefully be conceptualized.

Redefining culture

As indicated in Chapter 1, the distinction between people's activities and discernible patterns of action on the one hand, and what they are assumed to hold in their minds on the other, has been a central feature of post-structuralist anthropology. It has proved an extremely valuable analytical device, in that it has enabled anthropologists to explore the relationship between what people do and say and what they know, think and feel. Before the distinction was made, there was a tendency for analyses to imply that cultural norms, for example, unproblematically determine what people do, thus denying the element of choice which is considered essential to the concept of action. There was no satisfactory way of explaining how patterns of action were generated; of explaining why, for instance, if all the members of a society regard marriage with a cousin as the ideal, only a small percentage actually marry their cousins. The distinction between people's actions and what they hold in their minds made choice available for investigation. It became possible to show, for instance, how patterns of action are produced by political strategies which may contradict the norms that are held to govern behaviour (Holy 1979), and to demonstrate that the recognized pattern of kinship relations in a community can be shaped by people's economic activities (Leach 1961). Rather than assuming that different perspectives on the world give rise unproblematically to different ways of doing things, anthropologists have shown that similar patterns of action can co-exist with diverse ways of thinking (Keesing 1970). The distinction has proved sufficiently useful that I would wish to retain it, and to use the term 'culture', as it has been used by many anthropologists in recent decades, to refer to what exists in people's minds.

However, I would also wish to depart from the recent orthodoxy in cultural theory and suggest, agreeing in part with Ingold, that not everything that exists in people's minds is 'constructed'. At least some of what we know, think and feel about the world comes to us directly through our experience, in the form of discovered meanings. Where I differ from Ingold's view is in insisting that these meanings, these 'perceptions', are part of culture. Meanings vary between cultures (in the more specific sense of the term) because those who hold them engage with the world in different ways; they act differently within it. Thus, while an Icelandic fisherman comes to know whales as an economic resource (Einarsson 1993), a whale-watching tourist might come to know them as a source of wonder and delight. Neither of these understandings is more accurate than the other. They derive from diverse experiences, generated through action, of what whales have to offer.

The role of culture in human–environment relations can now be clarified. Because culture consists of perceptions as well as interpretations, it does not create a barrier between ourselves and the 'real' world, but rather situates us within the world. It is indeed the case that we could not survive without it, for it is what makes the world meaningful to us. It is through culture that we identify objects as food or not food, sensations as pain or pleasure, emotions as fear or contentment. By enabling us to make these distinctions, culture makes possible the practical activities that ensure our survival. It is also through culture that we reflect on our actions and experiences, describe them to others and plan future courses of action.

The suggestion that culture is indivisible, that it encompasses all understanding, whether derived from perception or from interpretation, might be seen as generating even greater heresies than the suggestion that culture should be excluded from ecological analysis. First, it implies that culture is not wholly social in origin. That culture consists of socially produced knowledge has been taken more or less for granted by many anthropologists, but the suggestion that culture should include meanings that flow directly from our experience in the world implies that a social environment is not necessary for culture to exist. Second, it might be seen as blurring the distinction between human and non-human. Ingold pointed out that, in developing his model of direct perception, Gibson stressed the continuities between humans and other animals:

> If perception is a matter of discovering meanings rather than adding them on through some kind of cognitive processing, then the apparently unique cognitive capacities of humans ... will not lead them to perceive their environments in a radically distinct way from other animals.
>
> (Ingold 1992a: 52)

If culture is generated through perception as well as interpretation, then are we not led to the conclusion that it is not an exclusively human phenomenon? I find this conclusion anything but heretical; indeed, the position that human beings are unique in possessing culture has always seemed an absurd denial both of experience and of logic.

As we learn more about both human and non-human animals, it becomes increasingly difficult to sustain the view that culture is uniquely human (cf. Eckersley 1992: 50). Any attempt to define culture in a way that excludes perception, and to see it as a framework only for interpreting and sharing knowledge, seems like a last-ditch effort to hang on to its distinctively human status. If so, it is unlikely to succeed, for knowledge-sharing techniques among other animals are well known. Many species have been shown to educate their young on how to obtain food. Honey bees dance on their return to the colony, to indicate the location of a source of nectar, and gazelles similarly use a series of signals to inform members of their herd where food is located (Armen 1976: 64–5). Knowledge sharing is also common between species. Animals of different species stay together in order to benefit from each other's knowledge of both food sources and danger (Rasa 1985: 24–5). Human beings in tropical regions allow the honey guide bird to show them the way to wild bees' nests, and the bird in turn benefits from the human beings' ability to extract the honey. Chimpanzees have been taught American Sign Language (Gardner et al. 1989) and have then taught it to each other (Fouts et al. 1989). I suggest that we abandon any attempt to claim culture as a uniquely human characteristic, and with it the pretence that human beings are 'different' in a way that sets them significantly apart from the rest of the animal kingdom. Human beings are different in the sense that any species is different from the rest, in having its own way of living in the world and its own distinctive impact on the world.

Culture and environmentalism

If culture is the mechanism that situates us within the world and enables us to interact with it, then it is undoubtedly an important component of human–environment relations, perhaps the most important. But it remains the case that at least one influential approach to the study of human ecology, the ecosystem model, when strictly applied, excludes consideration of culture. This is be cause culture is an unobservable component of human–environment relations, and the ecosystem model only takes into account phenomena which, it is assumed, can be treated as more or less observable: people's activities and their environmental consequences. In order to argue that culture should be included in an understanding of human ecology, we need to establish that the ecosystem model on its own is inadequate.

Some of the attempts to do this in the past have been unconvincing. The argument that the inclusion of culture enables us to understand what is distinctively human about human ecology (Ellen 1982: 234) collapses if we accept that culture itself is not distinctively human. And the suggestion that its inclusion 'at least enriches our understanding' of material relations (Rappaport 1969: 186) is based on a rather personal assessment of what constitutes a rich understanding. The question is, while it remains possible to understand the participation of human populations in ecosystems without taking into account how those people perceive and interpret the world, are there good reasons for going beyond this level of understanding? If the purpose of the analysis is purely academic, the question of whether or not to include culture depends on the personal interests and preferences of the analyst. There are no analytical imperatives which require a certain depth or richness of understanding.

Once the analysis is given a practical purpose – to solve a particular problem, for instance, or to find new ways of organizing society – then the adequacy of the approach is judged, not in terms of the analyst's personal preferences, but in terms of what is necessary to effect a solution. Environmental discourse forms an appropriate context in which to argue that certain types of approaches to the understanding of human ecology are more or less adequate. If we are concerned with how to solve problems or avoid crises, we may need to understand more than if we want to know how an ecosystem operates. In this context, Rappaport's argument for the inclusion of culture in the study of human ecology becomes particularly important (Rappaport 1968, 1971). He suggested that a principal reason for including people's understanding of the world in a study of their ecological relations is to determine whether or not their knowledge is ecologically appropriate, whether it is adaptive or maladaptive (Rappaport 1971: 261–2). To use the more fashionable (but still contentious) term, it will establish whether or not particular knowledge is ecologically *sustainable*. By analysing the relationship between people's cultures (their ways of perceiving and interpreting the world) and the ecological impacts of their activities, we might be able to understand which cultures, and which cultural features, are ecologically sustainable, and which are not. Thus cultural theory has the potential to become 'part of our own adaptation, our own means for perpetuating ourselves and preserving those living systems to which we remain indissolubly bound and upon which we continue to be utterly dependent' (Rappaport 1971: 264). It is in this sense that anthropology, as the study of human ecology, could help us to define our environmental responsibilities and work towards their fulfilment.

Environmentalism as a cultural perspective

In the previous chapter I identified a second way in which anthropology might contribute to environmental discourse, by suggesting that anthropologists, like other social scientists, might become theorists of environmentalism. I also suggested that a distinctively anthropological way of doing this would be to treat it as a cultural phenomenon, and it is now possible to give a clearer indication of what is meant by this. The discussion in both chapters has identified three key features of culture as it is defined here. First, culture exists in people's minds and is expressed through what they say and do. Second, culture consists of perceptions and interpretations. Together, these encompass the full range of emotions, assumptions, values, facts, ideas, norms, theories, and so on, through which people make sense of their experience. Third, culture is the mechanism through which human beings (and, I would argue, other species as well) interact with their environments. Environmentalism was identified in Chapter 1 as a concern to protect the environment through human responsibility and effort. As such, I suggested, it is unambiguously a part of culture, part of the way in which people understand the world and their place within it. I also suggested that it be seen as a type of 'cultural perspective', and it is appropriate now to explain what is meant by this.

A distinction was made in Chapter 1 between culture in its general sense, in which it is a universal component of human experience, and 'cultures', as specific sets of assumptions, values, ideas, norms, and so on, that are associated with particular categories of people. In this sense, we speak of 'American culture', as the set of cultural phenomena broadly shared by residents of the United States or recognized by them as their own, and of 'Irish-American culture' as the set of cultural things shared by those members of that population who consider themselves Irish as well as American. However, it is often with considerable reservations that anthropologists describe a culture as 'shared', for it is obvious that American culture encompasses countless different ways of perceiving and interpreting the world: countless sets of assumptions, values and norms, many of which are incompatible with each other. This kind of complexity is not confined to industrial society. There are often many diverse ways of understanding the world even within a small village community. In one of the Kenyan villages where I conducted fieldwork in the late 1970s, some of the 700 or so inhabitants accepted the teachings of the Anglican Church, some believed that their fortunes were influenced by the spirits of their ancestors, and others regarded both the Anglican teachings and beliefs in ancestral spirits as the work of the Devil. Some valued a western-style education and employment in a town as the surest way of improving the quality of their lives; others shunned modernity as superficial and unsatisfying compared with a traditional life of subsistence farming in the context of a supportive kin group (see Chapter 4, below).

These distinct ways of seeing the world, which can be identified within a single culture, and which carry different implications for action, are what I understand as cultural perspectives. Unlike whole cultures, cultural perspectives can be expected to be more or less internally consistent, in that their different elements – assumptions, values, explanations, norms – will tend not to contradict each other. This is because, whereas the many different components of a culture are distributed throughout the members of a society, a perspective is normally held in its entirety by the same individual.[7] The relationship between cultural perspectives and cultures in everyday discourse is ambiguous. There are many circumstances in which cultural identities – 'British', 'American', 'Kikuyu' – are assumed to imply a certain way of understanding the world and acting within it. But there are also many circumstances in which such identities are understood to encompass a plurality of perspectives. I am suggesting that, for analytical purposes, it is useful to distinguish cultures from cultural perspectives. This is not only because what we might want to identify as a single culture can include many different perspectives. It is also because cultural perspectives are not necessarily confined within cultures. People who hold a Christian perspective, for instance, belong to many cultures, as do pacifists, democrats and environmentalists.

The freeing of cultural perspectives from the confines of particular cultures is a consequence of globalization, and more will be said about it in Chapter 5. For the moment, I simply want to establish that 'environmentalism' can be seen as identifying a type of cultural perspective, in which a concern to protect the environment through human responsibility is a central guiding principle. I suggest that this is a distinctively anthropological way of understanding environmentalism which can complement the approaches offered by other disciplines. In order to establish this, it is necessary to understand how environmentalism has been analysed by other social scientists. This is the task for the next chapter.

3

ENVIRONMENTALISM IN SOCIAL SCIENCE

> My aim is ... to ask whether sociological analysis leads us
> to expect the wrong things from ecological arguments.
>
> (Scott 1990: 81)

The products and by-products of environmentalist thought are all
around us. The campaign literature of environmental groups is
delivered to thousands of homes. Green slogans compete for our
attention from the packages on supermarket shelves. Television
programmes inform us about the threats of global warming, the
intimate details of the lives of plants and animals, the deficiencies
of government policies on energy and transport. The advertise-
ments that interrupt those programmes try to entice us with green
images. Bookshelves and catalogues display a bewildering array of
environmental literature, from official reports to fictional adven-
tures.[1] Development projects are subjected to environmental
assessments, companies and government departments to environmental audits, and the curricula of schools and colleges have been
invaded by courses on environmental science, law, politics and
management.

As the products of environmentalism have multiplied, so have
the attempts to describe and understand it. My task in this chapter
is less daunting; it is to present an analysis of the analyses, or
rather of some of them, in order to argue that an approach from
the viewpoint of cultural theory is both possible and useful. This
task is complex enough, however. In the 1970s, when public
interest in environmental issues was beginning to have significant
political impacts, the relevant body of social scientific literature
was small and relatively easy to digest because it focused on a few
key areas: changes in public values (Cotgrove and Duff 1980), the

69

social bases of environmental concern (Van Liere and Dunlap 1980) and pressure group politics (Kimber and Richardson 1974). In the mid-1990s it is enormous, diverse and extremely complex. The task of analysing it is made more difficult (but also more interesting) by the fact that the boundary between advocacy and analysis is often difficult to detect. In other words, social scientific studies of environmentalism cannot always be distinguished from literature advocating environmentalist points of view.[2] This is to be expected, for several reasons.

First, ideas are refined and advanced through critical analysis, so anyone wishing to further environmentalist thought is likely to do so through an analysis of existing ideas. In this sense, authors who see themselves primarily as advocates have also to be analysts in order to substantiate their views and give them credibility. Second, social scientists who become interested in environmentalism are often motivated by their own concerns for the environment and a personal desire to contribute to environmental discourse. Thus some authors who regard themselves, or may be seen by others, primarily as analysts use their research to advance or defend particular environmentalist perspectives (for instance, Eckersley 1992), or to suggest how environmentalist ideas might be made more practicable (Paehlke 1989, Goodin 1992). Finally, in environmentalism we are dealing with a part of culture and, as argued in Chapter 1, culture is both the object of our analyses and a phenomenon in whose creation we inevitably participate, even as we analyse it. In this sense it is impossible for analysts of culture, even if their motives are purely academic, not to contribute in some way to the development of the object being analysed.

In order to argue that cultural theory offers a distinctive way of analysing environmentalism, I need to compare it with other social scientific projects of the same kind; in other words, those analyses which have treated environmentalism itself as an object of study, and which have addressed questions about its nature. Sociology and political science have been the leading disciplines in this enterprise, and studies which fall within these fields form a central focus of discussion in this chapter. But, as was pointed out in Chapter 1, the boundaries among the social sciences are, to say the least, blurred, and some of them become indistinguishable when the veneer of specialist terminologies is chipped away. In what follows, academic niches are not important. Having said this, there is one major field of analysis which should at least be mentioned if I am to avoid the accusation of having ignored much of what seems relevant: environmental economics, whose contribution to environmental discourse has received more public attention than those of the other social sciences.

ENVIRONMENTAL ECONOMICS

Environmental economics is a rapidly growing field which encompasses several schools of thought, though it tends to be identified (as does economics in general) with the most influential of these, the neoclassical tradition.[3] This approach is primarily concerned with ways of enabling environmental values to be taken into account in economic activity. This has meant exploring techniques for assigning measurable values to environmental benefits, such as clean air, unpolluted rivers, pleasant landscapes and wildlife, and incorporating them into costing and pricing procedures, such as cost-benefit analyses and fiscal practices. Some of these techniques were already being developed by the early 1970s (see, for instance, Pearce 1972, 1974, Krutilla and Cicchetti 1972), but they have come to public attention only during the past ten years or so, as ways of making industrial economies sustainable have become central to environmental discourse. They have met with considerable criticism, not only from conservationists who have argued that environmental benefits are often seen as priceless, and that assigning monetary values to things such as pleasant landscapes and wildlife can only serve to undervalue them, but also from economists who have explored the limitations of the neoclassical model (Jacobs 1991, 1994) and argued that its valuation techniques are fundamentally unsound (Bowers 1990, Clift 1994). In response to these criticisms, neoclassical environmental economists have pointed out that environmental goods are assigned implicit values in much of what we do (Pearce 1991: 2–6), and that it is the failure to make these values explicit that has effectively undervalued the environment; things that are implicitly regarded as priceless are often treated as worthless in economic decision making.

Economists have been the most conspicuous social scientists to participate in environmental discourse because, on the whole, they have been the only ones to whom policy makers in industrial societies have been prepared to listen. Indeed, politicians throughout the industrial world have actively sought the advice of economists, while specialists in other disciplines have struggled to demonstrate the value of their skills. It is the quality that makes economics attractive to politicians which effectively makes it marginal to the discussion in this chapter. Economics, as Simmons has pointed out, is about means rather than ends. Economists are technicians, who explain how goals might be achieved, while supposedly remaining indifferent to the goals themselves (Simmons 1993: 44). This indifference to goals makes economics a favoured political tool. Economists can be called upon to examine how predefined political goals might be achieved, in the knowledge that they will not question the goals themselves. Sociology and political science are unpopular with politicians for precisely the converse reason: their practitioners see it as their role to question, not only political goals, but also the values and assumptions from which those goals are derived. While sociology and political science (and, for similar reasons, cultural anthropology) are inherently subversive, economics, at least in its neoclassical form, cannot be.

Environmentalism is about goals as well as means; it is about protecting the environment through human activity. As the brief summary above indicates, economics can be (and has been) enlisted to examine how this goal might be achieved, to consider what its achievement might mean in practical terms (see Pearce *et al.* 1989, Pearce, D. 1991), but it cannot provide an analysis of environmentalism itself, since this means examining the goals of environmentalism, the interpretations of reality from which those goals are derived, and, quite possibly, the perceptions which accompany environmentalist interpretations of the world. So while the contribution of economists to environmental discourse has been conspicuous, it has not enabled them to become theorists of environmentalism, since this is not the nature of their enquiry.

In fact the role of economics in environmental discourse is similar to that identified in the previous chapter for anthropology, as the study of human ecology. This is not surprising, given that economy and ecology both embody the material relations between human beings and their environments, and that the two concepts have been virtually inseparable in the work of some anthropologists (see, for instance, Sahlins 1972). It was suggested in the previous chapter that, by studying the relationship between people's understanding of the world and the ecological impacts of their activities, it might be possible to assess whether or not particular cultural perspectives are ecologically sustainable. Such knowledge could then be applied in a search for more sustainable ways of living (cf. Rappaport 1971: 264). This kind of role for anthropology would be a technical one, which would help to establish whether the means for achieving a sustainable way of living were available, without examining the goal itself. It would thus parallel the role of environmental economics, which considers ways of achieving environmentalist goals through economic activity, but does not analyse those goals.

ENVIRONMENTALISM IN SOCIAL AND POLITICAL THEORY

When scientists encounter a new object, they try to establish its place in the order of things by assessing its characteristics in terms of what is known and familiar. Is it genuinely new, or merely masquerading in new attire? Does it represent a new class of objects and, if so, is there perhaps more than one kind of it? How is it related to objects in the known universe? When environmentalism first gripped the public imagination in the 1960s and early 1970s,[4] and when, contrary to the expectations of some analysts (Bowman 1975: 93; Sandbach 1980: 1), it became clear that it was not going to go away, social scientists were faced with the problem of how to characterize it. Did it fit a known pattern of social events, or did it represent a genuinely new way of thinking and acting? Did it break the mould of traditional political allegiances or merely reproduce them in a new idiom? Was it an internally homogenous category, or was there more than one kind of environmentalism? The answers to these questions have formed the nexus of a debate within social science about the nature of environmentalism; they also set the agenda for the following discussion. The most pervasive points of argument in the debate have been the identification of two kinds of environmentalism, the status of environmentalism as a (new) social movement and as a political ideology, and the relationship of environmentalism to established cleavages in politics. I begin with the issue of two environmentalisms since this, for some analysts, is fundamental to the other issues.

Two environmentalisms

It appears that there have always been two environmentalisms, or at least since the beginning of this century when the battle of words between Muir and Pinchot, over the damming of a river in Yosemite National Park, laid the foundations of a split between the 'conservationists' and the 'preservationists' (see Norton 1991: 6–9). While conservationists wished to protect nature as a resource for human use, preservationists recognized a moral obligation towards nature itself and wished to protect it *from* human use. This distinction was easy to recognize because it was played out in action – people took sides – but the current environmental debate, throughout its development during the past thirty years or so, appears to have been characterized by less distinct and more variable cleavages. The result is that, while analysts have continued to recognize two environmentalisms, they have not always been the same two.

The most pervasive distinction in the literature is between an environmentalism which can be accommodated within the structures of contemporary industrial society and one which demands fundamental change to those structures (Milbrath 1984: 72). In this sense it is useful to speak of the two environmentalisms as 'conservative' and 'radical'; it is the nature of the conservatism and radicalism that appears to shift, often in quite subtle ways, from one analytical perspective to another, or even within a single analysis. Cotgrove made a distinction between those environmentalists (including conservationists *and* preservationists) whose policies offer no challenge to the dominant economic value system, and those who would wish to replace economic goals with 'welfare values which are incompatible with or in conflict with purely economic ends' (Cotgrove 1976: 24). In this formulation, the distinction is between different evaluations of the economic *vis-à-vis* other kinds of value. But he also followed Kruse (1974) in describing the division between two environmentalisms in terms of evaluations of technology; a faith in human ability to overcome environmental problems as opposed to a conviction that human ingenuity is subject to limits imposed by nature (Cotgrove 1976: 25). He offered yet another variation, a distinction between environmentalists who preach an holistic message based on ecological principles, and those who advocate a 'piece-meal tinkering' with industrial processes to bring about environmental improvements. The former is revolutionary and millenarian, the latter is reformist (Cotgrove 1976: 25). A later version of the distinction identifies 'catastrophists' as those who consider industrialization *per se* to be the cause of environmental breakdown, and 'cornucopians', who blame 'the exploitative and predatory nature of capitalism' (Cotgrove 1982: 7). In each case, the distinction is between a more radical and a more conservative environmentalism, but the idiom in which the conservatism and radicalism are expressed changes from one formulation to the next.

Cotgrove's second formulation is similar to O'Riordan's distinction between the 'technocentric' and 'ecocentric' forms of environmentalism (O'Riordan 1981 [1976]: 1–19). Technocentrists have faith in technology and assume that humankind is in control. They may wish to make industrial society more environmentally benign, through changes in policy and practice, but they do not question the goals of industrial development, nor the values which drive it; they thus represent a conservative form of environmentalism. Ecocentrists see humankind as subject to, rather than in control of, nature. They preach humility towards the natural world and respect for its processes and products. The practical implications of this view include low-impact technology and self-reliance, which could not be achieved to any significant degree without a radical overhaul of the foundations of industrial society.

An important component of both Cotgrove's and O'Riordan's conceptualization of the division was the observation that people hold different understandings and evaluations of science. Sandbach brought this into focus by distinguishing between an environmentalism which seeks to influence economic and technological change by presenting scientific arguments based on the analysis of ecological systems, and one which questions whether science itself is compatible with humanistic values (Sandbach 1980: 21–2). But in this formulation, ecology seems to have changed sides. Both Cotgrove and O'Riordan observed that an holistic understanding of ecology was the inspiration for the more radical mode, whereas for Sandbach it formed the rational basis of conservative environmentalism. This apparent contradiction shows how ecology, as a body of scientific knowledge, is amenable to different interpretations, and therefore plays a part in the pursuit of diverse, often contradictory, objectives.[5] It is seen both as a route through which human management of the environment can be improved, and as the basis for an alternative vision of our relationship with the rest of the natural world. Just as the complex structure of the eye, for one analyst, proves the existence of a divine creator, and for another denies it (Dawkins 1986: 5), so a knowledge of ecology leads some to a greater faith in our ability to control natural processes, while for others, like Douglas Adams' 'Total Perspective Vortex', it creates a sense of our relative insignificance in the natural order.[6]

The distinctions considered so far refer to environmentalism as it was understood by analysts before 1980. In more recent analyses the division into two environmentalisms has persisted, but the terminology used does not sit easily upon the earlier interpretations. Cotgrove, O'Riordan and Sandbach all referred explicitly to types of environmentalism. Dobson, rather confusingly in the context of this discussion, used the term 'environmentalism' to refer to just one side of the distinction; the more conservative mode, green with a small 'g', which assumes that the environment is a resource for human use, manageable through human ingenuity, and that environmental problems can therefore be solved 'without fundamental changes in present values or patterns of production and consumption' (Dobson 1990: 13). 'Ecologism', the contrasting radical mode (Green with a capital 'G'), is based on the understanding that the environment has a value of its own, independent of its use to human beings (Dobson 1990: 15). Our proper treatment of it therefore requires a fundamental change in the way we understand our relationship with nature; it requires us to see ourselves as one element in a complex ecological system, rather than as the centre of the universe. The logic of Dobson's terminology is clear. An environment is that which surrounds, 'and can exist ... only in relation to what is surrounded' (Ingold 1993: 31; 1992a: 40). 'Environmentalism' therefore only makes sense if we assume the existence of a centre. An ecosystem is viewed as if from without, as a complex of interacting organisms and other factors. An ecological perspective has no central focus (see above, Chapter 2), and it therefore makes little sense to refer to such a perspective as 'environmentalism'. However, despite its undeniable logic, Dobson's terminology has not been widely adopted, and most analysts continue to refer to kinds of environmentalism. The substance of his distinction, on the other hand, has been recognized by other analysts as the most important cleavage in current environmentalist thought. Eckersley characterized the two perspectives as 'anthropocentric' and 'ecocentric', respectively (1992).[7]

There are both shifts and continuities in the way the two environmentalisms have been characterized by analysts over the past twenty years. The main continuity is in the distinction between a conservative and a radical environmentalism; this cleavage can be detected in each of the formulations discussed above. The main shift is in the definition of the radical perspective. In the earlier analyses, it is difficult to identify a unity underlying the various expressions of radical environmentalism, other than the fundamental nature of its challenge to industrial culture (in other words, its radicalism). In the later analyses, a more developed 'ecologism' (to use Dobson's term) or 'ecocentrism' (to use Eckersley's) has emerged. The significant cleavage is clearly identified as an opposition between a perspective which values the natural world in terms of its use to human beings, and one which sees it as having value independently of human use or, indeed, of human existence. The most obvious explanation for this emergence is that it reflects a real trend in environmentalist thought, that the 'New Ecological Paradigm' (Lowe and Rüdig 1986: 516), which was undeveloped and unarticulated in the 1970s has, during the 1980s and early 1990s, become a coherent and well-defined ideology, partly through the work of environmentalist writers and ecophilosophers (Bahro 1982, Porritt 1986, Naess 1989, Merchant 1992), and also through the work of analysts such as those discussed here, whose thoughts, as I have suggested, feed into and help to shape the object of their analyses.

It is possible to detect, in the recent analytical literature, suggestions of an alternative interpretation. Atkinson pointed out that the debate over the desire to adjust the relative importance of human beings and nature 'suffered from a lack of rootedness in social conditions and practice' (1992: 202). Norton suggested that the dichotomy between the two environmentalisms has been exaggerated by theorists and ecophilosophers. While acknowledging the long-standing presence of two distinct world views, he argued that those who openly and conspicuously espouse one or the other should be seen as 'idealized arguers' (Norton 1991: 9), whose polarized perspectives are not reproduced in environmentalist policy and practice. Instead, a consideration of what environmentalists want and do reveals a remarkable unity. Norton did not underestimate the importance of a common environmentalists' dilemma, that of how to sustain and advance a moralist perspective on nature in the face of economic and utilitarian arguments, but he pointed out that only some environmentalists opt for one or other horn of the dilemma (1991: 10); it does not, therefore, divide environmentalists into two exclusive camps. Many, perhaps most, experience it as an internal, personal quandary which influences, sometimes in one direction, sometimes the other, their everyday decisions.

Norton's analysis raises the question of whether the identification of a fundamental split between two environmentalisms, with a coherent ecocentric position emerging over the past ten years or so, represents a rather narrow characterization of environmentalism. The literature on the divisions in environmentalist thought clearly says something about environmentalism, but it does not say everything, and it may say very little, about the everyday experiences of environmental activists and policy makers. In fact, there is a huge number of empirically grounded analyses of environmental movements, groups, protests and debates, and, especially during the 1970s, studies of the social bases of environmental concern.[8] But these have failed to influence the theoretical characterization of environmentalism and have, in turn, been little influenced by it. The gap noted by Lowe and Rüdig (1986: 513), between empiricism and theorizing, still remains.

One reason for this gap may be that those writers who have emphasized the dichotomy between two environmentalisms have focused on environmentalist thought rather than environmentalist policy and practice. They have drawn their material from environmentalists' own accounts of the way they understand the world. Much of this literature is, itself, strongly analytical and therefore tends to interpret through categories and boundaries. Environmentalists, like other ideologists, have been keen to draw attention to the differences between their views and those of others, in order to establish the nature of the 'true' faith. Unless they pay attention to the empirical studies, analysts of environmentalism have no reason to suppose that the practice is significantly different from the theory.

Environmentalism as a social movement

The term 'social movement' designates the principal category into which social scientists have slotted the new phenomenon of environmentalism. As a prelude to examining how they have done this, it is helpful to consider briefly the relationship between objects and categories. When scientists of any variety allocate a new object to a familiar category, they do so as part of the process of investigating its place in the wider scheme of things, however that might be conceptualized. The initial allocation is usually provisional; a close examination of the object may indicate that it would be better placed elsewhere. A set of broad categories thus forms an analytical framework within which the specific characteristics of objects can be examined and compared. But the categories themselves are not immutable; science leaves their boundaries open to question, and, to recall Bohannan's comment (quoted in Chapter 1), one person's black box is another's field of investigation. It is the continuous examination of their contents that results in analytical categories being redefined. Categories and their contents are thus held perpetually (though not continually) in suspense.

This has been the pattern of social scientific studies of environmentalism as a social movement. Some analyses, probably the vast majority, have taken for granted the status of environmentalism as a social movement. They have used the category as a broad framework within which to examine the special features of environmentalism, such as its relationship with science and its global character (Yearley 1992a, 1994), without questioning the boundaries of the category. Rüdig *et al.* noted this tendency in British writing on social movements:

A notable feature of much of British writing is the frequent but perfunctory use of the term *social movement* without exploration of its potential connotations or efforts to set it into relevant theoretical or conceptual contexts. Typically it is undefined and is often used quite promiscuously.
(Rüdig *et al.* 1990: 125, emphasis given)

This comment is presented as a criticism, and is valid as such in the context of their discussion of social movement theory. But in broader terms, every analysis needs to leave some concepts unquestioned. If everything were open to investigation, there would be no solid ground in which to anchor an interpretation, no way of tying it to a broader field of study. Thus, in two of the early empirical studies of environmentalism, Harry *et al.* (1969) and Devall (1970) used 'social movement' as nothing more than a convenient label. It served to locate the object of analysis within a broad typology of social phenomena, in order to relieve the reader of any concern about what kind of a thing was being discussed, and direct their attention to what most interested the analysts, in these instances, the social characteristics of conservationists.

In a similar way, McCormick (1989) referred to the phenomenon whose history he was describing as 'the global environmental movement', but paid no attention to the sense in which it might be called a movement. Numerous studies have used the label in a similar way to provide a context for analyses of environmentalism in different countries (for instance, Baker 1990, Diani 1990, Dalton 1992). The label signals that, in all these cases, something similar is being discussed, and that comparisons are therefore valid and possibly interesting, but suspends interest in how that broad something might itself be understood.

According to Yearley's (1994) analysis, this use of the category is more in line with the American interpretative tradition than that established in Europe. In the American tradition, 'social movement' is typically treated as an 'empirical generalization', recognized by its broad organizational features: 'more organized than protesting crowds or mobs, less formalized than political parties and more concerted than simple social trends' (Yearley 1994: 152–3). European theorists have tended to identify social movements in terms of 'their perceived capacity for major social transformation' (Yearley 1994: 151), perceived, that is, by the analyst, who is drawn to search for signs of transformative capacity.[9] For Touraine, it is present when one class struggles against another for control of historical processes (1981: 77). For Melucci it is present when norms are contested and sources of power are challenged (1980: 204). For Eyerman and Jamison it resides in what they call 'cognitive praxis', an attempt to generate new knowledge through communicative action (1991: 45ff.). A considerable amount of interpretation of observed reality is required in order to recognize any of these criteria, leaving no clear, non-arbitrary way of identifying social movements for analysis (cf. Yearley 1994).

In addition, although it is the *capacity* to transform that defines a social movement, there is a tendency to regard as 'true' social movements only those which *actually* transform (there being no other proof of transformative capacity than actual transformation). In other words, true social movements can only be identified retrospectively, not only after a movement has been analysed, but also after its social consequences have become clear. This effectively rules out the possibility of identifying a phenomenon as a social movement as it develops and as a framework in which to examine its special features. The European tradition, while it may have advanced our understanding of the role of social movements in a wider context, has therefore not produced the kinds of definitions which can form a useful framework for analysis. In a similar vein, Eyerman and Jamison made the observation that movements, by definition, are transitory, they live and die, and whatever innovations they introduce are either rejected or adopted by wider society (1991: 60). However reasonable this might appear, it could not be used as a criterion for identifying social movements empirically, unless we were to confine our studies to movements that had already died, and whose transitory nature was therefore confirmed.

Jamison *et al.* (1990) forged their own definition of social movements by combining transformational and organizational criteria, and in doing so claimed to bridge the divide between theorists in the European tradition (such as Touraine and Habermas), for whom social movements are sources of new collective identities, and those in the American tradition who see social movements as mechanisms for 'resource mobilization', and identify them empirically by their organizational features (Jamison *et al.* 1990: 1). However, their comparative analysis of environmentalism in Sweden, Denmark and Holland shows that their new composite definition is found wanting as an empirical tool. Environmentalism takes on different shapes in different countries, because environmentalists have to organize their activities according to the political context in which they operate. The analysis showed that in Sweden environmentalism did not develop a distinctive oppositional character, for two main reasons. First, there are financial incentives for new organizations to formalize their structure along the lines of established political groups, with the result that 'the borders between the established and the oppositional are blurred' (Jamison *et al.* 1990: 194). Second, it is difficult for new political actors to loosen the grip on Swedish political culture, of the long-established cleavage between the socialist and bourgeois blocs. Instead, new interests tend to be incorporated into those of the existing blocs and promoted through their activities. As a result, in Sweden, 'environmentalism can hardly be called a social movement' (Jamison *et al.* 1990: 198). Thus, despite their declared intention to combine transformational and organizational criteria, the analysts fall back on the organizational when identifying social movements empirically. Although environmentalists in all three countries share the same collective identity, environmentalism in Sweden is less of a social movement because it does not possess the appropriate organizational features.

The distinction between organizational and transformational criteria is significant in relation to the perceived existence of two environmentalisms. Both the conservative and the radical forms (or indeed, in some cases, a single undifferentiated environmentalism) have been seen as displaying the organizational features of a social movement. But almost by definition, only the more radical form has the capacity to transform society, and so analysts who have understood social movements in this way have tended to restrict their use of the term to the more radical form. Thus Cotgrove who, quoting Banks (1972), saw social movements as self-conscious attempts 'to introduce innovations into a social system', suggested that 'something more like a coherent movement emerges' if we focus only on the groups that fundamentally challenge dominant economic values (Cotgrove 1976: 24). However, it would probably be more accurate to say that the transformative capacity of radical environmentalism has more often been seen as identifying it as a 'new' social movement (Yearley 1994). More will be said about this when discussing the relationship of environmentalism to established political allegiances.

Environmentalism as a political ideology

Social scientists have treated 'political ideology', like 'social movement', as a category within which to examine the distinctive features of environmentalism. Again, the term is left undefined and 'used quite promiscuously' by some analysts and subjected to quite close scrutiny by others, though this does not always yield a clear definition. Cotgrove, following Mannheim (1966), defined ideology as 'beliefs and values which are justifications for the status quo, the preservation of existing institutions and the interests which they serve' (Cotgrove 1982: 101–2). As such, they contrast with environmentalist perspectives which he regarded as 'utopias', visions of a better society. And yet he also referred to environmentalist ideologies (Cotgrove 1982: 10), and identified the function of an ideology as 'legitimating or justifying courses of action' (1982: 88), regardless of whether the actions concerned support or oppose the status quo.

Dobson, following Donald and Hall, also defined ideology in

82

terms of its function: political ideologies provide 'the concepts, categories, images and ideas by means of which people make sense of their social and political world, form projects, come to a certain consciousness of their place in that world and act in it' (Donald and Hall 1986: x, quoted in Dobson 1990: 12). In this sense, ideology fulfils both cognitive and practical functions; it enables people to understand the world and their place within it, *and* forms a basis for action. Paehlke provided a more purely substantive definition: an ideology is 'a worldview both value laden and comprehensive' (1989: 5), but he also saw the practical component of ideology as definitive. His aim was to develop 'a political theory with ideological potential' (1989: 3), a potential which he identified as lying in the ability of environmentalism to present an effective challenge to the dominant political order.

From these and other studies it is possible to identify three features of environmentalism which analysts have seen as signifying its status as a political ideology: its comprehensiveness, its coherence and its practical potential. The comprehensiveness of environmentalism lies in its ability to present a vision of a complete alternative society, a 'post-industrial' and 'sustainable' society (see Cotgrove 1982: 105ff.; Dobson 1990: 5, 16; Paehlke 1989: 140ff.). Not surprisingly, some analysts identify this feature only in the more radical form of environmentalism. By definition, radical environmentalism rejects a managerial and piecemeal approach to environmental change and seeks a comprehensive overhaul of society's values and institutions. Thus for Dobson, 'ecologism' is an ideology, whereas the more conservative perspective (which he calls 'environmentalism') is not. Paehlke, however, made little of the radical/conservative distinction, and identified environmentalism in terms of a single though wide-ranging set of values (1989: 144–5). He observed that 'the opponents of environmentalism apparently saw its ideological potential before its advocates did', in that they recognized that the values espoused by environmental campaigners (respect for nature, a need to reduce waste) held far-reaching implications for social change (1989: 6).

The internal coherence of environmentalism has been examined at some length by Goodin (1992) who, though he did not identify environmentalism explicitly as a political ideology, analysed it in ways consistent with the concepts of ideology discussed above. For Goodin the distinction between conservative and radical environmentalism (expressed as 'shallow' and 'deep' ecology; 1992:

42ff.) is less significant than the relationship between what environmentalists value and the kinds of actions they advocate. A theory of value implies a theory of agency, in the sense that what is seen as valuable should be protected through action. Goodin identified nature or 'naturalness' as the core environmentalist value (1992: 30ff.). People value nature, he suggested, because it provides them with a context in which to set their own projects and activities and, in so doing, enables them to see some sense and pattern in their lives (1992: 37).[10] He argued that, although this theory of value has clear implications for the kinds of public policies that environmentalists might advocate, it does not necessarily hold implications for individual lifestyles. The need to see personal lives set in a larger context demands that the context itself (nature) be protected, but it also demands that personal lives be somehow distinguishable both from the larger context and from each other. It is therefore 'logically coherent', according to Goodin, for environmentalists to advocate policies which protect the natural world, while refusing to adopt a green personal lifestyle (1992: 81–2).

Goodin's analysis would seem to hold out some promise for the practical potential of environmentalism as a political ideology. Individuals are more likely to support environmentalist goals if they are not expected to give up their cherished patterns of activity. Not so Dobson's analysis which, in exploring the implications of radical ecologism, emphasizes the practical difficulties of pursuing 'Green' objectives in a society which appears receptive only to a more conservative 'green' message. He pointed out that in Britain, Green activists tend to speak with a green voice in order to make their message more palatable, with the result that the true voice of ecologism is not heard in public (Dobson 1990: 207–13; cf. Yearley 1992b: 141). What Paehlke would call the 'ideological potential' of radical environmentalism is thus destroyed by the perceived need to compromise. In contrast, Paehlke's own analysis seems to suggest that some degree of accommodation between environmentalism and other political perspectives is necessary in order for the ideological potential of environmentalism to be fulfilled. Paehlke saw this potential in the ability of environmentalism to present a realistic alternative to 'neoconservatism', which he saw as the dominant ideology in Anglo-American democracies during the 1980s (1989: 217). The ability of environmentalism to achieve this, he suggested, depends to some degree on its relationship with other established perspectives in the political spectrum.

Environmentalism and the political spectrum

Social scientists have been interested in the relation of environmentalism to the established political ideologies for two main reasons. First, as part of a broader interpretation of social processes, they have considered its status as a 'new' social movement. 'Old' social movements are those derived from class politics, which reproduce the struggle between labour and capital. New social movements are those which take politics out of a class framework (Yearley 1994: 152). Thus the women's movement and the peace movement are typically seen as 'new' social movements. Second, radical environmentalists have claimed that they offer a genuinely new political perspective, that breaks away from or transcends the old division between right and left (Spretnak and Capra 1985: 3). They claim that the similarities between the established ideologies of communism and capitalism are more significant than their differences (Porritt 1986: 44) and that the old order of right and left needs to be replaced by a new opposition of green against the old, grey politics of industrialism (Icke 1990). Social scientists have considered the place of environmentalism on the political spectrum specifically in order to test this claim.

Analysts have presented at least four responses to the question of how environmentalism is related to the left–right spectrum in politics: that the division between left and right is not a useful analytical framework, that environmentalism's perceived place on the spectrum will vary according to the perspective of the perceiver, that environmentalism really does offer a genuinely new departure from the left–right spectrum, and that the division between left and right is actually reproduced within environmental politics.

Eckersley saw the main thrust of radical environmentalism as emancipatory, and suggested that ecocentrism can be seen as seeking 'emancipation writ large', in the sense that it allows all human and non-human entities to develop 'in their own way unhindered by the various forms of human domination' (Fox 1989: 6, quoted in Eckersley 1992: 53). Her analysis explores the place of ecocentrism within the broader field of emancipatory thought and, since contributors to this field 'cluster to the left' of the traditional political spectrum, she did not consider this spectrum to be a useful framework (Eckersley 1992: 27).

The value of the left–right spectrum as an analytical framework has also been questioned by others, on the grounds that there is no universal agreement on what is meant by left and right. Paehlke argued that a line between left and right, though it captures the popular perception of ideology, is not a particularly appropriate shape for depicting established political perspectives, in that it fails to acknowledge both the view that the extreme poles have much in common, and the deep rifts that divide apparently adjacent ideologies, such as communism and democratic socialism (Paehlke 1989: 184–5). Dobson pointed out that left and right may be taken to mean different things. If the left is seen as favouring equality and the right as favouring hierarchy, then ecologism, which seeks a kind of equality among all beings, human and non-human, leans to the left. If, on the other hand, the right is seen as favouring minimal intervention, and the left as favouring the management of nature for the maximal benefit of all human beings, then ecologism, 'which is in principle averse to anything but the most timid engineering of the social and natural world' appears firmly on the right (Dobson 1990: 30–1). It all depends how right and left are defined, and what criteria are used to identify environmentalism itself.

In view of these ambiguities, Dobson found it useful to distinguish between the left–right dichotomy and that between communism and capitalism. Environmentalist critics of established politics tend to treat these as more or less synonymous, arguing that environmentalism transcends the left-right spectrum though its attack on industrialism, as the basis of both capitalism and communism (Dobson 1990: 29–30). By distinguishing the two pairs, Dobson showed how the 'Green' claim that capitalism and communism are similar in their environmental consequences is, from the perspective of the left, a right-wing view. By attacking industrialism, environmental politics is failing to confront capitalism, therefore helping to sustain it. From this left (socialist, rather than communist) viewpoint, ecologism belongs to the right (Dobson 1990: 31–2, 175–7). Paradoxically, from this perspective, the more conservative environmentalism identified by Cotgrove (1982) appears more left-wing. While the radical 'catastrophists' saw industrialism as the cause of the environmental crisis, the 'cornucopians' saw the greed of capitalism as the main problem (Cotgrove 1982: 7).

ENVIRONMENTALISM IN SOCIAL SCIENCE

The clearest indication of how environmentalism can be seen as
a genuinely new departure from the established political spectrum
is offered by Paehlke. Again, the way in which this spectrum is
defined is crucial. Paehlke observed that traditional politics is about
distribution – who receives what – and that interests are generally
interpreted in these terms (Paehlke 1989: 188). The left–right spectrum, insofar as it is useful, represents a range of views about
distribution. Environmentalists do not ignore distributive issues,
but they give a higher priority to matters of technology – how
resources are used and how our relationship with the rest of the
natural world is organized. Thus, once environmentalism is
included within the political spectrum, the distributive axis
between left and right is no longer an adequate representation of
that spectrum (Paehlke 1989: 189–90). But Paehlke also made the
point that, in order to fulfil its potential as a political ideology, and
offer a realistic alternative to neoconservatism, environmentalism
should break away from its 'neither left nor right' image, and
be prepared to engage in distributive politics. In other words,
environmentalism can only become an effective player in the political arena if it is seen to be concerned with the kinds of issues that
have traditionally fuelled political debate in the industrial world.
Such is the 'central tactical dilemma' (Scott 1990: 93) that haunts
environmentalists and undermines their aspirations to become an
effective political force while remaining truly 'Green' (Dobson
1990: 207–13; Yearley 1992b: 141).

Paehlke's analysis can be seen as having rather contradictory
implications for the status of environmentalism as a new social
movement. 'Old' social movements, which were concerned with
the distribution of economic resources among classes, helped to
establish the distributive character of political discourse. If
environmentalism defines interests in terms other than distribution,
and therefore appeals to social groups which are not differentiated
along distributive lines, its status as a 'new' social movement,
which takes politics out of a class framework, appears to be sub-
stantiated. And yet it makes some sense to argue that it is not
distribution itself that distinguishes old and new politics, but the
question of what is being distributed. It could be argued that
the new social movements – the women's movement, the peace
movement, the environmental movement – are also about distribution, but not of material wealth. Instead, they seek to distribute
access to power, rights and freedoms more equitably throughout

87

the human and (in the case of environmentalism) non-human world. Seen in these terms, it is the economic basis of old politics that distinguishes it from the new, not its concern with distribution.

The observation that old and new social movements might be seen as sharing a concern with distributive issues would seem to lend weight to Scott's argument that, instead of transcending the left–right cleavage as some activists and analysts claim, environmental politics reproduces this division. Scott observed, for instance, that the German Green Party (Die Grünen) developed out of a number of citizens' initiatives with diverse ideologies and that left and right political perspectives had already crystallized within this movement by the time the Party was launched in 1979 (Scott 1990: 85). He went on to argue that this diversity is represented in environmentalism generally, because its supporters have drawn on existing ideologies in formulating their message. In consequence, environmentalism as a whole has been difficult to locate on the left–right spectrum precisely because the different points on that spectrum are reproduced within environmental politics (Scott 1990: 93ff.).

Thus it is difficult to generalize about where analysts have placed environmentalism in relation to the established political spectrum. Perhaps all that can usefully be said is that it depends on a number of factors. For instance, it depends on what criteria are used to characterize both environmentalism and the established spectrum: whether they are seen in terms of a concern with distribution, with emancipation, or with intervention in natural processes. It also depends on whether the analyst is examining environmentalist ideas (Dobson and Eckersley), assessing the practical potential of such ideas (Paehlke) or analysing actual (if limited) political achievement (Scott). Once again, we seem to be faced with the reality that, the closer one comes to practical involvement in politics, the harder it is to sustain the claim that environmentalism offers something different.

ENVIRONMENTALISM IN ANTHROPOLOGY

So far, this chapter has concentrated on some of the frameworks employed by sociologists and political scientists to understand environmentalism. It is now appropriate to consider what anthropology has to offer. Several anthropologists have turned their attention to environmental issues in recent years, but the best-established and most consistent application of cultural theory in this field is presented in the work of Douglas and those who have used her ideas. Since this approach is widely known both within and outside the discipline, it provides an appropriate starting point from which to explore an anthropological approach to environmentalism.

Douglas' theory of culture

Expressed simply, Douglas' theory states that culture is determined by social organization. She used 'culture' to refer to people's understanding of the world – what they think, feel and know – in a manner comparable with that outlined in Chapter 1 as being typical of post-structuralist anthropology. 'Social organization' refers to the way people run their social relationships: the degree of freedom they accord each other and the level of constraint they impose, the patterns of authority they establish, the extent to which they act in groups or as individuals. Her approach thus conforms to the broad pattern established in post-structuralist anthropology. Culture, assumed to exist in people's minds, is distinguished from actions and patterns of behaviour (society, social structure, social organization) in order to focus on the relationship between them.

However, she differs from most other post-structuralist anthropologists in the way she conceptualized this relationship. Others saw the relationship between culture and social organization as dialectical, and set themselves the task of exploring the workings of the dialectic through human choice. Douglas saw it as deterministic, and thus appeared to deny the possibility of choice playing a role, though on this point, her work is ambiguous, as we shall see. For Douglas, a particular form of social organization gives rise directly to a particular way of understanding the world. The influence of Durkheim, which Douglas fully acknowledged, is clearly visible here, though she felt that 'Durkheim did not push his thoughts on the social determination of knowledge to their full and radical conclusion' (Douglas 1978: xi, quoted in Wuthnow *et al.* 1984: 80). Douglas' approach to culture has been to explore the paths down which such thoughts lead. Environmentalism is just one of the many fields she has visited on the way.

One of the central pillars of Douglas' approach to culture is a model which defines forms of social organization in terms of two variables, which she called 'grid' and 'group' (Douglas 1970). 'Grid' represents the regulation of activity, 'group' represents the degree of social cohesiveness. Grid is high when people's actions are strictly controlled by authorities, and low when they are free to act as they please. Group is high when people show allegiance to collectivities, and low when they act primarily in their own interests. These two variables combine to produce diverse forms of social organization. High grid and high group produce a hierarchical form; freedom of action is tightly constrained from the centre, and activities are directed towards collective interests. Low grid and low group produce a 'market' form of organization; people are free to act in their own interests and pursue personal gain. Low grid and high group produce an egalitarian or 'sectarian' form of organization; people pursue collective interests but do not tightly regulate each other's activities. High grid and low group produce a society in which people do not pursue collective interests, but also have no freedom of action to pursue their own interests. Although Douglas originally used this model to develop a loose typology of whole societies (Douglas 1970: 86–91), she also recognized, as did others who have used her model, that the different forms of social organization might exist in combination in any one society (Douglas and Wildavsky 1982).[11]

The essence of Douglas' theory is that the different forms of social organization give rise to different ways of understanding the world, different cosmologies or, to use the term suggested in Chapter 2, different 'cultural perspectives'. If a society is homogeneous in its organization it can be expected to hold a single cultural perspective; its whole culture will consist of one perspective. A society that embodies several forms of organization will be culturally heterogeneous; it will support and maintain a number of cultural perspectives. Douglas' theory makes connections between specific forms of organization and specific perspectives, through the following line of reasoning. The moral order – what people take to be right or wrong, appropriate or inappropriate – protects the social order – the existing form of social organization. The moral order is sanctioned through fears of dangers and threats – things that people assume will befall them if the moral order is violated. A simple illustration of this is the belief, held in many societies, that sexual misdemeanours, such as incest or adultery, cause the transgressors or members of their families to become ill and die;[12] fear of the sanction protects the structure of the family.

There are many dangers about which societies and social groups could be concerned: illness, war, witchcraft, divine retribution, crime, environmental damage. But societies and groups tend not to be equally concerned about all these things; they tend to fear some more than others, and some not at all. Douglas' theory asserts that societies and groups select those fears which most closely reflect their social order, enabling people's fears and concerns to be explained in terms of their forms of social organization. In an entrepreneurial context, in which individuals compete for personal gain, the most feared dangers are likely to be the mechanisms through which individuals harm each other: witchcraft and sorcery, gossip, crime and litigation. Among the Cewa of Zambia, for instance, contests for political office were often accompanied by sorcery accusations, usually between close maternal kinsmen, among whom competition was most intense (see Marwick 1965). In western liberal democracies, attempts to discredit opponents by revealing (or perhaps fabricating) financial or sexual misdemeanours have become a normal part of political life. Not surprisingly, some of the most successful entrepreneurs occupy roles which offer individuals protection against these threats, or retribution should their fears be realized: insurance and security companies, the legal profession, diviners and witch-doctors.

Hierarchists might be expected to worry most about losing their power and are therefore likely to promote fears which help to sustain that power. A hierarchical priesthood may invoke divine retribution as a threat to enforce continued submission to their authority. In traditional Australian Aboriginal societies, the continuation of life was seen as depending on the expertise of ritual elders, for only they knew how to perform the sacred ceremonies which guaranteed the supplies of essential resources (see Chapter 4, below). For other members of the population, an ever-present fear was that of incurring the anger of these elders, who could order the execution of those they considered guilty of sacrilege (violating sacred norms or objects), and who could withhold ritual knowledge from anyone whom, because of some misdemeanour, they considered unworthy to hold it, thereby blocking their access to power.

Douglas' theory establishes a category of phenomena in which environmental concern can be placed. Fear of pollution, resource depletion, species extinction and so on become, like other fears, mechanisms through which society protects its institutions. In this sense, concern about environmental pollution in industrial society is the functional equivalent of the fears of ritual pollution expressed in many other societies (Douglas 1966, 1972). They do the same job: they protect the moral order on whose fulfilment the continuation of social order depends.

Surprise theory and the myths of nature

Douglas' grid–group model has been adopted by several analysts investigating the diversity of people's responses to environmental change. In Chapter 1, I pointed out that ecologists have been found to conceptualize 'nature' in different ways: as robust, fragile, capricious or robust within limits. These four 'myths' of nature have been associated by the 'surprise theorists' (Douglas 1992: 262) with the forms of social organization described in Douglas' grid–group model and the cultural perspectives that Douglas has suggested are associated with those forms (Thompson and Tayler 1986, Timmerman 1986, James et al. 1987). Hierarchists (high grid–high group) believe nature to be robust within limits; egalitarians (also referred to as 'communards'), with a sectarian form of organization (low grid–high group), believe it to be fragile; entrepreneurs, who favour market organization (low grid–low group), see nature as robust; and fatalists (high grid–low group) see it as capricious. Thus fatalists see little point in planning, since it is impossible to predict how the environment will respond. Entrepreneurs act on the understanding that, whatever they do, the environment will recover. They are thus free to pursue personal profit, unconstrained by worries about environmental consequences. Hierarchists, on the understanding that the environment will tolerate a certain amount of abuse but no more, urge caution and central control. Egalitarians worry that even the slightest additional burden placed on the environment might push it over the edge into inevitable decline.

These associations of forms of social organization with cultural perspectives and myths of nature are useful to the surprise theorists in enabling them to identify possible responses to environmental change. Douglas' summary of these responses is as clear as any:

Supposing in the event nature turns out to be really ephemeral and the biosphere splits and slides away; then the communards will not be surprised. Saying 'We told you so' will be small comfort to themselves and to the surprise holders, in this case the entrepreneurs and the hierarchists. But supposing in the event nature turns out to be robust enough to take all the punishment we mete out to her. Then the surprise-holders will be the communards. They will find that they didn't need to reduce their style of life, that they have gained little while their opponents have made large fortunes. And so it goes on. The only people who will get no surprise are the fatalists because they made no bets.

(Douglas 1992: 265)

In the surprise theorists' models, environmental dangers thus appear as those most likely to be feared by egalitarians (communards), which makes environmentalism a cultural perspective most likely to be associated with sectarian forms of social organization (low grid–high group), but also present (with a lesser sense of urgency) among hierarchically organized groups (high grid–high group). This accords closely with the observations made by Douglas and Wildavsky (1982) in their study of environmentalism in America.

Cultural theory and American environmentalism

Douglas and Wildavsky set out to explain why environmentalism became an important part of American culture during the 1960s and 1970s. They identified, in American society, three of the forms of social organization defined by the grid–group model; hierarchy, market and sect. Hierarchical and market forms of organization (characterized, respectively, as high grid–high group, and low grid–low group) are established central components of American society, while sectarian organization (characterized by low grid and high group) is more typical of the 'border' or, to use a more common term, the 'periphery'. Sectarian groups tend to develop in opposition to central institutions.

The chief characteristic of sects is that their membership is voluntary (low grid); they are held together by commitment to communal interests (high group). Douglas and Wildavsky suggested that the rise in environmental concern in America in the 1960s and 1970s was related to a growth in sectarian organization.

Sects sustain themselves by opposing the centre. Environmental concerns are an appropriate mechanism for doing this because they question the values and assumptions on which the continuation of hierarchical and market forms of organization depend, such as the supremacy of science and technology and confidence in established laws and procedures (Douglas and Wildavsky 1982: 126ff.). By sustaining fear of pollution and other forms of ecological damage, environmental groups kept their members with them, so ensuring their own continuation: 'these ideas and these dangers respond to the problems of voluntary organization: they are the daily coinage of debate in groups that are trying to hold their members without coercion or overt leadership' (Douglas and Wildavsky 1982: 11). Environmentalism thus developed as a means whereby sects, groups held together by voluntary association, sustained themselves; an environmentalist perspective was produced or determined by this form of social organization.

Douglas and Wildavsky recognized that, rather than explaining the rise of environmentalism in America, this argument merely shifted the focus of the enquiry. If environmentalism developed in order to sustain sectarian groups, the central question becomes, why did this form of social organization become important in America in the 1960s and 1970s? The analysts answer this question by pointing to historical and technological factors that helped to shape post-war American society. For instance, the broadening of access to higher education, together with the development of labour-saving technology, produced a large number of educated people for whom industry had no room. This surplus fed the development of the service sector, which, they suggested, is less tolerant than industry, both of hierarchical control and of the pursuit of individual gain.[13] Faith in individualism as a guiding principle was undermined by the exposure of social injustice, particularly racism, and faith in the bases of central authority was shaken by events such as the Vietnam War and Watergate (Douglas and Wildavsky 1982: 158–64).

As well as relating environmentalism in general terms to the spread of sectarian organization, Douglas and Wildavsky drew attention to the fact that some environmental groups are more sectarian than others. They pointed out that the older, well-established conservation organizations, such as the Sierra Club and the National Audubon Society, tend towards hierarchy. David Brower, as Director of the Sierra Club during the 1950s and 1960s, involved the organization in several large-scale campaigns against environmentally damaging developments, with two significant consequences: the membership of the Club grew from 7,000 to 77,000, and its tax-exempt charitable status was withdrawn by the Internal Revenue Service. The resulting split in the Club's leadership led to Brower's resignation as Director. Shortly afterwards he became a founder member of Friends of the Earth, which was organized along less hierarchical lines and adopted more sectarian principles (Douglas and Wildavsky 1982: 130–3).

Points of convergence?

Although my purpose here is to argue that cultural theory can provide a complementary understanding of environmentalism to those offered by social and political theory, it would be misleading to suggest that there is no overlap among these fields. Some of the studies conducted by sociologists and political scientists have much in common with an anthropological approach. There is a striking similarity between some of the analytical concepts used by social and political theorists and those used by anthropologists. Take another look at Donald and Hall's description, quoted by Dobson (1990: 12), of the functional character of ideology: 'the concepts, categories, images and ideas by means of which people make sense of their social and political world, form projects, come to a certain consciousness of their place in that world and act in it'. If the phrase 'social and political' were removed, it would become an acceptable description of what many anthropologists in recent decades have understood by culture. Paehlke's understanding of ideology as a comprehensive, value laden world view (1989: 5) is also close to what anthropologists would call a cultural perspective. Eyerman and Jamison's concept of 'cognitive praxis', the generation of knowledge through communicative action (1991: 45ff.), which they see as the essential feature of social movements, is similar to the way in which anthropologists view the process of cultural change, which they assume to be going on all the time in all social contexts (see Riches 1979).

It is not surprising, then, that the insights provided by social and political analyses of environmentalism appear similar in some ways to those provided by Douglas' cultural approach. For instance, in describing the rise of sectarian organization in America, and relating it to the emergence of environmental concern,

Douglas and Wildavsky, it could be said, effectively presented an account of environmentalism as a social movement. Their interpretation appears similar to that of Jamison *et al.* (1990) who, by examining how environmentalists organize their activities in different political circumstances, also pointed to the conditions under which environmentalism might become a social movement. But the similarities are only superficial, for an important element in Douglas and Wildavsky's framework, that cultural perspectives (or ideologies, or world views) are caused by forms of social organization, is not shared by the social and political analyses. Thus for Jamison *et al.*, specific conditions lead people, who are already concerned about the environment, to organize their activities in certain ways, but for Douglas and Wildavsky it is the organizational form that generates environmental concern, that turns people into environmentalists. As indicated above, it is this causal or deterministic element that sets Douglas apart from most post-structuralist anthropologists and which is seen by many as the main difficulty with her approach to culture. I shall return to this point in the next section.

There is also some similarity between Douglas and Wildavsky's framework and the social problems approach which Yearley (1992a: 47ff.) used to analyse the development of environmentalism in Britain. Both share the assumption that public concern for an issue is generated and sustained, not by 'objectively' existing conditions, but as a result of claims made by groups and individuals (Kitsuse and Spector 1981). Yearley showed, for instance, how the Royal Society for the Protection of Birds (RSPB), throughout the hundred years of its existence, has generated and sustained public sympathy for birds by drawing attention to the problems they face (Yearley 1992a: 61ff.). The problems have changed over the years. Concern for the impact of the plumage trade was replaced by concern for the impact of egg collecting, of pesticides, of the live-bird trade, of afforestation in Scotland and deforestation in the tropics. What has remained constant is the fact that it has been the efforts of the group that have kept public concern alive. However, while Douglas' theory of culture would lead us to assume that the RSPB did this for the purpose of sustaining itself, Yearley made no such assumption. This difference highlights a second major difficulty with Douglas' approach to culture, as the discussion in the next section will show.

Doubts and contradictions

I have used Douglas' model as an illustration of how cultural theory has been used in the analysis of environmentalism, but I would not wish to argue that her approach to culture is the most appropriate. In fact, there are contradictions in it which make it impossible to swallow whole, and it is important to identify these in order to be able to select from it what is valuable. The most controversial feature of Douglas' theory is the assertion that forms of social organization cause or determine cultural perspectives. Determinism was seen as one of the major evils of the various structuralist approaches in anthropology (in particular, structural-functionalism which, like Douglas' model, was heavily influenced by Durkheim) and which post-structuralist anthropologists sought to leave behind. The main problem with determinism is that it appears to deny the possibility of choice and therefore of change, since change is assumed, in post-structuralist approaches, to result from people choosing to act or think differently.[14]

Like the structural-functionalists before her, Douglas denied that her model precluded change, and indeed used it to interpret changing situations, such as the rise in American environmentalism. But in doing so, she contravened the logic of her theory. The theory states that cultural perspectives change as a result of changes in social organization (see Douglas and Wildavsky 1982: 192). In other words, the *social* change is prior to, and causes, the change in *culture*. Social change, in turn, is the result of new conditions. For instance, the emergence of a highly educated sector of American society with no role in industry provided the conditions in which a sectarian form of social organization could flourish. But how did the increase in sectarian organization actually take place? According to Douglas and Wildavsky's analysis, it happened when people lost faith in existing institutions. In other words, the social change, the rise in sectarian organization, depended on a prior *cultural* change, a loss of faith in existing social forms.

It is also clear from their analysis that Douglas and Wildavsky did not intend to deny the possibility of choice. In fact, choice is presented as playing a pivotal role in the generation of both cultural perspectives and forms of social organization: 'people select their awareness of certain dangers to conform with a specific way of life' (Douglas and Wildavsky 1982: 9); 'the selection of dangers and the choice of social organization run hand in hand' (1982:

97

186). Sectarian organization is founded on choice – the voluntary association of people in groups which persuade (not compel) their membership to remain with them. Thus, the hard determinism of Douglas' theory of culture appears to give way, in the analysis of American environmentalism, to a softer, more flexible representation of the relationship between social organization and culture, in which choice is central to the generation of cultural perspectives and social forms. Once choice is admitted into the interpretation, several specific questions arise which are not directly addressed by Douglas and Wildavsky's analysis. Why, for instance, do people choose one form of social organization in favour of another? Why was sectarian organization considered an appropriate alternative to the established institutions in which faith had been lost? And once sects had been 'selected', why were environmental threats considered more appropriate than other kinds of danger as a mechanism for holding them together?

In another way, Douglas' theory of culture departs, not from the views of most post-structuralist anthropologists, but from the rather specific perspective on culture developed in the first two chapters of this book. In stating that social organization determines culture, Douglas' theory implies that culture determines (or defines) reality. Indeed, her views are often taken to be typical of what I have described (in Chapter 2) as the more moderate form of cultural constructivism: the view that culture imposes meaning on an otherwise meaningless world. For Douglas (as for Durkheim), the source of meaning is society itself. The content of cultural perspectives is determined, not by what exists in the 'real' world, but by the form of social organization they are required to sustain. People's knowledge of what constitutes dirt, for instance, or of what is or is not edible (Douglas 1966), or of animal categories (Douglas 1957), is generated by their social structure. There is no room here for knowledge to arise from any source other than society, for people to discover things about the world that are not derived from their social conditioning (cf. Richards 1993); no room for direct perception.

This is the logical entailment of the view that knowledge is socially determined, and yet Douglas' own analyses, again, seem to deny this logic. The 'real' world, unconstructed by society, is assumed to enter human consciousness: 'The perils of nuclear wastes and carcinogenic chemicals are not figments of the imagination' (Douglas and Wildavsky 1982: 1–2, cf. 40). It would not be

98

possible to say this without assuming that we have access to a world independent of cultural construction, that not all knowledge is socially determined. The same point can be illustrated using Douglas' analysis of the dietary laws listed in the Old Testament (Deuteronomy, chapter 14 and Leviticus, chapter 11). Pigs, among other species, were not allowed to be eaten because they were seen as unclean. The reason for this, according to Douglas, was that they only possess one of the features which identified animals as edible – they have cloven feet, but they do not chew the cud. Thus, pigs straddle the boundary between cloven-footed, cud-chewing (and therefore edible) animals and the rest. The prohibition against eating pork served to protect these cultural categories (Douglas 1966). But whatever the social function of these categories and the rules that protect them, the categories themselves, as Douglas has acknowledged in her more recent work (Douglas 1990) are defined on the basis of empirical observation. People first had to observe the ways in which pigs differ from other animals before they could select these criteria as socially significant. People cannot select from a meaningless reality; knowledge of the world as meaningful is a precondition for whatever influence social organization might exert on our cultural understanding.

Notwithstanding the inconsistencies and contradictions discussed above, Douglas' theory states that social organization will always be the prime mover in cultural change. The implication of this for environmentalism as a cultural perspective is that it exists to serve the purpose of generating or sustaining some organizational form. Like most functionalist explanations, this model appears to make some sense in some situations, but is clearly denied by others, which leads us to be highly sceptical about its general explanatory value. It is possible to envisage an environmental organization whose participants, in order to perpetuate the group, select and promote those concerns that appear most likely to keep their members with them. But there are also many environmental groups that are created in response to specific problems and then disperse once opposition becomes either futile or unnecessary. Given Douglas and Wildavsky's argument that environmental concerns are appropriate for sustaining sectarian forms of organization, it is ironic that the groups which seem the most likely to perpetuate themselves are those that tend towards hierarchy. A large organization with central facilities, established political connections and many paid employees is much less easily dismantled than an informal group with little established political or economic commitment. Indeed, some form of hierarchical organization seems to be implied in the idea that fears are selected and promoted for social purposes, for such an enterprise, in order to work, surely needs both activists and an attentive following.

The only alternative interpretation consistent with Douglas' theory is that each environmentally concerned individual is 'really' worried about something else; that environmentalism is an expression of some more fundamental and more significant fear about society and is not, as environmentalists themselves believe, about the physical threats posed by polluted air and water, or the loss of valued landscapes and species. Anthropologists used to explain witchcraft and sorcery and other apparently 'irrational' beliefs in much the same way, by arguing that they were really expressions of something else, inevitably something that made more sense in terms of the anthropologists' own cultural perspective. One of the most important advances of post-structuralist anthropology has been that we no longer consider it our role to legislate on what counts as reality for the people whose cultures we study.

WHAT CULTURAL THEORY CAN OFFER

What is the purpose of all this theorizing? Why have social scientists been concerned to classify environmentalism as a social movement, an ideology or a cultural perspective? These categories constitute part of the social scientist's known and familiar world into which the new and unfamiliar needs to be slotted if it is to be understood. Establishing the status of environmentalism as a social movement is seen as increasing our understanding of it because we know, more or less, what a social movement is; we have certain expectations of it. If environmentalism can be shown to fit into this category, then we can reasonably expect the same things of environmentalism. This approach is one of the principal ways in which scientific knowledge of the world is assumed to advance. But it carries an inherent and inescapable limitation: the understanding of what is new and unfamiliar is restricted by what is already known. Most scientists, social or otherwise, will have experienced the frustration of this limitation at an individual level; the feeling that their own knowledge is not adequate to make sense of their data, the frantic search through the literature, the mining of other scholars' knowledge, in order to extend the boundaries of their own familiar world, in the hope of turning up a more satisfactory approach or explanation.

The reason why social scientists call for interdisciplinary approaches to the environment or any other issue is because they recognize that this limitation also exists at the level of whole disciplines. Although the boundaries between disciplines are hazy, each is nevertheless a product of its own tradition. Anthropology developed as the study of 'other' cultures with non-industrial, mostly land-based economies whose members live in small communities. Anthropologists consequently have an elaborate array of concepts for discussing economic exchange, kinship relations, ritual and so on, but they are ill equipped to discuss large-scale economic and social processes. Sociology and political science, on the other hand, have tended to focus on social and political processes that operate within and between contemporary industrial states. This bias is revealed in the call for '*internationally* comparative and interdisciplinary approaches' to the environment (Jamison *et al.* 1990: vii, emphasis added). To an anthropologist, the assumption that nations will be the appropriate units of comparison seems restrictive, and an interdisciplinary approach based on this assumption would threaten to exclude anthropology, in which nations have never been as significant as cultures, societies or communities.

The question of whether or not an interdisciplinary approach to environmental issues is a realistic option will be considered in the final chapter. For the moment, my purpose is to indicate what I understand by an anthropological approach to environmentalism, in order to define the parameters for the analysis presented in the following chapters. Although Douglas' model is seen by some outside the discipline as providing the anthropological slant on environmentalism, it does not represent a consensus among anthropologists and, as we have seen, there are serious problems with it, but it also demonstrates what I regard as one of the main strengths of a cultural approach.

Causality, explanation and interpretation

The Durkheimian influence in Douglas' theory of culture makes it, in part, a survival from a previous era of anthropological thought. The battle against causal theories in anthropology was fought during the 1960s and 1970s. The assumption that social and cultural phenomena are somehow causally linked to each other belonged to the old structuralist and functionalist models which the 'revolution' in anthropology (Jarvie 1974) sought to overthrow. As explained in Chapter 1, the purpose of narrowing down the concept of culture and confining it to what people hold in their minds was to open up the possibility of examining how it is related to people's activities and forms of social organization. It was precisely because many anthropologists considered a causal model inadequate for understanding this relationship that the shift in thinking occurred. Social and cultural systems, once treated as machine-like entities composed of functioning parts, came to be seen as the emergent products of human activity, 'the statistical outcome of multiple individual choices' (Leach 1960: 124). The central importance of choice in this new paradigm made causality an inappropriate analytical concept. Choices are made, it was assumed, *in order that* goals might be achieved and not *because* certain conditions prevail (see Stuchlik 1977).

The abandonment of causality had a significant effect on the way anthropology is viewed by its practitioners. In the early part of this century it had struggled, alongside other social sciences, to establish its status as an explanatory and predictive discipline. The assumption that cultural phenomena have causes – be they environmental, as in some of the models discussed in Chapter 2, or social, as in Douglas' model – enabled anthropologists to claim that, by identifying those causes, they were explaining culture in some final and definitive sense. Once the concept of choice became central to analyses of culture, anthropologists felt less able to claim that those analyses produced definitive explanations. This was not because a concept of choice is incompatible with explanation, but because the task of explaining how a cultural feature is generated and sustained becomes so much more complex once choice is involved. Countless individual decisions contribute to the processes that sustain any one cultural feature, and many analysts feel uncomfortable generalizing about something as variable as human choice. Anthropologists have not given up the effort to explain cultural features, and some regard this as their ultimate goal, but since the 1970s many have seen their task as interpretative rather than explanatory (see Geertz 1973). Their role has been to reveal how cultural perspectives make sense, by showing how they are related to the activities of those who hold them, and how their various components – assumptions, values, norms, goals – relate to one another. This is the approach adopted in the analyses presented both in the next chapter and in Chapter 6.

As the discussion in Chapter 1 indicated, many anthropologists would also dissent from Douglas' model in another way. For Douglas, social organization was primary and cultural perspectives the secondary products of social forces. Many anthropologists would see the relationship between the cultural and the social as a dialectic. What people know, think and feel forms a basis for their social activities, and these activities generate experiences which both sustain and modify their cultural perspectives. I have taken this formula as the starting point for developing a model of culture appropriate for exploring anthropology's contribution to environmental discourse. But, in Chapter 2, I suggested a departure from it. I argued that culture does not relate only to people's social activities and does not, therefore, consist only of what they learn through their interaction with others. Instead, it consists of all the meanings through which we understand the world, whether they are communicated to us by others or discovered through our active engagement with our surroundings (in the process referred to as 'direct perception'). It is partly because we acquire some of our culture outside social contexts that it makes little sense, in my view, to regard our understanding of reality as being 'socially constructed'.

This model makes culture the mechanism through which we interact with our environment. It also allows for the possibility (which the constructivist model logically does not) that individuals from very different social backgrounds might come to understand their environments in quite similar ways. This is important for examining environmentalism as a perspective that can be shared and communicated beyond the confines of what anthropologists have called cultures. It acknowledges that, in a world in which communication transcends the boundaries of communities, societies and nations, perspectives can effectively become 'transcultural'. These ideas are explored further in Chapters 5 and 6.

Broadening the limits of comparison

A great deal of social scientific analysis proceeds through comparison: the characteristics of social and cultural phenomena are identified by comparing them, and the factors that generate and affect them are isolated by comparing the contexts in which they occur.

In such analyses, categories such as 'social movement' and 'political ideology' have the role of defining the limits of comparison. By defining environmentalism as a social movement, we are stating that it is valid to compare it with other social movements. Through this comparison, our understanding of environmentalism itself and social movements in general is assumed to advance. One of the most striking features of anthropological analyses, which sets them apart from those of other social scientists, is the breadth of material on which they draw for comparison. Instead of comparing, say, political processes in (more or less) similar nation states (like Jamison *et al.* 1990 and Pridham 1994), an anthropologist is more likely to draw on ethnographies of distant communities in Africa or New Guinea to elucidate what is happening in contemporary Europe or America. This points to what I see as one of the most significant insights provided by Douglas' model and cultural approaches in general. For Douglas, ritual pollution and environmental pollution are phenomena of the same kind. It makes sense, therefore, to ask whether they are generated by similar forces or play similar roles in human society. While not sharing her deterministic assumptions, I applaud the breadth of vision that makes such comparisons possible.

If environmentalism is identified, for the purpose of studying it, as a social movement or a political ideology, we are precluded from considering what else it might be, how else a concern to protect the environment might be expressed. Our analysis is constrained by what we know about social movements and ideologies. If environmentalism is identified as a cultural perspective, we can ask (as Douglas and Wildavsky did) under what conditions it might be expressed as a social movement or an ideology. These phenomena are seen as types of environmentalism, or forms it might take. Of course, the analysis is still constrained – it is the purpose of a theoretical perspective to constrain analysis – but it is constrained by different parameters. It is shaped by our understanding of culture, which is universal in human experience, rather than our understanding of social movements or political ideologies, which are less widely distributed.

If culture in its general sense is the mechanism through which we interact with our environment, then specific cultures and cultural perspectives can be treated as distinct forms of this relationship, and environmentalism as one such form. In other words, environmentalism is one of many ecological alternatives employed by people – it is a basis for interacting with the environment – and we can advance our understanding of it as such by isolating its essential cultural features. The established anthropological technique for doing this is cross-cultural comparison. Just as treating environmentalism as a social movement provides a basis for its comparison with other social movements, so treating it as a cultural perspective enables us to compare it with other cultural perspectives, in order to identify more closely its distinguishing features. I suggest that, in the broad spectrum of cultural perspectives, there will be some that are overtly environmentalist in character, others that are capable of accommodating environmental concerns, and yet others that effectively exclude or are hostile to such concerns. If we can determine which is which, and why, then we might go some way towards understanding what constitutes environmentalism; which particular assumptions and values make it a legitimate and practicable way of understanding the world. This is the task for the next chapter, in which the environmentalist credentials of a range of cultural perspectives are examined and compared.

4

ENVIRONMENTALISM AND CULTURAL DIVERSITY

> Different societies, and different ages, re-invent Nature in
> their own image, sometimes benignly, sometimes with hos-
> tility, but rarely with indifference.
>
> (Ellen 1986: 9)

I suggested, in Chapter 1, that anthropology's contribution to
environmental discourse might take two forms. Through its tradition of studying human culture in all its diversity, anthropology
can provide insights into how people understand and interact with
their environments. In this sense, anthropology is the study of
human ecology, and its relevance to environmental discourse is as
great as that of any branch of ecology, if not greater, given that
human activities are taken to be the major cause of environmental
damage. Anthropology can also contribute directly to the development of environmentalist thought, by examining environmentalism
itself as a cultural phenomenon, as a particular way of understanding the world. Chapter 2 established the theoretical background
for the first of these tasks, by considering how anthropologists
have understood the role of culture in human–environment
relations. Chapter 3 examined the theoretical background for the
second task, by showing how an anthropological analysis of
environmentalism as a cultural phenomenon differs from the types
of analysis offered by other social sciences.

In this chapter the two tasks are combined. A range of different
ways of understanding the environment are compared with one
another and with ideas drawn from western environmentalist
thought. The purpose of this cross-cultural comparison is to build
conceptual bridges (Richards 1992a: 153) between environmentalism and other ways of knowing the world, in the hope of under-

standing both more clearly. The discussion begins by examining a misunderstanding referred to in Chapter 1, the environmentalist myth that non-industrial cultures are ecologically benign.

THE MESSAGE OF THE KOGI

In 1990, a BBC television documentary enabled the Kogi people of Colombia to give a message to the world.[1] The Kogi live on the Sierra Nevada de Santa Marta, a mountain rising to nearly 19,000 feet above the city of Santa Marta in northern Colombia. They are descendants of the complex pre-Colombian society which was gradually destroyed following the Spanish invasion of the early sixteenth century. Their oral tradition tells how refugees fled from the consequences of the invasion high into the Sierra, where the Kogi continue to live under the guidance of their ritual specialists, the Mamas (Ereira 1990: 135–44).

According to Kogi tradition, the world was created by the Mother, with the Sierra at its centre. The Mother's son Serankua created humans. 'They were made to look after the world, to care for everything in it. Animals and plants were placed not under their dominion but in their care' (Ereira 1990: 118). Later, Serankua created

> another kind of human being, a Younger Brother to the original people . . . a creature with a butterfly mind, which paid no attention to the Mother's teaching . . . . This Younger Brother was not to remain in the Sierra: he was ejected. He was given a different way of knowing things, a can-do technological knowledge, and exiled to lands designated for him across the sea.
>
> (Ereira 1990: 118)

The Kogi see themselves as the Elder Brothers, who have continued, through their rituals and offerings, to care for the world. The Spanish invaders and their descendants are the Younger Brothers, who have returned from their designated lands across the sea and who exploit the Earth's resources with a careless disregard for the consequences of their actions. The Elder Brothers' concern is portrayed in an interpreted Kogi divination:

A human being has much liquid inside. If the liquid dries up we fall with weakness. The same thing can happen to the earth, weakness makes you fall, weakness.

So the earth today catches diseases of all kinds. The animals die. The trees dry up. People fall ill. Many illnesses will appear, and there will be no cure for them. Why?

Because Younger Brother is among us, Younger Brother is violating the basic foundation of the world's law. A total violation. Robbing. Ransacking. Building highways, extracting petrol, minerals.

We tell you, we the people of this place, Kogi, Asario, Arhuaco: that is a violation.

(Ereira 1990: 196)

Until recently, the Kogi had felt no need to inform the Younger Brothers of their concern, but they had observed that the highest parts of the Sierra were drying out and the vegetation was dying. If the Sierra, the heart of the world, was dying, then everything would surely end.

So now I am sending this message over there. I want to give some advice to the Younger Brother. If they go on like this, they will see what will happen. I do not know yet on which day the world will end. But from being plundered so much, of oil and everything else, it will end.

(Ereira 1990: 227)

The Kogi message created a brief but noticeable flurry of excitement in the media. The film maker gave several radio interviews, and some of the questions and comments contained a hint of disbelief. A similar degree of suspicion could be detected in informal conversations among my fellow anthropologists. Some, it seemed, found it difficult to accept that the Kogi could be as isolated, or as primitive, or as ecologically wise, as they appeared.[2] The source of these suspicions is of interest. The Kogi appeared suspect because they seemed to fit too neatly (for the sensibilities of anthropologists, at least) a popular western stereotype. If environmentalists had wanted to invent a primitive society to bring an important message to the world, they might well have created a people very like the Kogi.

THE MYTH OF PRIMITIVE ECOLOGICAL WISDOM

The understanding that non-industrial peoples possess a kind of primitive ecological wisdom is widely held within industrial society (Rayner 1989), and has a prominent place in environmentalist thought. It is 'part of civilized humanity's image of the noble savage' (Peoples and Bailey 1988), part of the romantic tradition which idealizes the natural, and from which some of the values central to environmentalism are derived (see Thomas 1983: 301–2). I suggested in Chapter 1 that, within environmentalist thought, the model of primitive ecological wisdom has the character of a myth, in the sense that it is dogmatically asserted. As the work of Douglas (1972) and others has indicated, this is to be expected of ideas that support cherished theories, arguments and institutions. The myth of primitive ecological wisdom is not just an incidental part of the romantic package carried by some environmentalists. It is fundamental to the radical environmentalist critique of industrialism, for without the assumption that non-industrial societies live sustainably in their environments, there would be no grounds for arguing that industrialism is the cause of environmental destruction.

The logic of this argument would lead us to expect all non-industrial ways of living to be regarded as ecologically sound, but there is a tendency for certain societies and kinds of society to be presented far more prominently than others as models for a better, environmentally benign, way of life. While hunters and gatherers, shifting cultivators and rainforest peoples are proclaimed as 'paragons of ecological virtue' (Ellen 1986: 10), settled agriculturalists and transhumant nomads are virtually ignored. This is the result of several selective pressures.

First, in accordance with the romantic tradition of idealizing the natural, the most ecologically sound ways of living are assumed to be those that conform most closely to what is seen as a natural existence. In turn, the most natural ways of living are assumed to be those that appear to transform the environment least, that leave it as close as possible to its raw state. This has focused attention on the hunting and gathering communities, whose activities do not appear radically to modify their environments (Ellen 1986: 10). We now know that this is a false impression, partly because hunting and gathering often incorporate practices that have substantial long-term impacts on the environment, such as the systematic

109

burning of vegetation to improve conditions for game species, and partly because most contemporary hunter-gatherers do not practise a 'pure' hunting and gathering mode of subsistence (see below). Nevertheless, the idealized image persists, and hunter-gatherers are identified as the archetypal primitive environmentalists.

Second, because the image of primitive ecological wisdom is born of a comparison with industrial practice, it tends to be shaped by issues of concern within industrial society. For instance, intensive agriculture has been a target for environmentalist criticism for several reasons: because it requires the use of chemical fertilizers and pesticides which are seen as polluting and damaging to health; because it converts diverse landscapes into monocultures, destroying wildlife habitats in the process; and because, particularly under large-scale bureaucratic control (in the European Union, for instance), it often produces a surplus, which is seen as wasteful. Shifting cultivation by non-industrial peoples is often highlighted as an ecologically sound mode of subsistence because it differs in appropriate ways from intensive agriculture. It typically allows the soil to recover, often for several seasons, before re-use, and uses the land's natural fertility, contained in the vegetation growing on site, rather than adding nutrients produced elsewhere. In addition, the plots are small and several different crops may be grown in rotation with fallow periods. The result is a diverse environment which apparently provides what people need without waste and without damage to other forms of life.

Third, proximity to industrial society, in both an historical and a geographical sense, has directed the spotlight towards some non-industrial societies rather than others. Modern American society, with its high levels of consumption (Redclift 1984: 29, 35) is seen by many environmentalists as the embodiment of all that is ecologically unsound (see, for instance, Holmberg et al. 1993: 8). The most apt and striking contrast, for those seeking an ideal model, is provided by the indigenous North American peoples, both because their ways of living were destroyed and supplanted by modern America, and because their continued presence in American society provides a ready source of alternative principles. Udall referred to American Indians as the 'first ecologists' (1972: 2). The westward expansion of white America is seen by environmentalists as having replaced a range of relatively peaceful, ecologically benign cultures with an aggressive, ecologically destructive one. Thus the ideals of contemporary environmentalism can be linked to the events of nineteenth-century America, in much the same way as the ideals of racial equality can be linked to the history of the slave trade. At the same time, the published words of American Indian philosophers are seen as a source of environmental wisdom (see Neihardt 1972 [1932], Erdoes 1976) and icons from American Indian mythology, such as the Rainbow Warrior,[3] have been adopted by environmental activists.

Fourth, and following from the last point, environmentalists tend to advocate a greater respect for the indigenous peoples of any region, than for those inhabitants whose origins lie elsewhere. The aboriginal societies of North and South America, of Australia, Malaysia and the Pacific Islands, are revered as the rightful, most appropriate guardians of those regions' resources. The members of the radical environmental group Earth First! identify with the original inhabitants of whatever region they are operating in. In North America, they look to American Indian spirituality as a way of interacting with the rest of the natural world (Taylor 1991: 259). In Britain, Earth First! activists look back to the pre-Christian era as 'a time when people were more respectful of the Earth' (Burbridge 1994: 10), and seek to protect archaeological sites threatened by development.[4] One reason for identifying with pre-Christian peoples is that some Earth First! activists blame the Judaeo-Christian tradition for what they see as the alienation of modern human society from the rest of the natural world (Taylor 1991: 258). But the greater respect for indigenous peoples shown by environmentalists in general might be seen, again, as part of the romantic tradition which idealizes the natural, and which is echoed in contemporary scientific ecology, by the greater value placed on indigenous species over introduced species, and on pristine natural habitats over habitats altered by human effort.

Finally, environmentalist thought has focused more on the human inhabitants of some ecosystems than of others, because those ecosystems have themselves been the centre of environmentalist concern for various reasons. The rainforests, for instance, have been seen by environmentalists both as particularly endangered and as particularly important. They are seen as endangered because of the speed with which they are being destroyed (IUCN et al. 1991: 124). They are seen as important because they help to stabilize both the climate (by taking in carbon dioxide) and the soil (by preventing erosion), because they hold the greatest biological diversity (biodiversity) of any ecosystem, because they might hold many undiscovered medical cures, and so on. In seeking to conserve the rainforests, environmentalists have drawn attention to those communities who live there apparently without destroying them, such as the Indians and the rubber-tappers (*seringueiros*) of Amazonia (Hildyard 1989, Cowell 1990), and the Penan of Malaysia (Manes 1990: 122–3), and have contrasted their modes of subsistence with the destructive commercial pursuits of cattle ranchers and commercial timber companies. On the other hand, the ecological importance of tropical grasslands has had a much lower profile in environmental discourse, and environmentalists have therefore seen little need to focus attention on the human communities (mainly nomadic pastoralists) who have traditionally used these ecosystems.

If the understanding that non-industrial societies possess a primitive ecological wisdom has, for environmentalists, a mythical status, there might seem little point in subjecting it to empirical testing. The results, if they happen not to support the myth, might fall on deaf environmentalist ears. But the effort is worth making if, as I have suggested, anthropology is to contribute to the development of environmentalist thought. After all, the point of testing the myth is not to suggest that non-industrial societies have nothing to teach the industrial world about how environmental responsibilities might be defined and implemented. It is to demonstrate the value of a more sensitive awareness of how human societies understand and interact with their environments. In this enterprise, the potential roles of anthropologists as students of human ecology and as theorists of environmentalism come together.

Questioning the myth

Anthropologists have already said quite a lot about the myth of primitive ecological wisdom; their views have occasionally even reached the national press (Smith 1995). The central argument in Ellen's 'exemplary demystification' (Rayner 1989: 1) was that 'green primitivism' is based on an illusion created by several factors. Certainly, some cultures seem to idealize harmony with the environment (Ellen 1986: 10), but non-industrial communities are often held in a state of apparent balance with their environments by factors other than their ideology. For instance, small populations do not exert much pressure on the environment, but they may be kept small by factors other than deliberate planning, such as infertility and disease. Douglas described the acute concern of the Lele that their population was dying out due to attacks by sorcerers (1972: 137). Even when family size and the spacing of children are deliberately controlled, it is more likely to be for practical reasons than to avoid population pressure on the environment, and it may be achieved through abortion or infanticide (Ellen 1986: 11).

Relative isolation is another factor that helps to minimize the pressure exerted by some communities on their environments. People who interact regularly with outsiders are often involved in patterns of exchange that require them to produce a surplus of wealth. An isolated community needs to provide only for its own subsistence, and the absence of any incentive to produce more may keep the economy sustainable (Ellen 1986: 12). On the other hand, people who might wish to produce more may be prevented from doing so by a limited technology. Sillitoe wrote of the Wola people of the New Guinea Highlands, 'It is their agricultural technology, coupled with a modest population density, rather than their cultural ideology, that protects the Wola environment in the long term' (1993: 172).

In addition to the argument that the apparent harmony between some non-industrial societies and their environments is due to factors other than their ideologies, several anthropologists have pointed to incompatibilities and misunderstandings between environmentalism and specific non-industrial cultures. Harries-Jones described the grievances of Ontario Indians against environmentalists who are said to have misappropriated Indian culture, by transforming 'Indian respect for land and communitarianism into a cult-like vision of new-age "spirituality"' (1993: 49). Feit demonstrated the incompatibilities between attitudes to animals expressed by animal rights activists and those traditionally held by Cree hunters (1991).

The combined message of all these arguments and observations would seem to be that non-industrial peoples do not think like environmentalists. Some of them may live their lives in ways that are environmentally sound, but ecological balance, where it exists, is an incidental consequence of human activities and other factors, rather than being an ideal or a goal that is actively pursued. In other words, the practices in which some non-industrial peoples engage may be environmentally benign, but their cultures, their ways of understanding the world, are not. If this is a valid inference from anthropologists' observations on the myth of primitive ecological wisdom, it could be a highly significant, if rather pessimistic, contribution to environmental discourse. Environmentalists look to non-industrial peoples, not only for models of ecologically sound practice, but also for appropriate ways of thinking about the environment. But if, in fact, no appropriate ways of thinking exist in the human cultural repertoire, if non-industrial peoples are prevented from destroying the environment, not by their ideologies, but by conditions beyond their control, then the reality facing the environmentalist cause looks considerably less favourable.

However, the conclusion that no environmentally benign cultures exist outside the industrial world is just as much a misleading generalization as is the myth of primitive ecological wisdom. The best way of demonstrating this is by examining a range of cultural perspectives on the environment, and considering how far the assumptions on which these perspectives are based, and the actual and potential values generated by them are compatible with those of environmentalist thought.

DIVERSE CULTURES, DIVERSE ENVIRONMENTS

Cross-cultural comparison is a tricky exercise; the discussion on cultural relativism, in Chapter 1, indicated some of the difficulties. Essentially, comparing different cultures means translating diverse ways of understanding the world into a single framework which is itself, of course, yet another cultural perspective. It is easy to distort the cultures being compared in the process of making them fit the comparative framework. Some would no doubt argue that distortion is inevitable in the act of translation itself, that we change the meanings intended by others simply by expressing them in a different language. These difficulties need to be acknowledged and addressed, but we should not allow them to become obstacles to cross-cultural analysis. Communication across cultural boundaries is an everyday reality, and lamenting on its limitations is not the best way for anthropologists to contribute to contemporary public discourse. A few categorical statements at the outset should help to clarify any confusion that might arise from the following comparative analysis.

As the model of culture presented in Chapter 2 implies, I do not regard a distinction (much less a dichotomy or an opposition) between nature and culture as a useful analytical device. On the contrary, I see nature as the overarching scheme of things to which culture and everything else belong. Some cultures, however, including that in which I have been brought up, do appear to recognize a fundamental opposition between nature and culture, or at least to make distinctions which anthropologists have felt justified in interpreting in these terms. In the following analysis, anything that resembles an opposition between nature and culture belongs strictly to one or other of the cultural perspectives being compared, and not to the analytical framework.

If a distinction between nature and culture were being used as an analytical device, then it would be appropriate to refer to the cultural perspectives being compared as different ways of understanding nature, as Ellen did in the quotation that opens this chapter. Instead, I refer to them as ways of understanding the environment. But I also acknowledge that some of the perspectives discussed below do not translate easily into many people's commonsense understanding of 'the environment'. In particular, some of the forces identified as existing in the environment, such as witchcraft and anger, are human, while others, such as God and the ancestors, would normally be glossed as spiritual. Is it not a misrepresentation of the perspectives being compared to refer to these forces as part of the environment?

I would argue that it is much less of a misrepresentation to regard these forces as environmental than to present them in more conventional ways. Formulating analytical definitions of any category is difficult, because no term is culturally neutral. But I suggest that 'the environment' can be defined in a way that is more widely applicable than categories such as such as nature and culture, spiritual and non-spiritual. As Ingold pointed out, an environment is that which surrounds (1993: 31; see Chapter 3, above). Identifying an environment therefore entails making a conceptual distinction between it and whatever is surrounded. But this is the *only* conceptual distinction it entails. Identifying an environment does not require us to distinguish between the human and the non-human, the material and the spiritual, the dead and the living. I suggest that virtually all people distinguish themselves, as individuals, from the things that surround them, and these things include their fellow human beings, gods, spirits, animals, plants, and whatever else enters their perception. Defining the environment simply as 'that which surrounds' makes all relations ecological. In the following analysis, I compare the ways in which people understand the phenomena that surround them and impact on their lives. It is therefore appropriate to refer to the knowledge described as knowledge of the environment.

The choice of examples for comparison has been governed by several factors, some of which will become clear as the analysis proceeds. I have tried to include some of the cultures that are commonly picked out by environmentalists as ecologically benign (such as hunter-gatherers and North American Indians), and some drawn from a category, settled cultivators, that have received little such attention. I have also drawn on the work of fellow anthropologists and other scholars who have had a particular interest in understanding the environmental knowledge of the communities they have studied. This is partly for convenience; it is easier to accept another analyst's interpretation than to start from scratch with 'straight' descriptive material. But it is also because I assume that, when the purpose of the analysis is specifically to understand people's knowledge of their environment, it is likely to be more culturally sensitive than when environmental knowledge is being presented, say, as a background to something else, such as an analysis of the kinship system or political organization. One example, Kasigau, is included because it is familiar to me as my own fieldwork community.

Hunter-gatherers in a giving environment

For many years, hunter-gatherer[5] societies were generally seen, both within and outside anthropology, as those who fulfil their material needs from wild sources (Woodburn 1980: 95; 1982: 432). Associated with this image was the assumption that hunter-gatherers modify their environments to a lesser degree than societies using other modes of subsistence, and that, of all human societies, they therefore conform most closely to a 'natural' existence. Within anthropology, this assumption led to contemporary hunter-gatherers being treated as sources of information on the origins of institutions (for instance, Durkheim and Mauss 1963), while outside the discipline it helped to generate and sustain the myth of primitive ecological wisdom. Although this image of hunter-gatherers has persisted in environmentalist thought, it has been replaced in anthropology by a far more sensitive understanding based on detailed ethnographic accounts.

116

It has been argued that it is no longer satisfactory to distinguish contemporary hunter-gatherers from other societies in terms of their mode of subsistence (Bird-David 1990, 1992b). Ethnographic descriptions produced during the past twenty years or so indicate that hunter-gatherers fulfil their needs from many other sources as well as hunting and gathering. Some groups appear to have a history of sporadic cultivation interspersed with hunting and gathering (Keesing 1981: 122). Some engage in trade or take wage employment with neighbouring communities (Harpending 1976, Hart 1978). Some groups depend simultaneously on several sources. The Nayaka people of the Gir Valley in southern India, whose economy has been described in detail by Bird-David (1992b: 24–38), have for years combined hunting and gathering in their forest environment with rice and coffee cultivation, paid employment on a coffee plantation and, more recently, for a timber company. For some hunter-gatherers, hunting has long since ceased to be a purely subsistence activity. In particular, the fur trade gave indigenous hunters of North America a role in a worldwide economy (and consequently made them vulnerable to fluctuations in the international fur market; see Wenzel 1991).

The knowledge that hunter-gatherers use a variety of subsistence techniques casts doubt on the distinctiveness of hunting and gathering as a type of economy, but Bird-David has argued that hunter-gatherer communities can still be seen as distinctive, in the manner in which they understand and relate to their environment (Bird-David 1992b: 38ff.). Her argument focuses particularly on those hunter-gatherers who have what Woodburn called 'immediate-return' systems (Woodburn 1980). In other words, they tend to consume whatever they need when it is available to them rather than storing it for future use. Drawing on her own experience among the Nayaka, and comparative material on the Mbuti of Zaïre and the Batek of Malaysia,[6] all of whom have immediate-return systems, Bird-David argued that these groups trust their environments to fulfil their needs by giving freely to them without imposing obligations or asking for any return (1990: 190–1). She also showed how this 'cosmic economy of sharing' (1992a) permeates Nayaka social relations. Whatever is asked for is expected to be given freely. Individuals who use items 'belonging' to others (in the specific Nayaka sense) without first asking permission, cause offence by depriving the 'owners' of their right to give (1990: 193).

A giving environment can be seen as supporting a hunting and gathering economy by providing the wild plants and animals needed for human survival. This is the conventional image of hunter-gatherer societies held by anthropologists and others. But there is nothing in the hunter-gatherers' own understanding of the environment to suggest that its generosity is restricted to these particular gifts. A giving environment might be expected to provide any kind of opportunity for people to meet their needs. It might, for instance, provide a nearby coffee plantation on which to earn money, and local stores from which to purchase items that do not grow wild in the forest. It might also provide a commercial market for things that were once collected for direct consumption alone, such as timber and animal hides. Thus, when hunter-gatherers engage in trade or cultivation or take paid employment to meet their needs, they are not acting in a manner contrary to their underlying ethos; they are taking the opportunities that their environment provides, in full accordance with their understanding that the environment will always provide what they need (Bird-David 1992b: 39–40). Bird-David suggested the term 'procurement' to describe the relationship between hunter-gatherers and their environment:

> 'to procure' (according to the *Shorter Oxford Dictionary*) is 'to bring about, to obtain by care or effort, to prevail upon, to induce, to persuade a person to do something'. 'Procurement' is management, contrivance, acquisition, getting, gaining. Both terms are accurate enough for describing modern hunter-gatherers who apply care, sophistication and knowledge; whose activities range from collecting what the environment gives to prevailing upon it, persuading it and managing it in order to get resources.
>
> (1992b: 40)

The most significant general point to emerge from Bird-David's analysis of hunter-gatherer economies is that an economy, any economy, can be seen as having both cultural and technological components, and that it is the cultural component that makes an economy distinctive (see Gudeman 1986). In Bird-David's analysis, what distinguishes the hunter-gatherer economy is not so much its technological character – communities which have been classified as shifting or settled cultivators also engage in a variety of modes of 'procurement', including hunting and gathering. The

118

hunter-gatherer economy is distinctive in that it depends upon a *giving* environment rather than some other kind.

This line of argument points to the possibility of dissolving the conventional classification of human economies (or human *ecologies*) in terms of technology (hunter-gatherers, pastoralists, shifting cultivators, settled agriculturalists, industrialists and so on) and characterizing them instead in terms of the type of environment on which they depend – the environment as understood by their participants. As well as giving environments, we might be able to identify passive environments, protective environments, fragile environments, vindictive environments and so on. By examining a wide range of human cultures, it might be possible to discover many more than the four 'myths of nature' associated by the surprise theorists with Douglas' grid–group model (see Chapter 3).

Like hunting and gathering, cultivation is beset by popular misconceptions. In the general sequence of cultural evolution, the beginning of agriculture is often taken to be the point at which human beings gained control over the environment. This is not just a popular notion. Within anthropology, the ethos of control has been seen as central to a cultivating mode of subsistence: 'The creed of gardeners, whether Western, Oriental or Islamic, is that by bringing nature under control they can direct its productivity to their benefit' (Sillitoe 1993: 172). If this is so, then the criterion that distinguishes a hunter-gatherer economy from one of cultivation could be that the first depends on a giving environment while the second depends on a passive environment amenable to human control. The ethnography, however, does not bear this out, as the next two examples indicate.

The Dogon: respecting the powers of the environment

The Dogon village of Tireli is located at the foot of the Bandiagara escarpment near the border between Mali and Burkina Faso in West Africa. The environmental knowledge of Tireli's residents, and particularly their relationship with trees, has been described by van Beek and Banga (1992). The village, a permanent settlement with a long history, is surrounded by bushland. Here the Dogon grow millet, their main staple crop, subjecting different parts of the bush (scree slope, flood plain, drift sand and fixed dunes) to different cultivation patterns. They also grow onions and tobacco, keep sheep and goats, hunt bush animals and eat the fruit of several trees, though trees are more important for other purposes – as fuel, building and fencing materials, and as a source of medicines and manure (in the form of leaves) for their crops (1992: 59–68).

The bush is seen as dangerous, being the home of spirits, which may attack people, and of animals, rocks and trees, which are also feared because of their power. Indeed, the bush is the source of all power, knowledge and life: 'The bush is the *fons et origo* of everything that makes life possible, e.g. the animals all know the future; they have a perfect awareness of man's activities: his intentions, mistakes, transgressions and frailties, and know what the future holds for humans' (van Beek and Banga 1992: 67). Animals are used in divination, and hunting is a magical skill, since only strong magic can outwit the animals. Trees can confer life on human beings, through their medicinal powers, and wealth, but can also bring death if not treated properly. Trees and rocks are known to move around. In fact everything in the bush moves; the villages are the only fixed points in a fluid landscape. Subsistence depends on harnessing the power of the bush through work and turning it to human purposes, but in this very process, that power is diminished, 'used up and worn down': 'in changing things of the bush to things of men, the truly fertile, life-giving aspects are lost' (1992: 71).

Respect is an essential component of the relationship between the Dogon and their environment, as it is of their social hierarchy. If millet is not treated with respect, it will disappear from the granary; the consumption and cultivation of millet is subject to taboos. Trees are particularly respected; wood is not wasted and, wherever possible, small branches are cut. Wooden objects, apart from firewood, are not burned but left to deteriorate once they are no longer useful. The felling of a whole tree is a serious decision, never taken by one individual alone, and may require an offering. Some trees are planted, in the areas nearest the village, for fruit and shade (van Beek and Banga 1992: 69–70), but, for the most part, the Dogon take what they need from the bush without trying to replace it. Indeed, it would be inappropriate for them to try to replenish what is the source of all power and life.

Kasigau: at the mercy of environmental forces

Kasigau is a large hill rising out of the plain about 40 miles south of Voi in southern Kenya. I describe the community as it was in

1977–79, when I carried out fieldwork there. Five villages are situated on the lower slopes, and the villagers' fields, where they grow maize and a few other crops, occupy a band of flat plain around the base of the hill. Beyond this is bushland, parts of which are occupied by cattle ranches, a mining operation and Tsavo National Park. Most households keep chickens and goats and some have cattle; animals are both a store of wealth and a source of food. Education and the market economy of modern Kenya have brought new opportunities to the Wakasigau (people of Kasigau). Some find casual employment locally. Those with a secondary school education find work in offices in Voi or Mombasa, or as teachers in local primary schools. A very small proportion of the population with specialized training become civil servants, secondary school teachers or medical workers; some work in the commercial sector in Nairobi and occasionally travel further afield.

Life for the Wakasigau is often described by them as difficult, though easier for some than for others. Farming remains the basis of the economy, and the seasonal round of sowing, weeding, harvesting and grinding is seen as an endless chore. Food is far from scarce, but its production entails long days of hot, tiring work. In addition, there are many dangers to cope with. The rains might fail and ruin the harvest. Monkeys raid the maize crops and large animals occasionally trample them. Snakes, which are common, are a real threat to life. Goats and cattle might be lost to lions or to illness. Human ailments are a constant worry and an everyday topic of conversation. The changing times have brought new trials. Young people, it is often said, no longer respect their elders. They go to the towns and fall into bad company. Girls become pregnant before marriage. Assistance once given freely by kin now often has to be paid for.

The Wakasigau do not regard themselves as being in control of these events; they live in a world where things happen to them. Although a few specific illnesses are attributed to personal transgressions, such as incest or adultery, many misfortunes are blamed on sorcery, or spirits, or the anger of ancestors or living persons (cf. Harris 1978). Each village has its reputed sorcerers, whose crimes are usually thought to be motivated by jealousy. Spirits take possession of individuals and demand offerings, causing illness and misfortune if their wishes are not met. Chronic illness is sometimes taken as a sign that an ancestor feels neglected. All these agencies belong to what might be called 'traditional' Kasigau culture, and there is a range of traditional medicines and charms to guard against them.

By the time of my fieldwork, Kasigau had been influenced by Christianity for fifty years or more and the vast majority of the population had undergone Anglican baptism. About 10 per cent of adults (and a considerable but fluctuating number of children) claimed to be born-again Christians, some within the Anglican Church and others in several small non-Anglican fellowships (see Milton 1981, 1982). Some of those who claim to be Christian still use the traditional explanations of and cures for misfortune, but others, particularly the non-Anglican born-again Christians, have replaced the plethora of bad forces with a single one, Satan. Instead of sorcerers, wild animals and spirits being evil or dangerous in and of themselves, they are seen as instruments of Satan, against whom the only sure defence is a steadfast faith in God.

A second modern influence on Kasigau culture is the essentially British formal education that has been transmitted through the schools since the 1930s.[7] Exposure to western science has led some people to express disbelief in sorcery, spirits and the harmful effects of anger. Those inclined to think in this way have largely abandoned traditional means of combating illness and misfortune, and instead use the modern health facilities provided in the least remote of the villages.

The presence of several different frames of reference within Kasigau culture is neatly illustrated by the following incident. A well-educated man, a devout member of the Anglican Church, was walking along a path that joined the two hamlets of his village when he was confronted by a cheetah. The animal did not attack, but in his surprise the man stumbled and cut his leg. No one could remember a cheetah having appeared in the village before. The 'traditionalists' assumed that some sorcery was at work, that the animal had been sent to cause harm. The non-Anglican born-again Christians prayed for the evil influence of Satan to leave their community, and assumed that the man's own faith in God had saved him from greater injury. The man himself thought it likely that bush fires on the plain below had driven the animal out of its normal range. He considered it nonsense to suggest that it had some evil intent because it was, after all, just an animal.

It would be impossible to identify a single Kasigau perspective on the environment. It has become a plural culture, with a variety of experiences and influences generating several diverse ways of understanding the world. But what many people in Kasigau share is an understanding that they are at the mercy of forces largely beyond their control. Traditionalists feel put upon by a range of personal agents. Herbal medicines, charms and ritual offerings give some protection against specific threats, but there are always others waiting in the wings. Christians see themselves as pawns in a struggle between good and evil. The most effective protection is a strong faith in God, but this is difficult to maintain in the face of worldly temptations, and in any case is no guarantee against misfortune, for the ways of God are a mystery. If Christianity is supposed to have ushered in a new era of human dominion over the natural world, there was little sign of it in Kasigau. If anything, Christianity brought a new fatalism; nothing happened except at God's command, and God's will was unquestionable.

Power and protection

The environment that dictates the fortunes of people in Kasigau is clearly very different from that whose powers are respectfully harnessed by the Dogon, and different again from that which generously meets the needs of hunter-gatherers. But all three environments share one important feature: they are all more powerful than the human communities that interact with them. It would be a mistake to see human beings as totally powerless in the face of these environments. The hunter-gatherers, as Bird-David pointed out (1992b), prevail upon, persuade and manage their environments in order to get what they need. The Dogon help to ensure their continued subsistence by showing the environment proper respect. The Wakasigau can employ both traditional and modern means for protecting themselves against attack from environmental forces, and they can put their faith in God, the most powerful of those forces. But in each case, the power of human beings to exert an influence on environmental processes is overshadowed by the environment's power in their lives; the balance of power lies with the environment, not with the people.

Compare this with the concern which, I have suggested, identifies a cultural perspective as environmentalist, the concern that the environment be protected through human effort and responsibility. This presupposes that people are in a position to protect the environment, that it is amenable to their protection, which implies that the balance of power lies with the people, not with the environment. This can be illustrated using a brief description of the values and assumptions of nature conservation.

Nature conservationists: protecting a fragile environment

The nature conservation perspective is a familiar part of the cultures of many industrial societies, and is expressed through the words and actions of some of the most high-profile environmental organizations, some of which have a long history.[8] Conservationists define the environment as 'nature', and the living part of nature as 'wildlife'. Nature is seen as separate from the processes and products of human activity, but not necessarily or universally separate, for in accordance with the myth of primitive ecological wisdom, the alienation of humanity from nature is seen as a consequence of industrial development: 'as social structures became more complex, and technologies improved, human beings were able increasingly to insulate themselves against nature' (Diamond *et al.* 1987: 325).

Insulation against nature made industrial societies blind to the impacts of their activities on the environment, but science has revealed the character and extent of these impacts. Populations of animals and plants have been reduced and many have become extinct as a consequence of human activity. Their habitats have been destroyed for development and through the effects of industrial pollution. But as Yearley pointed out (1992a: 143-4), science does not provide a moral basis for action. The nature conservation perspective depends on the integration of scientific knowledge with moral principles which derive from the values attached to 'natural' things. Nature is seen as inherently good; natural processes and circumstances are consistently valued more highly than those that result from human activity. Nature is at its most valuable when it is untouched by human hand. In selecting sites as nature reserves, conservation groups and authorities choose those that are closest to their 'original' state: primary woodland rather than secondary woodland, pristine peatland rather than areas that have had peat removed from them and have recovered. Wildlife species that are indigenous to an area are seen as more important than those introduced by people.

The most highly valued of all nature's characteristics is its diversity, which is seen as a source of spiritual and economic benefit to human beings (IUCN *et al.* 1991: 28). But this is not the only, nor necessarily the most important, reason why conservationists value nature's diversity. The greatest possible variety of life is seen as beneficial to the process of evolution, to which human beings and all other life forms are assumed (on the basis of scientific knowledge) to owe their existence. The more diversity there is, the greater the chance that some life forms will be able to adapt to changing conditions, ensuring the continuation of life itself. Anything that threatens nature's diversity jeopardizes this process. The most serious human impacts on nature, in the minds of conservationists, are those that threaten nature's diversity; hence their concern over the disappearance of species and habitats.

The very fact that this is happening is taken by conservationists as an indication that nature is not capable of defending itself against humanity. The biosphere is finite; 'our planet is much smaller, and infinitely more vulnerable, than we ever thought', and threatened species are 'flashing warning lights'. The counter argument, that nature is, in fact, robust, is seen as an attempt to absolve our guilt and abdicate our responsibility (Diamond *et al.* 1987: 21–2). Conservationists therefore act on behalf of nature, and encourage others to do the same. They 'stand in for nature' (Yearley 1993) in those situations in which nature's interests would otherwise be ignored: they represent the whales in debates over commercial whaling, and argue the case on behalf of species whose habitats are threatened by land-use proposals. They also take over the management of natural processes when nature is failing to sustain itself against the impact of human activity.[9] It would be misleading to suggest that conservationists see nature as totally powerless, for they often draw attention to instances in which nature appears to fight back – soil erosion and floods are nature's response to deforestation – but the balance of power, in the conservationists' perspective, rests with human beings.

Thus, while hunter-gatherers, the Dogon and the Wakasigau live in powerful environments, nature conservationists live in an environment that is fragile and needs their protection. This type of divergence of cultural perspectives was neatly demonstrated by Richards, studying Mende cultivators in the Gola Forest region of Sierra Leone. After discussions with local students about conservation, he suggested that they try to translate conservation slogans into Mende.

'Save Gola Forest', apparently the simplest slogan under consideration, was the one that caused the greatest difficulty. 'Save' was generally understood in the sense of to care for or to protect. In local thought that would imply to care for the forest as if it were someone's property.... But to Mende, forest is not property, nor should it be allowed to become so, because it is a basic resource upon which the whole society depends.

(Richards 1992a: 151)

The Mende were not in a position to protect the forest, not only because it was not property, but also because the forest, in their view, cared for and supported *them*, in the way that patrons support their clients. The closest local approximation to 'Save Gola Forest' was a phrase that meant 'get away from behind (stop living under the protection of) Gola Forest'. The forest was compared to a patron with too many clients, and the only conceivable way of 'saving' it was to relieve it of this burden (Richards 1992a: 151–2).

The cases discussed so far suggest that, in looking for non-industrial cultures that conform to the myth of primitive ecological wisdom, we should examine those in which human beings are seen as wielding some power over the environment. In her analysis of hunter-gatherer economies, Bird-David distinguished between the giving environment and the reciprocating environment (1990: 191). While the giving environment provides unconditionally, the reciprocating environment provides in return for the fulfilment of obligations. Thus a reciprocating environment is amenable to human influence. It was the reciprocal character of their relationship with their environment that brought North American Indian societies to the attention of environmentalists.

Indigenous hunters of North America: interacting with a reciprocating environment

In comparing traditional American Indian and European attitudes towards 'nature', Callicott made the following generalization:

most American Indians, lived in a world which was peopled not only by human persons, but by persons and personalities associated with all natural phenomena.... the typical traditional American Indian attitude was to regard all features of the environment as enspirited. These entities possessed a

126

consciousness, reason, and volition, no less intense and complete than a human being's. The Earth itself, the sky, the
winds, rocks, streams, trees, insects, birds, and all other animals therefore had personalities and were thus as fully persons as other [sic] human beings.

(Callicott 1982: 305)

He based these general comments on a range of sources, particularly the words of the Sioux spokesmen, Black Elk (Neihardt 1972
[1932]) and Lame Deer (Erdoes 1976), and the observations of two
ethnographers of the Ojibwa, Jenness (1935) and Hallowell (1960).
The rationale of Indian environmental knowledge was that everything that has power has life, and everything that has life has spirit,
consciousness and personhood. Power was evident, not only in
the observable characteristics of animals and plants, but also in the
movement of water and the decomposition of rocks into soil. All
living things are related in a family, of which the sky and the earth
are father and mother respectively (Callicott 1982: 302–3). This
relatedness of living things has moral implications that inform the
interactions between indigenous Americans and other persons in
their environment. The Cree hunters of Quebec, whose economy
and environmental knowledge have been described in detail by
Tanner (1979) and Scott (1989; see also Feit 1973), provide an
appropriate illustration.

The Cree and the animals they hunt belong to a single moral
community whose members recognize and fulfil obligations
towards each other. The Cree are aware of the needs and sensibilities of the animals and take them into account in their activities.
Similarly, the animals are aware of the needs of humans and provide for those needs as considerate kin are expected to do. Individual hunters are helped by animal friends, with whom they
form long-term relationships (1979: 139–40). Gifts are exchanged
between the human domain (the dwelling) and the animal domain
(the bush). The animals give themselves as food to the Cree.
Offerings of tobacco are made in return, and gifts of food placed
in the fire are carried back to the bush via the smoke ascending
through the chimney (Tanner 1979: 172–4). The distribution of the
meat and the treatment of inedible parts of the animal are important in the fulfilment of human obligations towards the animals
(Scott 1989: 203–4).

The extent to which the animals are really seen as choosing to give themselves is not entirely clear from the ethnography. Cree hunters go to considerable lengths to outwit their quarry (Scott 1989: 199), and some Cree myths present hunting as a struggle between hunter and animal (Tanner 1979: 149). Hunting is also likened to a sexual relationship in which the hunter seduces the animal with charms and songs. Reluctant animals may be tricked into giving themselves up against their will (Bird-David 1993: 113). On the other hand, a hunter who has no success should not be too disappointed, because 'it is wrong to expect more than is offered freely by a partner in reciprocity' (Scott 1989: 204), and the reciprocal nature of the relationship is stressed repeatedly in Tanner's description.

This element of reciprocity is crucial in distinguishing the type of environment experienced by the Cree from the other examples presented above. At first sight, it might appear that the Cree live in a giving environment very similar to that which, according to Bird-David's analysis, is experienced by hunter-gatherers with immediate return systems (such as the Nayaka, the Batek and the Mbuti). But these communities receive gifts unconditionally from their environments, whereas the Cree understand that their environment will cease to give if its generosity is not returned. The Cree environment might also appear superficially similar to that of the Dogon, who also received sustenance from the bush in return for respect. But the Dogon environment is unambiguously more powerful than the Dogon themselves, and power diminishes as it flows from the bush to the human sphere. The Dogon can take power from the bush, but they cannot give it back. In contrast, Tanner's description of the Cree hunt indicates that power is first transferred from animal to human, and then returned to the environment:

he [the hunter] acknowledges the animal's superior position, and following this the animal 'gives itself' to the hunter, that is, it allows itself to assume a position of equality, or even inferiority, with respect to the hunter.

... at the stage of divination [which precedes the hunt], the animal is on friendly terms with the hunter, but is far more powerful than him. The act of killing, on the other hand, becomes an exchange between 'persons' at a reciprocal or equivalent level. Finally, after the kill, ... the hunter must

128

observe rules... which... symbolize a final shift in the social model of the man–animal relationship.

(1979: 136, 153)

The power received by the Cree from the environment is returned in the form of ritual observances which, among other things, have 'the purpose of regenerating further animals' (Tanner 1979: 153). The Dogon feel unable to replenish the bush (van Beek and Banga 1992: 71), but the Cree see their own activities as doing precisely that. By giving back the power that it gives them, they ensure that it will provide for them in the future. This way of interacting with the environment is taken further in the next example.

Indigenous Australians: perpetuating the environment

Australian Aborigines have attracted a great deal of attention from anthropologists over the years, from the classic ethnography of Spencer and Gillen (1968 [1899]) to detailed analyses of their art and knowledge (Munn 1973, Morphy 1991) and studies of how they understand and come to terms with life in modern Australia (Sansom 1980, Bell 1983). Aboriginal culture has proved difficult to translate into terms that are easily comprehensible to outsiders (Keesing 1981: 333–4). The following brief account, taken mainly from Strehlow's ethnography of the Aranda-speaking peoples of central Australia (1970), makes no attempt to interpret its more complex components, but outlines only what is necessary to make a comparison with the cases presented above.

The environment in which indigenous Australians lived was created (Bird-David suggests 'procreated'; 1993: 114–16) by ancestral beings travelling through the country. As they travelled, they made the landscape of hills and valleys, rocks, pools and streams, the plants and animals that inhabit the landscape, and the elements on which all life depends. Many ancestral beings are themselves embodied in landscape features located at their journeys' end. They also created ceremonies to ensure the perpetuation of the environment, and sites where ceremonies should be performed. The ancestors named things as they created them, and the Aborigines continued to create by naming things in song, or painting them on rocks and bark, and by re-enacting the ancestral journeys in dance. The continuation of life depended on the correct performance of the creative acts invented by the ancestors. Thus the economic survival of Aboriginal communities was in the hands of ritual experts who knew the ceremonial cycles.

Responsibility for the continual recreation of the environment was distributed among Aboriginal clans and sub-clans according to their ancestral ties. All living Aborigines were considered to be reincarnations of ancestral beings, and each clan was responsible for continuing the work that its ancestors initiated. So, for instance, one clan might be responsible for perpetuating rain, another for perpetuating kangaroos, another for perpetuating honey-ants, and so on. These responsibilities were communal in the following sense:

> each Aranda local group was believed to perform an indis-pensable economic service not only for itself but for the population around its borders as well. Thus, the Eastern-Aranda Purula-Kamara local group of Ujîtja was believed to have the responsibility of creating rain for the whole of the surrounding countryside by the performance of the Ujîtja rain ceremonies .... In the same way, the members of kanga-roo, euro, emu, carpet snake, grass seed, and other totemic clans were regarded as having the power of bringing about the increase of their totemic plants and animals not only within their local group areas, but throughout the adjoining regions as well.
>
> (Strehlow 1970: 102)

If the population of a particular species declined, those respons-ible were blamed for not having performed the ceremonies cor-rectly. One euro (wallaby) clansman commented of the bandicoot clansmen, 'their ceremonies are useless. Euros are to be found everywhere, and it is we who create them. The bandicoots have vanished long ago' (Strehlow 1970: 103). A serious consequence of missionary influence among the Aborigines has been the disap-pearance of the traditional ceremonies, resulting in a long and steady decline in the state of the environment. On this point, it is worth quoting Strehlow at length:

> in present-day Central Australia one of the commonest Aboriginal criticisms made of the new order introduced by Europeans is that the whole country has been economically ruined by the wholesale destruction of all the indigenous forms of ritual activities. Ever since Central Australia's first

major drought of 1927–29 the Aboriginal population has attributed the ensuing lengthy successions of poor and dry years to the disappearance of the older generations of ritually wise and traditionally educated elders who alone knew fully how to create rain and how to promote the increase of plants and animals. . . . During the grim eight-year drought which ended in 1966, many sophisticated Aboriginal agnostics and some Christianized young leaders privately joined together in the same chorus of abuse: 'The old men always said that the rains would fail to come, that the animals and trees would die, and that men and women would fall ill, if the sacred songs were no longer sung and if the sacred acts were no longer performed. And what they said has come true. We young folk who know nothing about the old traditions are helpless to save the country; and the white people are just as useless.'

(Strehlow 1970: 111)

The idea of saving the environment thus appears to be entirely compatible with the cultural perspective held by at least some indigenous Australian societies. Unlike the Wakasigau, the Dogon, the Mende and those hunter-gatherers who live in an unconditionally generous environment, Australian Aborigines felt able, as long as they retained their knowledge of traditional ceremonies, to replenish the resources on which they depended. When their environment declined, it was seen as the result of their own failure.

The argument that the development of an environmentalist perspective depends on the way power is allocated within the human–environment relationship can be sharpened by presenting one final example. The Gaia theory[10] holds an ambiguous position within environmentalist thought. I suggest that this ambiguity can be attributed to the fact that the theory itself is ambiguous about the location of power.

Gaia: getting by with a little help from her friends?

Lovelock, who originated the Gaia theory, stated its central idea as follows: 'that the physical and chemical condition of the surface of the Earth, of the atmosphere, and of the oceans has been and is actively made fit and comfortable by the presence of life itself' (1979: 152). In other words, it is living organisms that keep the planet in a condition able to sustain life. This makes the Earth a single complex living system, a superorganism (Yearley 1992a: 145), to which Lovelock gave the name of the Greek Earth goddess, Gaia. One of the implications of the theory is that, for the future of life on Earth, it is the health of the system as a whole that matters, not the health of any particular species. Indeed, a particularly troublesome species, which threatens the health of the system, might be shrugged off, disposed of. Thus the planet's future as a living system is a separate issue from the future of humanity (Lovelock 1988: xvii). This has made Gaia a pivotal idea in the tension between anthropocentric and ecocentric environmentalist views.

The Gaia theory has received mixed responses from environmentalists. Some have embraced it as inspirational, and as a rationalization for their moral concern for the Earth as a whole, but have used it more as a basis for the spiritual expression of environmentalism than as a guide to practical action. Conservation scientists, in particular, were slow to acknowledge it. This is not surprising given that it challenged their conventional wisdom, 'which held that life adapted to the planetary conditions as it and they evolved their separate ways' (Lovelock 1979: 152). But in recent years, its scientific status has been treated more seriously (see the contributions in Schneider and Boston 1993), and some of the most scientifically orientated environmental organizations give the occasional nod in Gaia's direction (for instance IUCN et al. 1991: 27).

I suggest that these responses have been mixed because the implications of Gaia for human action are not clear. The theory seems to suggest that Gaia is in charge, and that she can look after her own interests; she does not require people to protect her. But we cannot be sure of this, for scientists tell us that living systems are vulnerable. The understanding of the Earth's history generated by geology suggests that, if the Earth is a superorganism, it might have vital organs and expendable parts. Periodically, the living system of the planet has lost about 30 per cent of its territory to glaciation, and has recovered each time. This suggests that Gaia's vital organs are not in the temperate regions but in the tropics, or perhaps in the wetlands or on the continental shelves (Lovelock 1979: 129ff.). Although Lovelock saw his role as that of explaining how Gaia works rather than prescribing courses of action, he did suggest that we might try to protect these regions if we want to minimize our impact on the planet's ability to support life. He also suggested ways in which, as individuals, we might try to live in harmony with Gaia (Lovelock 1988: 225ff.). So the Gaia theory is ambiguous on the matter of where power is located in the human–environment relationship, and therefore on the matter of what we can do. Its implications are such that environmentalists have felt unable or unwilling to ignore it, but suggest neither that Gaia is totally in control of her own destiny, nor that her future is fully in our hands.

THE LESSONS OF CROSS-CULTURAL COMPARISON

At the beginning of this chapter I suggested that, by comparing a range of cultural perspectives on the environment, we might come to understand how environmentalism differs from, and is similar to, other ways of understanding the world. As a starting point for the comparative analysis, I chose to examine the myth, commonly held by environmentalists and others within industrial society, that non-industrial societies possess a primitive ecological wisdom that enables them to live in harmony with their environments. It is time to consider what the comparison reveals, both about the myth and about the character of environmentalism as a cultural perspective.

Reassessing the myth

The cases outlined above are not, of course, intended to be representative or exhaustive. They merely illustrate a range of perspectives that exist within the human cultural repertoire. But they are sufficient to indicate that the myth of primitive ecological wisdom is not well founded. Clearly, there are some non-industrial societies that hold themselves responsible for protecting their environment. The Kogi, the Australian Aborigines and some indigenous American societies all see it as their obligation to perform tasks that will ensure the continuation of the environments on which they depend. But there are also non-industrial societies which do not recognize a human responsibility to protect the environment, and which probably could not do so without changing some of their basic assumptions about the nature of the environment and their relationship with it. Whatever the differences between cultural

133

perspectives that encompass environmentalist principles and those that do not, they apparently have little to do with the dividing line between non-industrial and industrial societies.

Why, then, do environmentalists continue to believe that non-industrial cultures are environmentally benign? I suggest four reasons for the persistence of the myth. The first concerns its nature as a myth, as a dogmatic assertion not easily refuted. The myth persists because environmentalists have good reasons for wanting to believe in it. The idea that non-industrial cultures are kind to the environment enables radical environmentalists to argue that industrialism *per se* is responsible for environmental destruction. It also enables them to believe that there are viable alternatives to a destructive economy, that by relinquishing industrialism we might create a truly sustainable way of life.

Second, environmentalists remain largely ignorant about the ways in which non-industrial peoples understand and interact with their environments; they therefore have no grounds for doubting the myth. Rayner pointed out that this is the fault of anthropologists: 'If Mrs Thatcher, the Green Movement, or Joe Public persist in misconceptions of the lesson that anthropology can teach us about human relationships with the natural environment, anthropologists are largely to blame' (Rayner 1989: 1; cf. Milton 1989: 30). Like many other academic specialists, they have failed to communicate their knowledge to an audience beyond their own colleagues. They have couched their findings in language that non-specialists find difficult to understand, and published them in journals that most people never hear of.

Third, environmentalists fail, as anthropologists used to, to distinguish between culture and the things people do. The actual impacts of non-industrial societies on their environments depend on how they use those environments to meet their needs; whether they harvest wild food from the forest or clear areas of forest to grow crops, whether they fell whole trees for firewood or merely cut a few branches from each, whether they exploit the resources of one area to exhaustion or move around, spreading their demand more thinly over a larger territory. Without distinguishing between what people think, feel and know about the world (their culture) and the things they do, it is easy to make the mistake of assuming that societies which appear to have little impact on their environments must necessarily have environmentally benign cultures. And yet, as Ellen (1986) and others pointed out, there are other factors that reduce the impact of people on their environment, such as geographical isolation, low population density and limited technology (see above). Once we distinguish between a society's culture and its members' actual uses of their environment, it is possible to see that low environmental impact can exist alongside a culture which espouses no environmentalist principles.

This point can be illustrated using the example of hunter-gatherers with immediate-return systems, who think of their environment, according to Bird-David's analysis, as a generous donor that unquestioningly meets their needs. Since they do not *expect* its generosity to run out, they might well continue to take from the environment whatever it can give until its supplies are exhausted. In terms of the surprise theorists' model, outlined in Chapter 3, hunter-gatherers who are accustomed to living in a giving environment are likely to act as if 'nature' is robust. It might come as quite a shock to western environmentalists to learn that some of the least environmentally damaging societies are culturally closer to industrial entrepreneurs, in some ways, than to themselves!

The final reason why the myth of primitive ecological wisdom persists among environmentalists is that, within the context of global environmental discourse, non-industrial societies have themselves helped to perpetuate the myth by adopting the image that industrial society has constructed for them. There are good political reasons why they should do this. In particular, by allowing themselves to be depicted, in the global arena, as environmentally benign, they win the support of environmentalists throughout the world against the political elites in their own countries in their efforts to retain or regain their traditional freedoms. This point will be discussed more fully in Chapter 6.

Identifying environmentalist cultures

It is not my intention here to try to explain why some cultures contain or can accommodate environmentalist ideas and principles while others do not, though this is a question to which cultural theory could and should be addressed; indeed, it is the question addressed by Douglas and her colleagues, whose work was discussed in the last chapter. Here, I want to identify the kinds of questions we should ask in order to determine whether a particular culture or cultural perspective might be capable of accommodating environmentalist ideas. These questions concern the way people

135

define their environment and their relationship with it, the way they value it, the manner in which they allocate moral responsibility and the timescales within which they plan and evaluate their activities.

The first question is that identified in the comparative analysis above: where does the balance of power lie in human–environment relations? Societies and groups which see the balance of power as lying with the environment are unlikely to be able to envisage taking a protective role towards it, while for those who see the environment as amenable to their influence or manipulation, a protective role is not precluded. The clearest illustration of this contrast is provided by Richards' comparison of Mende and conservationists' understandings of the rainforest. For the conservationists, the forest is a passive object, 'an endangered asset ... without human agency it can have no future' (Richards 1992a: 138). For the Mende, as we have seen, it is more like a patron who supports and protects them. They could envisage the possibility of relieving it of this burden, but not of actively protecting it (Richards 1992a: 151–2). The fact that people see themselves as living under the power of their environment, rather than vice versa, does not mean that they will have no concern for it if it appears threatened. But it does mean that they are unlikely to see protection of the environment as something they themselves can accomplish. Instead, they might watch helplessly as the desert advances or the forest disappears, or hope that some external agency (a divine power, a central authority or international organization) might intervene.

Second, there is the question of whether the environment is assumed to be vulnerable or resilient (or, in the surprise theorists' terminology, 'fragile' or 'robust'). This question identifies one of the features separating environmentalists within industrial society from those whom they oppose. The understanding that the environment can be dominated and manipulated by people is shared by both parties. But a great deal of industrial development has taken place apparently on the assumption that the environment can withstand whatever is done to it, whereas environmentalists assume that it cannot. The Kogi would recognize this view. For them, it is the careless disregard of the Younger Brother that has placed the very heart of the world in jeopardy. They do what they can, through their ritual observances, but their only hope is that the Younger Brother will recognize the vulnerability of the Earth and cease his destructive ways.

Third, there is the question of how the environment is valued. It may be seen as both vulnerable and amenable to human influence and power, but there may still be no imperative to protect it if it is not considered important. Insofar as people view their environment anthropocentrically – in terms of its use and value to them – their assessment of its importance will be affected by the extent to which they see themselves as dependent upon it.[11] If they do not need it for their own survival and comfort, they are less likely to be concerned if it is threatened. In Chapter 1, I drew attention to Dasmann's distinction between ecosystem people (small, traditional communities or people who have opted out of industrial society), who rely on the resources of a single ecosystem, and biosphere people (industrial society), who draw on the resources of the entire biosphere. I pointed out that ecosystem people might be expected to value their immediate environments highly because they depend upon them. Biosphere people might be expected, not only to attribute less value to their immediate environments, because the resources on which they depend come from elsewhere, but also to attribute less value to those distant environments whose resources they use. These environments, because they are distant, do not impinge on their lives, and if their resources fail, they can always move on to exploit some other, equally distant environment. This particular characteristic of biosphere culture is illustrated by the observation that industrial societies have often exported their worst environmental impacts by locating their most polluting activities well outside their own borders (see Yearley 1992a: 157ff.).[12]

The answers to these questions will indicate whether a particular society or group of people is likely to regard protection of the environment as possible and/or necessary, or to be able to accommodate such a view. We may need to ask other questions to determine the likelihood of their actually adopting environmentalist principles. For instance, how is moral responsibility allocated within the society? People who acknowledge that they have the power to protect the environment, and that it is important to do so, might still see it as someone else's responsibility. Environmental campaigners often find it difficult to persuade even a concerned and attentive public to take personal responsibility for environmental change. Within a liberal democracy, the public and the government tend to delegate responsibility to each other. The public assume that they elected the government for that very purpose, while the government tend to treat an apparent lack of public concern as reason not to act; they act only when public protest or voting patterns prompt them to do so. In Britain, for instance, the government's first significant efforts to demonstrate a concern for the environment came only after the Green Party had won 14.5 per cent of the vote in the 1989 European Parliament Elections (Dobson 1990: 2; Yearley 1992a: 1–2).

Or, how is the relationship between events and time understood? If time is seen as a linear dimension within which change is irreversible, this adds an extra impetus to environmental concern. It is particularly important to protect the environment *now* because there may be no other chance to do so. This kind of thinking is implied in such environmentalist slogans as 'Tomorrow is too late' and 'Extinction is for ever'. This impetus is missing if events are seen as repeating themselves in a cyclical pattern. Our understanding of past climatic changes, in which successive ice ages have given way to warmer periods, helps to insulate us, to some extent, from the fear that we might ultimately be responsible for irreversibly changing the Earth's climate. The changes provoked by human activities seem less alarming when set in the context of the larger, 'natural' pattern. In a similar way, the understanding that mass extinctions have happened repeatedly in the past (see Leakey and Lewin 1992: 354), followed each time by a recovery of biological diversity, enables us to reassure ourselves that our impact might not be so final after all. One of the reasons why environmentalists have felt ambivalent towards the Gaia theory is that it presents us with the larger pattern and so offers this kind of reassurance.

Even when people are convinced of the need for environmental protection and have identified a timescale within which it has to be accomplished, they might not be able to relate their own activities to that timescale. In societies with 'immediate return systems' (Woodburn 1980), people do not expect to have to concern themselves with future needs, but consider only what is necessary to satisfy them for the present. And it has often been observed that the electoral systems of liberal democracies operate on a timescale that is incompatible with concern for the long-term future. Those with the power to effect the kinds of policy changes that might ensure long-term environmental protection have only four or five years to persuade the electorate that they should remain in power for another, equally short, spell.

The environmentalist critique of industrialism

If the myth of primitive ecological wisdom supports the environmentalist critique of industrialism, where does the refutation of the myth leave this critique? One of the main components of the cultural case against industrialism is the argument that it is industrial society's idealization of growth, and of the consumption patterns that sustain growth, that help to support an environmentally destructive economy. The myth of primitive ecological wisdom rests, to a large extent, on the assumption that non-industrial societies are different from industrial societies in this respect; that they do not idealize growth or aim to maximize material consumption.

This image of non-industrial societies is quite close to Sahlins' model of the 'original affluent society' (1968). He argued that some non-industrial societies, particularly those with hunting and gathering economies, experience a degree of 'affluence', not because they possess so much but because they require so little to satisfy their material needs. But he did not imply that this lack of desire for material wealth was universal in the non-industrial world; to have done so would have flown in the face of evidence. There are many well-known cases in the ethnographic literature of lavish wealth and conspicuous consumption as a source of prestige and power. In many pastoral societies, in which animals are the main store of wealth, people aim to maximize the size of their herds, and large numbers of animals are given in marriage transactions (see, for instance, Evans-Pritchard 1940). Trobriand Islanders aimed to produce a huge surplus of yams from their gardens; some to be given away to kin and political patrons, some to be left conspicuously to rot in the yam houses as testimony to their owners' wealth and power (Malinowski 1935). Among the Kwakiutl of Vancouver Island, potlatch feasts, at which huge amounts of wealth were distributed, were an important source of prestige; 'There was keen competition among members of the elite to outdo each other in their largesse' (Howard 1986: 149; for a full account see Codere 1950).

Cross-cultural comparison of attitudes to wealth, and of other assumptions and values related to people's uses of their environments, clearly indicate that industrial culture is not unique in these respects. Thus it cannot be industrialism *per se* that is the cause of environmental destruction. This does not, of course, refute the argument that most large-scale environmental destruction is the result of industrial processes. Still less does it imply that a cultural shift away from industrialism will not be effective in fostering more benign ways of interacting with the environment. But it does mean that environmentalists need to be cautious in selecting their models for sustainable living from the non-industrial world.

Cultural diversity and survival

It seems fitting to round off a discussion on cultural diversity by commenting on its value. In outlining the nature conservation perspective, I referred to the fact that biological diversity is considered important because it is seen as the raw material on which the process of evolution depends. The less diversity there is, the greater the chance that life itself could be wiped out as a consequence of environmental change. It is worth pointing out that a parallel argument is made about human cultural diversity, both by anthropologists and by environmentalists. Different ways of understanding and interacting with the world provide different possibilities for human futures (cf. Keesing 1981: 506). If some cultural perspectives ultimately prove to be unsustainable (as environmentalists argue will be the case for industrialism), then human survival will depend on the existence of alternatives. Thus, while advocating that all societies strive to become sustainable, some environmentalists argue that the world needs 'a variety of sustainable societies, achieved by many different paths' (IUCN *et al.* 1991: 8).[13]

The discussion in this chapter has indicated that the identification of environmentally sustainable cultures is likely to be a complex and uncertain business. It is also difficult to imagine that the selection of such cultures could take place in a systematic and deliberate way. It could be that sustainable ways of living will simply be those that are left, once the unsustainable economies have burned themselves out, so to speak, or that sustainable cultures might eventually emerge out of whatever degree of devastation is created by unsustainable economies. Whatever the case, it seems reasonable to argue that, if we care about the long-term survival of the human species, we would do well to protect our cultural diversity as an important resource. This leads directly to the subject of the next two chapters, for if the process of globalization is taking place as some social scientists describe it, then it presents a serious threat to cultural diversity.

5

GLOBALIZATION, CULTURE AND DISCOURSE

Ah Love! could you and I with Fate conspire
To grasp this sorry Scheme of Things entire...
  (*Rubáiyát of Omar Khayyám*, Fitzgerald 1947: 146)

'Cultures' do not hold still for their portraits.
                                        (Clifford 1986: 10)

It would seem appropriate, in a study of environmentalism, to discuss globalization.[1] Environmentalists make constant reference to things global. Environmental protection is considered to be a global responsibility and global warming one of the major environmental problems. Environmental campaigners encourage us to 'think globally' while acting to protect our local environments. In its organization, too, environmental discourse has acquired global proportions. The biggest ever gathering of national leaders took place at the Rio Earth Summit in 1992 (Grubb *et al.* 1993: 1). The largest environmental NGOs, such as Greenpeace and the World Wide Fund for Nature (WWF), operate throughout the world. Rainforest communities of Amazonia and Malaysia, indigenous peoples of Australia and North America, mountain villagers of the Andes and northern India, as well as middle-class Americans and Europeans, all enter environmental discourse to claim what they see as their traditional rights or to express their altruistic concerns. If any cultural phenomenon can rightly be called 'global', then surely environmentalism must qualify.

But the issue is not as simple as it seems, for globalization, like most concepts in social science, is open to different interpretations. Does it refer to the way the world is seen or imagined, or to things going on in the world? Does it, for instance, describe the emergence of a concept of the 'world-as-a-whole' (Robertson 1990:

20), rather than, or as well as, a series of separate locations, or does it refer to the fact that we can now communicate easily with all parts of the world (Ahmed and Donnan 1994: 1)? Or are these processes considered to be part of the same broad phenomenon? In other words, does 'globalization' refer to the tendency for global communications to generate a sense of the global, or vice versa? As one would expect, the ways in which social scientists conceptualize and interpret globalization are dependent on their theoretical interests.

In this chapter I shall argue that, appropriately defined, a concept of globalization can provide a useful framework for understanding some features of environmentalism as a cultural phenomenon. This means developing an understanding of globalization that is consistent with cultural theory, one that enables us to ask questions about what happens to culture under conditions of globalization. In particular, following the discussion at the end of the last chapter, I am interested in how globalization affects cultural diversity. Most social scientists who have studied globalization have approached it from directions other than cultural theory. This does not necessarily mean that existing models of globalization cannot be used to develop a cultural approach, but it does mean that a careful scrutiny is needed to decide what is useful in the existing literature, and what is not. In particular, it is important to understand not only how globalization is defined, but also how culture is understood by those analysts who have focused on globalization. The following discussion therefore aims to clarify three issues within the current social scientific literature: what is meant by globalization, what is understood by culture in studies of globalization, and how the relationship between them is envisaged.

There are several models of globalization that could be extracted from the literature, but three seem to dominate and are clearly distinguishable, particularly in terms of the attention they pay to culture. First, there is the idea that globalization is the emergence of a world system, usually an economic or a political system. This model is most thoroughly developed in the work of Wallerstein, who is considered to be the leading exponent of 'world systems theory', though he himself did not see the object of his study in terms of 'globalization' (Robertson 1992: 141). The idea of a world system is also central to the study of international relations. Second, there is the idea that globalization is the creation of a particular kind of social condition as a direct consequence of modernity (Giddens 1990); globalized social relations flow inevitably from institutionalized ways of acting in the modern world. These models, the manner in which they have been used by writers on environmental issues, and their treatment of culture, are discussed briefly in the following sections. The third model, which sees globalization as a dual process whereby the world becomes a single place (Robertson 1992), is discussed later in the chapter.

THE STUDY OF WORLD SYSTEMS

Although, as has been pointed out, the concept of a system need imply only the existence of relationships (Wuthnow 1983: 61), analysts who have studied world systems have usually taken it to mean more: that the set of relationships is both structured and bounded in some way, so that a change in one brings about a change in others.[2] Wallerstein described a 'world system' in general terms as having 'boundaries, structures, member groups, rules of legitimization and coherence' (1974: 347). He also stated that a traditional economic system 'that became tied to an empire by the payment of tribute as "protection costs" ceased by that fact to be a "system"' (1979: 5, quoted in Chirot and Hall 1982: 84). In other words, once a system leaks, once it has relationships beyond its boundaries, it is no longer a system in itself, but becomes part of a wider system.

Wallerstein identified two types of world system: world empires, characterized by political relationships; and world economies, characterized by economic relationships (1979). In his models, the constituent units of both types of system were nation-states, though it has often been pointed out that the major players in the world economy include other units as well, such as transnational corporations, banks and other financial institutions (Nash 1981: 413ff.; Giddens 1990: 71; Chatterjee and Finger 1994: 136). World empires, for the moment at least, appear to be a thing of the past, whereas the world economy seems destined to exert an ever increasing influence on people's everyday lives. In its most popular form, what has come to be known as 'world systems theory' is concerned with modelling the global capitalist economy (see Wallerstein 1974, 1979, 1980).[3]

The structure which holds the world economy together consists of an industrialized core or centre and an undeveloped, or less developed, periphery. In this respect, world systems theory is similar to dependency theory, which preceded it (see Frank 1967, 1969). The periphery supplies the centre with the raw materials and labour it needs to fuel its own expansion. Because expansion is the centre's principal and overriding goal, it always pays back to the periphery less than it receives. Some nation-states may belong, at any one time, to an intermediate category called the 'semiperiphery'. Less powerful, in economic terms, than the centre, but more powerful than the periphery, semiperipheral states can play an important role in managing the political discontent of the periphery, and in providing relatively cheap resources for the centre when its production costs become uncomfortably high (Chirot and Hall 1982: 85).

Although generally referred to as theory, the world systems model is more historical than theoretical in orientation. It is essentially a description of a unique historical process, the rise of modern capitalism (cf. Wuthnow 1983: 59). There is thus just one case from which to derive generalizations, and no others on which to test them. As a general model for world-system construction, it remains speculative, at least for the present. The historical character of world system models has important consequences for the way globalization is conceptualized. If globalization is the process whereby the world system is created, and if the world system is an historically unique condition, then globalization must itself be an historically unique process. While it may be possible to conceive of different ways in which globalization *might* occur, these could not be tested because there is only one way in which it *has* occurred.

However, an alternative image of a world system is presented by analysts of international relations (Bergesen 1990). The absence of world empires does not mean that there is no worldwide political system; international relations theory models the development of the global political network, just as 'world systems theory' has modelled the development of the global capitalist economy. Giddens summarized the political model as follows:

> Sovereign states, it is presumed, first emerge largely as separate entities, having more or less complete administrative control within their borders. As the European state system matures and later becomes a global nation-state system, patterns of interdependence become increasingly developed. These are not only expressed in the ties states form with one

145

another in the international arena, but in the burgeoning of inter-governmental organizations. These processes mark an overall movement towards 'one world', although they are continually fractured by war.

(1990: 66)

It was once widely thought that this process would ultimately lead to the creation of a world state. Few would now predict this, though the progressive surrender of sovereignty by individual states to international bodies is still seen as characterizing the system. For instance, the European Union has restricted the independence of its member states by setting common standards in several areas, including environmental protection and food production, and worldwide the development of national defence capabilities is restricted by international treaties designed to prevent the abuse of nuclear power.

Like world systems theory, international relations theory is historical in orientation, and must therefore run the gauntlet of alternative interpretations of 'what really happened'. Bergesen, for instance, criticized both international relations theory and Wallerstein's world system model for the primacy they give to the nation-state. He argued that, instead of nation-states with separate identities interacting to create a world system, they only emerged as distinct units once a world system was in place (Bergesen 1990; cf. Giddens 1990: 67). In other words, state identities were born out of the interaction that took place within empires and within the global economy.

The world system and the environment

While not referring directly to the work of the world systems and international relations theorists, many writers on environmental issues employ the concept of a world system in their analyses. In particular, the environmental problems experienced by people in less-developed countries, in the form of deforestation, soil erosion, pollution, desertification, and a general inability to meet their own basic needs from their environment, are seen as the result of the participation of those countries in the global economy. The widespread African famine of the mid-1980s is often cited as an example:

Triggered by drought, its real causes lie deeper. They are to

146

be found in part in national policies that gave too little attention, too late, to the needs of smallholder agriculture and to the threats posed by rapidly rising populations. Their roots extend also to a global economic system that takes more out of a poor continent than it puts in.

(World Commission on Environment and
Development 1987: 6)

The global system of which some of these environmental analysts write is similar to that depicted by world systems and international relations theorists in that it is driven by the actions of nation-states. Environmental problems are seen as the outcome of economic and development policies pursued by states. It is also similar to Wallerstein's model (and to dependency theory) in that it has a centre and a periphery. The centre consists of the affluent and developed states of the 'North', the periphery is the less developed 'South'. The North's pursuit of economic growth is seen as the cause of environmental degradation in the South. The North has used the raw materials and labour of the South, has lent funds and supported development projects in the South, and has set the conditions of international trade, all on terms that favour its own economic expansion. Southern states have pursued policies which replace subsistence agriculture with schemes to generate cash, simply in order to repay their debts. In many areas, the very environments on which people depended for their survival have been destroyed: rainforests have been felled for the world timber trade or replaced with cattle ranches to supply the international beef market, large cash-cropping and industrial projects have used up or polluted local water supplies. It has often been observed that the character of environmental concern has been shaped by these centre–periphery differences. In the North, environmentalism has often been about the quality of life, in terms of a pleasant and diverse countryside and clean air, while in the South environmentalism is about life itself, about people's ability to survive in a degraded environment (see Redclift 1984: 47–8).

The understanding of environmental problems in terms of a global system of economic and political relations has given rise to several well-known analyses and critiques of that system (for instance, Meadows et al. 1972, Global 2000 1982, IUCN et al. 1991). The United Nations commissioned several reports which examined, with varying degrees of emphasis, the links between the

147

global economy, environmental degradation, human survival and international security, and proposed solutions (Brandt Commission 1983, WCED 1987). These reports have tended to argue for a continuation and enhancement of economic growth in order that the South might be made richer, enabling it to pay for a way out of its environmental and economic difficulties. This view will be discussed more fully in Chapter 6.

Culture in the study of world systems

Culture has been an important focus for debate among world system analysts. Early critics of Wallerstein argued that it was more or less absent from his understanding of how the world economy was produced. Chirot and Hall saw the refusal of world systems theory to take account of culture as a serious failing in its attempt to understand social change and economic progress (1982: 101). Such comments quickly became obsolete, however, as world system analysts developed an interest in the ideological basis of the world economy, and in the role of 'ideological communities' (Wuthnow 1983); for instance, in the form of both established and new religions, in shaping the world system by either supporting or opposing the capitalist ethos (see Wuthnow 1978, 1980, Wallerstein 1983). By the mid-1980s, Robertson and Lechner were able to write, 'Culture has . . . become a significant consideration in world-system theory. Indeed we are approaching the point where it has become an accepted part of world-system theorizing to include culture as a critical variable' (1985: 109). More recently, Wallerstein has identified culture as a principal mechanism through which national identities are created and contested within the world system (1990a).

The incorporation of culture into world system models might appear to suggest that they could be useful in developing a cultural theory approach to globalization. In order to assess their value in this respect, we need to know whether the concept of culture employed in world systems theory is compatible with those employed by anthropologists in their development of cultural theory. In the literature on world systems, culture is sometimes identified with 'ideas' (Chirot and Hall 1982: 101). Many post-structuralist anthropologists would no doubt find this perfectly acceptable, since it matches their own terminology (see Chapter 1). In the work of some world system analysts, 'culture' appears to be more or less identical with 'ideology'. Anthropologists might consider this restrictive (Hannerz 1989: 205), but as indicated in Chapter 3, what some social scientists understand by ideology is not far removed from the concept of culture that has predominated in post-structuralist anthropology. So the 'restriction' of culture to ideology in world systems theory does not necessarily indicate that it is incompatible with an anthropological approach. Some world system analysts focus on religion as a field in which to examine the relationship of culture with the world system (Wuthnow 1978, 1980). There appears to have been no intention to identify culture with religion (which anthropologists would certainly find restrictive), but it is difficult to avoid the impression that religion was somehow seen as unambiguously cultural, and therefore as a safe, uncontroversial route through which to bring culture into the debate.

Both the equation of culture with ideology and the focus on religion are symptoms of a more fundamental and, from an anthro-pological viewpoint, more problematic feature of world systems theory (and, indeed, of other approaches in social science): the identification of politics, economics and culture as distinct areas within the broad field of study. In the early development of world system models, politics and economics were distinguished as the integrating mechanisms of the two types of world system, empires and economies (Wallerstein 1979). Culture was included later as a third mechanism. Robertson and Lechner thus identified 'three major arenas of struggle' within the world system, 'the economic, the political, and *the cultural*' (1985: 109, emphasis given). The growing interest in culture among world systems theorists, which reflected the trend taking place throughout sociology (noted in Chapter 1), apparently resulted from a realization that politics and economics together did not account for all the processes that could be observed operating within the world system. Culture therefore had to be conceptualized as something other than politics and economics, and tends to be treated as a residual category, incorpor-ating everything that politics and economics do not.

The separation of politics, economics and culture within world system models renders them incompatible with an anthropological approach, for it makes the concept of culture implied in world systems theory different from that used by anthropologists. It is impossible, from an anthropological viewpoint, to conceptualize culture in such a way that it does not include at least some aspects of politics and economics, or to conceptualize politics and economics in a way that does not make them at least partly cultural. Anthropological thought never treated culture as a phenomenon distinct from, but of the same order as, politics and economics. In the functionalist and structuralist eras, culture was the all-encompassing category that included politics, economics, religion and all other institutionalized spheres of human thought and activity. When anthropologists began to distinguish, for analytical purposes, between culture and social processes, between what people know and the ways in which they organize their activities and relationships, this distinction cut across the substantive parts of each system, so that it makes sense to talk of political culture and political activity or organization, and of economic culture and economic activity or organization, but never of politics, economics and culture.

Interestingly, Wallerstein declared a wish to abandon this framework:

> The sooner we unthink this unholy trinity, the sooner we shall begin to construct a new historical social science that gets us out of the many cul-de-sacs in which we find ourselves. Emphasizing 'culture' in order to counterbalance the emphases others have put on the 'economy' or the 'polity' does not at all solve the problem; it in fact just makes it worse. We must surmount the terminology altogether.
>
> (1990b: 65)[4]

He went on to claim that world system analysis is part of his search for a better terminology. But the logic of this claim is suspect, for the framework he wishes to dismantle is the one that supports his model. If the trinity of economics, politics and culture were dissolved, the whole edifice of world systems theory would collapse; unthinking the trinity requires us to unthink the model.

GLOBALIZATION AS A CONSEQUENCE OF MODERNITY

The idea that globalization is a condition arising out of the institutions of modern life was advocated by Giddens (1990). He defined globalization as, 'the intensification of worldwide social relations which link distant localities in such a way that local happenings are shaped by events occurring many miles away and vice versa' (1990: 64). Countless examples could be offered in illustration, and it seems appropriate to mention two which have clear environmental implications. The furnishing of suburban homes in industrial societies is linked to the displacement of rain-forest communities in Brazil and Malaysia from their traditional lands, through the commercial harvesting of tropical hardwoods which destroys their environment. In the 1980s, the economies of Canadian Arctic communities suffered as a result of the high-profile campaign in Europe against the killing of baby seals. The import of baby seal products was banned by the European Community and some consumers threatened to boycott Canadian fish products until the seal hunt was stopped. Greenpeace, which played a prominent role in the campaign, later apologized to Arctic communities for the damage caused to their economies (see Wenzel 1991).

For Giddens, this intensification of social relations takes place in four dimensions: the world capitalist economy, the nation-state system, the world military order and the international division of labour (1990: 71). He criticized both world systems theory and international relations theory as having produced only partial models of globalization, since they each concentrate on only one of the four dimensions: the capitalist economy and the nation-state system respectively. It could be argued that Giddens' model is nothing more than an integration of these two images of the world system. If the capitalist economy and the international division of labour are both seen as economic dimensions[5] and the nation-state system and military order as political dimensions, then Giddens' model could be said to represent a world system in which politics and economics, the two integrating mechanisms treated separately by other analysts, are combined. But this view would contradict his understanding of the processes that lie behind globalization. The four dimensions of globalization correspond, in Giddens' model, to what he identified as the four institutional dimensions of modernity: capitalism, surveillance ('the supervision of the activities of subject populations'), military power and industrialism (1990: 55–9). Capitalism and industrialism, in his view, are distinct dimensions. Capitalism has to do with relations among people, specifically between the owners of capital and the providers of wage labour. Industrialism has to do with relations between people and the material world; it is the production of goods through the use of machines (1990: 55–6).

For Giddens, modern institutions are inherently globalizing. They enable social relations to operate over distances in time and space that would have been inconceivable in a pre-modern world. For instance, money, as a universal medium of exchange (enabling anything to be exchanged for anything), as a store of wealth and a measure of credit and debt, 'provides for the enactment of transactions between agents widely separated in time and space'. It is thus what Giddens called a 'disembedding' mechanism, in that it lifts transactions out of a particular context (Giddens 1990: 24). Modern means of communication have had a similar impact. They have lifted discourse out of local contexts and enabled it to take place over enormous distances of time and space. Transport technology has freed agricultural production from the seasonal constraints that operate in specific locations. It is now possible to guarantee (more or less) the supply of any commodity at any time (see Goodman and Redclift 1991: 96).

The consequences of modernity for the environment

It has been argued that environmental degradation is a routine consequence of modernity. The needs of the environment have been persistently subordinated to the needs of modern institutions, such as capital, bureaucracy and consumption, resulting in 'the breaching or rupture of eco-systemic tolerances in a systematic and reiterated fashion' (Saurin 1993: 47). The globalizing tendencies of modernity mean that degradation takes place on a global scale. Because industrial processes are not, thanks to modern technology, tied to particular times and locations, pollution can occur anywhere, and the means of transporting the material products of modernity to markets around the world add further to the degradation of the 'global commons', the oceans and the atmosphere.

Not only do modern institutions routinely generate environmental damage, they also make it difficult for us to do anything about it. Saurin's (1993) analysis identified (albeit implicitly) three aspects of this problem. First, the separation of actions from their consequences by a series of intervening processes makes it difficult to identify the cause of environmental damage. Awareness of this difficulty has promoted 'life-cycle analysis' as a means of assessing the environmental impacts of specific products and industrial processes (Elkington and Hailes 1993). Every stage in the manufacture and use of a product, from the means of obtaining raw materials to the manner of the product's eventual disposal ('cradle to grave'), is examined for its environmental consequences.

Second, the distancing of actions from their consequences also makes it difficult to allocate moral responsibility for environmental damage. The involvement of a large number of actors in an industrial process makes it easier for each to abdicate responsibility for the outcome of that process; there is always someone else to blame. In addition, the agencies involved in industrial processes are often impersonal – they are companies, governments, licensing authorities. Accordingly, responsibility is also impersonalized, and the moral significance of personal actions is suppressed: 'With most of the socially significant actions mediated by a long chain of complex causal and functional dependencies, moral dilemmas recede from sight, while the occasions for more scrutiny and conscious moral choice become increasingly rare' (Bauman 1989: 25, quoted in Saurin 1993: 50). Awareness of this difficulty has prompted environmental campaigners in recent years to concentrate on increasing people's understanding of the distant consequences of their actions, and persuading them to take personal responsibility for those consequences, particularly through the choices they make as consumers.

Finally, the diffuse nature of environmental degradation – because, as a routine consequence of modernity, it occurs wherever and whenever modern institutions have an impact – makes its management in practical terms extremely difficult. Thus, it is 'not carelessness nor even a lack of awareness of degradation that constitutes the major barrier to ecological sensitivity and propriety, but the inability to contain the diffused manufacture of degradation' (Saurin 1993: 47). Despite the apparently spectacular growth in the awareness of environmental problems within industrial societies, any movement towards solutions tends to be piecemeal and very slow. This is one of the major sources of frustration among environmentalists.

The consequences of modernity for culture

Robertson accused Giddens of neglecting culture in his model of globalization (Robertson 1992: 142). While it is true that Giddens did not employ a clearly defined concept of culture, he did not ignore the cultural components either of modernity or of globalization. According to Giddens, modern society is characterized by certain kinds and uses of knowledge. One of the differences between 'pre-modern' (what I have called 'non-industrial') and modern cultures is that, in the former, knowledge remains embedded in the context of its use, while modernity removes knowledge from that context through the creation of 'expert systems' (Giddens 1990: 27–9). This is a direct consequence of the industrial division of labour. Knowledge of how electrical appliances work is located away from most of the everyday contexts in which they are used, so that users need to call in experts when the appliances need repair. In industrial society many people who cook and eat vegetables do not know how to grow them, and most of those who grow them do not know how to produce the fertilizers and pesticides that are supposed to ensure their quality.

Where knowledge remains embedded in the context of its use, as it does in 'pre-modern' societies, it is derived directly from practice. Actions are assessed and legitimized in terms of what has been done before and what is known to work. In modern (or industrial) societies knowledge is often generated outside the practical context and therefore has to be legitimized with reference to independent principles and assumptions, usually in terms of scientific rationality. The cultural component of globalization is seen in the way in which this perspective comes to dominate other ways of understanding the world. Scientific rationality cannot afford to admit the legitimacy of other cultural perspectives. If it were to do so, the 'experts' would lose their expert status. This point will be considered further in Chapter 6, in the discussion of opposing views within the global environmental debate.

This argument implies that culture (as knowledge) is one of the instruments through which the globalization of modernity has progressed, and that cultures, as distinct ways of understanding the world, have been among the victims of globalization. But this view is not universally held in social science.

GLOBALIZATION AND CULTURAL DIVERSITY

Social scientists have already had quite a lot to say about what happens to cultural diversity under global conditions, whether those conditions are conceptualized as a world economic or political system, or as a worldwide network of intensified social relations. The question most often asked is whether globalization is eroding cultural differences and moving towards the formation of a single global culture (Smith 1990), or whether it is capable of accommodating or even generating cultural diversity. Not surprisingly, given their interest in cultural diversity, anthropologists have entered this debate. Hannerz identified in the literature two diametrically opposed views on what happens to culture under global conditions: the view that globalization generates cultural diversity and the view that it leads to increasing cultural homogeneity (Hannerz 1992: 223–5).

Cultural diversity in a globalized world

According to Wuthnow, 'the expansion of core economic and political influence promotes cultural heterogeneity' (1983: 66). This is not to say that the traditional cultures of peripheral regions necessarily survive incorporation into the global economic system; indeed, they are invariably and irreversibly altered by this process. Rather, the interface between the global economy and traditional cultures generates new cultural forms which differ both from the cultures of the core and from those of the periphery. This process has been described many times in the anthropological literature. The best-known instances are probably the 'cargo cults', which grew out of the contact between indigenous Melanesian societies and European and Australian colonists during the late nineteenth and early twentieth centuries (see Worsley 1957, Jarvie 1964). In some cases the most fleeting experience of industrial culture, in the form of an aircraft or steamship appearing where they had never been seen before, was enough to generate new religious ideas and practices. In other cases cults developed out of the Melanesians' more prolonged experience of the colonists both as employers and as missionaries.

Wallerstein also saw the world system as a source of cultural diversity (see Hannerz 1992: 224–5), not only through the generation of new forms at the interface between centre and periphery, but also through the creation of national cultures and through the creation and reinforcement of divisions (between elites and masses, for example) within nation-states. Wallerstein identified culture (in its general sense) with ideology, and treated it as the arena within which participants in the world system struggle for power (Wallerstein 1990a). Particular cultural phenomena, such as national and ethnic identities, symbols, principles and values, are used by those seeking to uphold their interests, justify their privileges and explain their disadvantages within the world system. As societies are incorporated into the world system, their members are drawn into this struggle, with the result that new divisions, new allegiances and oppositions, are created within them.

At first glance this model appears compatible with that, familiar to post-structuralist anthropologists, of the process in which culture is continually created and re-created by people acting in pursuit of their own goals (see, in particular, Barth 1966, Stuchlik 1977). But the view that the spread of a single economic or political system throughout the world does not lead to some degree of homogeneity remains tenable only as long as the expanding economic or political system itself is excluded from the sphere of culture. This is acceptable, indeed fundamental, in world systems theory, but for reasons explained above, it makes no sense in anthropology. Instead, anthropologists would be more likely to see the generation of a global political or economic system itself as an instance of increasing cultural homogeneity, because for them such a system must in part be cultural. To put it crudely, if the global economy is turning more and more people into capitalists, then it must, in this respect at least, be making them culturally more similar, for capitalism itself is in part a cultural phenomenon.

Cultural homogeneity in a globalized world

The view that cultural diversity is disappearing is exemplified by what Hannerz called 'radical diffusionism' (1989: 206) or 'global cultural diffusionism' (1990: 225). While 'diffusion' indicates movement, it does not imply anything about the direction of that movement. In theory, culture might flow in any direction, along any channels of communication, but radical diffusionists have tended to opt for the world system model of globalization, and to assume that the direction of diffusion is determined by the structure of that system. They have assumed that cultural influence, like political and economic influence, flows outwards from the centre to the periphery, and that the cultures of the centre eventually swamp those of the periphery so that ultimately nothing is left of them (Hannerz 1989: 207). This view is reflected in many of the terms used to describe contemporary cultural change: 'westernization', 'cultural imperialism', 'Americanization', and even more monstrous labels such as 'McDonaldization' (Ritzer 1992) and 'cocacolonization' (Hannerz 1989: 200).

Like world systems theory, radical diffusionism is a model of an historical process rather than a general theory. It therefore tends to be assessed against interpretations of what is 'really' happening. It is easy to understand its popular appeal, for it seems to depict accurately much of what can be observed at a superficial level. American hamburger chains really are opening branches all over the world, African villagers really can buy Coca-Cola in their local stores and American sit-coms can be seen on television throughout much of the globe. But even superficially, it is possible to identify many cultural features which appear to flow against the tide, from periphery to centre. Chinese, Indian and Mexican food, West Indian music, eastern therapies, are all popular in Europe, America and other 'central' regions. Environmentalism provides many examples of counter-flow; the myth of primitive ecological wisdom has fostered the view that industrial peoples have much to learn from non-industrial cultures. The motifs of indigenous American cultures, such as the Rainbow Warrior, have been adopted as icons of environmental activism (see Chapter 4). By hugging trees to protect them from developers, protesters in Britain mimic the actions of participants in the Chipko movement of northern India (Weber 1988), and echo the sacrifice of the Bishnoi who, according to legend, were prepared to die for their trees (Sankhala and Jackson 1985).

The observation that culture can flow from periphery to centre, as well as from centre to periphery, undermines one important element of the radical diffusionist argument, the assumption that the centre will eventually take over the periphery. But it does not imply anything about the view that the world is heading for cultural homogeneity. Cultural sameness can result just as much from a reciprocal exchange of cultural features as it can from a one-sided colonial expansion. There are good reasons to be suspicious of the view that cultural differences are disappearing, especially when it masquerades as a serious social-scientific proposition. It can be argued that such a view can only be sustained as long as observations remain superficial, and that if we look more closely at the evidence, a different picture emerges. Hannerz went so far as to suggest that the conviction that cultures are becoming less diverse has led to the kind of detailed cultural analysis typically conducted by anthropologists being ignored (Hannerz 1989: 207).

Many of the observations of increasing cultural homogeneity focus on commodities, and on things which are produced primarily, say, for consumption in industrial societies, but which are also exported to non-industrial or less industrialized countries, where they are assumed either to compete successfully with locally produced culture, or to occupy (or perhaps create) a niche which local culture does not provide for. The most obvious examples include television programmes, films, foods and clothing. This kind of cultural flow is driven by producers, who are constantly seeking out new markets, and who can often 'dump' products in peripheral regions at very little cost to themselves (Barber 1987, Hannerz 1992: 235). But the observation that the same commodities are available all over the world does not tell us very much about cultural homogeneity or diversity, since it says nothing about how those commodities are perceived and used (or not used) in the societies that receive them. The evidence provided by ethnographic studies suggests that when commodities are adopted into a society from elsewhere, they become 'indigenized' (Appadurai 1990: 5); they acquire a place in local understandings of the world. A casual observer might note simply that designer clothes from Paris have colonized Brazzaville. A closer look reveals that they are worn (with their labels conspicuously displayed) as part of a specifically Congolese strategy for accumulating prestige (Friedman 1990: 314–17).

The process whereby cultural imports take on new meanings and forms as they are adapted to local purposes is one with which anthropologists are very familiar, and it happens, not only to material commodities, but to the full range of institutions, ideologies, doctrines, symbols and so on that can possibly be communicated across cultural boundaries. A well-known ethnographic film shows how Trobriand Islanders have adapted the game of cricket to their own purposes, enabling it to take on some of the functions of traditional inter-community warfare. The so-called literary religions, each supposedly united through its own unchanging doctrine, have acquired multiple personalities as a result of their spread across the world, so that Islam in Morocco is different in character from Islam in Java (Geertz 1968), while Buddhism in Thailand is shaped partly by its complementary relationship with local spirit cults (Tambiah 1970). In the face of this kind of evidence, the suggestion that cultural diffusion necessarily produces homogeneity appears wildly inaccurate.

Anthropologists thus have good reasons for departing both from the view that global conditions necessarily generate cultural diversity and from the view that such conditions generate cultural homogeneity. The first is only tenable as long as what some analysts have seen as the integrating frameworks of world systems – namely, politics and economics – are excluded from culture, and this conflicts with anthropological definitions of culture. The second view is contradicted by ethnographic evidence, which indicates that some new cultural differences are being generated under global conditions, and some existing ones are being sustained. Is it possible, then, to identify a distinctively anthropological perspective on cultural change within the global context, one which employs a concept of culture with which anthropologists can feel at ease and which is consistent with their ethnographic findings?

GLOBALIZATION AND CULTURAL THEORY

The question, 'What happens to culture under global conditions?', is about the relationship between cultural phenomena and their context. It requires us to distinguish between 'culture' and the 'global conditions' in which it exists and evolves, and asks how they relate to each other. Anthropologists are well equipped to address this question. Throughout the history of the discipline they have devoted a great deal of attention to the relationship between culture and its context. Ecological anthropologists, whose work was discussed in Chapter 2, have identified this context primarily as the 'natural' environment, but have also acknowledged the role of the social environment in shaping culture (see, for instance, Sahlins 1961). Many more anthropologists have treated the social environment as the principal context in which culture exists. Like Douglas, whose work was discussed in Chapter 3, they have sought to understand the relationship between specific cultural perspectives and the processes, interactions and patterns of organization that constitute their social context. For reasons discussed in Chapter 1, anthropologists have tended to avoid analysing large-scale processes. They have tended not to take the entire globe as the relevant context in which to study culture, preferring to focus on small groups or clearly defined communities. But there are a few exceptions, and Hannerz (1989, 1990, 1992) and Appadurai (1989, 1990) have gone some way in developing anthropological models for understanding cultural change in a global arena.

Studying culture in a globalized world

Both Hannerz (1989: 201) and Appadurai (1990: 19) employ the concept of flow to describe how culture behaves in contemporary global conditions. Like a river crossing territorial boundaries, culture flows between social units, through numerous and diverse channels. Recent rapid developments in communications technology have opened the floodgates, so to speak, leaving culture to flow more freely than ever before. But this is not, in their view, a haphazard process. The movement of culture is organized, not always in a deliberate and targeted fashion, through human activity and the processes set in motion by such activity. For both Hannerz and Appadurai, understanding globalization means understanding the way cultural flow is organized within the contemporary global context. It means focusing on the spaces between social units, and identifying how culture is carried through these spaces.

Anthropology has often conveyed the impression that cultures are anchored to the ground, associated with territories occupied by specific communities or nations. But, for reasons that will be discussed below, this impression is more incidental than deliberate. Hannerz pointed out that, in reality, cultures and cultural things are carried by relationships, and as relationships have been freed from territorial boundaries, as a result of people's ability to travel and communicate more widely, so too have cultures (Hannerz 1990: 239). Pursuing this line of thought, Hannerz distinguished two types of culture: territorial cultures, which remain anchored in social units and are perpetuated through the activities of people who (to paraphrase the environmentalist slogan) both think and act locally, and 'transnational cultures', which move through the spaces between social units and are generated and perpetuated through the activities of cosmopolitans. Hannerz's response to the challenge of creating an anthropology of globalization was effectively to suggest that we make cosmopolitans our study community, and examine how their activities transmit culture through inter-societal space in a worldwide process of 'creolization' (Hannerz 1992: 264–6).

Appadurai offered a similar but more elaborate model which distinguished several conveyors of culture in addition to people. He identified five transnational landscapes through which culture travels, characterized respectively by the movement of people, technology, money, images and ideas (Appadurai 1990: 6–11). These are the vehicles which carry culture through inter-societal space, and they occupy different landscapes in the sense that they often do not move in conjunction with one another. While it is clear that money, ideas, technology and so on can be carried by people, they are more often launched (albeit by people's actions) on journeys of their own, across the airwaves, through the pages of books and newspapers or along fibre-optic cables. For Appadurai, the fact that the carriers of culture move independently of one another is fundamental in shaping global cultural processes (1990: 19), and gives the study of culture a new dimension.

Their central concern with culture sets the work of Hannerz and Appadurai apart from that of most other social scientists who couch their analyses in global terms. The central concern of world system analysts, for instance, is the operation and development of the global economy. Culture enters the analysis insofar as it is seen as having a role in that economy's operation. In an anthropological perspective, the emphasis is reversed. The world system is considered important insofar as it has a bearing on the character of contemporary cultural change. Hannerz, for instance, sees the relationship between centre and periphery within the world system as important in directing cultural change, though not in the straightforward manner suggested by radical diffusionism.

Given that culture is transmitted through communication, the most important function of whatever might be called the 'world system' or 'global condition', from the viewpoint of analysts trying to understand cultural change, is its provision of a network of channels through which communication both within and between social units can take place. Thus the character of the world system as a global capitalist economy, which world system analysts see as definitive, is relatively unimportant in the perspectives adopted by Hannerz, Appadurai and other anthropologists who take an interest in globalization (for instance, Komito 1994, Ahmed and Donnan 1994). What matters to them is the capacity of the world system, through its associated technology, both to provide for and to promote communication which transcends the barriers of time and space, and effectively frees cultural things from the contexts in which they were generated.

GLOBALIZATION, CULTURE AND DISCOURSE

The challenge to anthropology

Both Hannerz and Appadurai argue that the conditions under which culture exists in the contemporary world[6] cannot be adequately understood through traditional anthropological perspectives. These perspectives were developed in order to understand the workings of discrete social units, usually characterized by face-to-face interaction. The contemporary world is made up of units that are anything but discrete, and only a relatively small proportion of the interactions within and among them takes place through face-to-face contact. It is claimed that this requires anthropologists to find new ways of thinking about cultures (Appadurai 1990: 20). Hannerz pointed out that we have tended to see the world as a 'cultural mosaic, of separate pieces with hard, well-defined edges' (1989: 201), and that anthropologists have in the past been concerned largely with 'drawing the map of cultures as a mosaic' (1989: 211). In Chapter 1, I argued that both cultural relativism and the assumption that cultures are systems have encouraged us to think of cultures as bounded entities. In addition, cross-cultural comparison, which has long been the central device through which anthropologists have sought to generalize their findings, depends on the assumption that cultures have boundaries of some kind, since things cannot be compared unless they are first separated (cf. Appadurai 1990: 20).

In particular, the impression that cultures are tied to territories, through their associated social units, has reinforced the image of cultures as sharply bounded. This impression is the result of several factors. First, communities very often identify themselves by their location, and this tendency, quite understandably, is reproduced by ethnographers, who are usually concerned to present accurately the perspectives of those they study. Second, for practical convenience, anthropologists have often selected for study communities that are either spatially or socially discrete, those which either occupy a clearly defined territory, or which keep themselves discrete by minimizing their interaction with outsiders. Finally, even when communities selected for study are not discrete, anthropologists, again for practical convenience, have often treated them as if they were. The impression that cultures are the hard-edged pieces of a mosaic, whose boundaries can, in theory, be traced on the ground, is a product of the fact that anthropologists have preferred to do bounded ethnography (see Chapter 3, above).

162

This image of cultures as bounded units is not appropriate for studying cultural change in the global context, where 'cultures ... tend to overlap and mingle' (Hannerz 1990: 239). But I would question whether this represents a genuinely new way of thinking about cultures. Although the impression that cultures are bounded units has been strong and influential in anthropological thought, the nature of cultural boundaries has often been left undefined. Most cross-cultural comparisons are of selected phenomena, kinship terminologies, marriage rules, religious or political ideologies. In such comparisons there is no need to consider what the edges of a culture might look like. In addition, there are many studies in anthropology which deal explicitly with the cross-cultural communication of knowledge and which therefore, at least implicitly, assume that cultures are to some degree unbounded. Studies which have focused specifically on cultural boundaries have shown that their existence depends on their continual regeneration through action, and that they are negotiated and maintained through specific interactions (Barth 1969, Ross 1975, Donnan 1976). Thus, however strong may be the impression that cultures are regarded by anthropologists as bounded entities, the fact is that quite a lot of anthropological analysis could not have been done or even envisaged if this were the only way in which cultures had been conceptualized.

This does not mean that I regard the study of culture under global conditions as offering no kind of challenge to anthropology, but I suggest that this challenge is largely a practical one. In the global arena, it becomes particularly difficult to observe the processes which generate cultural change. As explained in Chapter 1, the analytical distinction between culture, as something that exists in people's minds, and social activities and processes has been seen as a distinction between what is and what is not more or less directly observable. In a small community whose members engage primarily in face-to-face interaction, anthropologists experience relatively little difficulty in observing, or at least getting to hear about, what they do and say. But the nature of contemporary communications technology makes it extremely difficult to observe more than a small part of what goes on in the global context. As Appadurai's model makes clear, culture is not transmitted primarily through face-to-face interaction, but through telephones, radio and television, books, newspapers and magazines, computers, fax machines and so on. Most of this communication takes place out of the sight of social scientists who might wish to analyse it, and takes such complex paths that it would be more or less impossible to keep account of even if it were more accessible.

There is no obvious way round this difficulty. If anthropologists confine their interest to what can be observed relatively easily, they will continue to study small communities and be able to say very little about what happens in the global arena. If they accept the challenge of analysing global processes, they may also have to accept a loss of analytical rigour. They may not be able to substantiate many of the connections they make in order to understand cultural change, and so may have to live with interpretations that are less well grounded in empirical observation than has been the case in the past. I suggest that this is a small price to pay for the opportunity of participating in, and commenting upon, global discourses.

GLOBALIZATION AS A DUAL PROCESS

In the opening paragraphs of this chapter I raised the question of whether 'globalization' refers to the way the world is seen or imagined, or to things going on in the world. This question asks whether globalization is going on within or outside culture. 'The way the world is seen or imagined' is a cultural phenomenon, part of people's understanding; 'things going on in the world' are part of 'observable' reality, and are therefore dialectically related to, but not a part of, culture. The two models of globalization discussed so far, the emergence of a world system and the creation, by modern institutions, of a global social condition, both locate the process outside culture. In both cases, culture can be seen to play a role in the globalizing process, but globalization is not presented as something that takes place within culture. A third model of globalization, developed by Robertson (1992), treats it as taking place both outside and within culture.

Robertson defined globalization as follows: 'Globalization as a concept refers both to the compression of the world and the intensification of consciousness of the world as a whole' (1992: 8). Without wishing to misrepresent Robertson's perspective, I suggest that 'the compression of the world' refers to something like the processes described in the other models. It means the bringing together of distant locations through their participation in a single economic or political system or network of communications, in such a way that events taking place in them influence one another. However, Robertson saw his concept of globalization as crucially different from those described in the other models. When globalization is seen either as the development of a world capitalist economy or as a social consequence of modernity, there is an implication that it flows across the world from its origins in 'the west', and can be described as 'westernization' or 'modernization'. Robertson saw this image of globalization as obstructive (1992: 55); it rules out the possibility that something else might be going on.

What makes the difference, in Robertson's view, is culture. Globalization is not just a process taking place in the world, in which culture plays a role. It is, in part, a cultural process, something that happens within culture as well as in the world outside people's understanding. Hence the second part of Robertson's definition: globalization also refers to 'the intensification of consciousness of the world as a whole'. This describes a change in what people think, feel and know about the world; it describes the development of what I would call 'a sense of the global'. But a sense of the global can take many different forms; people come to understand the world as a single place in many diverse ways. Ecologists and environmentalists, for instance, have come to see it as a single ecosystem, in which processes taking place in one location can affect the whole. Entrepreneurs have come to see it as a single market place, tourists as a single playground, and so on. There are also countless local cultural perspectives on 'the global'. The presence of this diversity, of competing ways of understanding the world as a whole, shapes the development of anything that might be called a world system or a global condition: 'cultural pluralism is itself a constitutive feature of the modern world system and . . . conceptions of the world system, symbolic responses to globalization, are themselves important factors in determining the trajectories of that very process' (Robertson and Lechner 1985: 103).

In Robertson's view, the presence and impact of diverse cultural models of the world as a whole means that globalization cannot properly be understood as a 'westernizing' or 'modernizing' process. Nor can it be seen as a process that moves relentlessly 'forward'. While some people are engaged in globalizing projects, such as the promotion of world trade or the development of global communications, others are engaged in 'deglobalization', 'attempts to undo the compression of the world' (Robertson 1992: 10). For instance, some environmentalists who see the globalization of the economy as environmentally destructive advocate moving towards greater self-sufficiency, a dismantling of international trade agreements and large centralized organizations. The cultural and social constitution of the world is shaped by the interaction between globalizing and deglobalizing tendencies. The interaction of these tendencies within global environmental discourse will be discussed in the next chapter.

Robertson's model of globalization as a process which is both 'subjective' and 'objective' (Robertson 1992: 9), taking place simultaneously within people's understanding of the world and in the ways their relationships are organized, parallels the distinction made by post-structuralist anthropologists between culture and social processes. 'The compression of the world' is a social process; it describes the intensification of social relations over long distances, the linking of individuals and communities in global systems of economic and political relations and worldwide communications networks. The development of 'a sense of the global', of an understanding of the world as a single place, is a cultural process, taking place within people's minds. Robertson's model is therefore quite compatible with cultural theory, as developed by anthropologists in recent decades, and can form a framework for examining how environmentalism, as a cultural phenomenon, is related to globalization.

Before discussing this further, it is necessary to clarify one more analytical concept. Until now, I have used the term 'discourse' without explaining what I understand by it. The concept of discourse can play a useful role in our understanding of globalization, so it is important to clarify its meaning.

CULTURE AND DISCOURSE

The concept of discourse has a long history in both social science and linguistics (Fairclough 1992), though in recent decades its use in social theory has been shaped largely by the work of Foucault (1972, 1979). Within social science, discourse, like culture, has both general and specific meanings. In its general sense, it refers to the process through which knowledge is constituted through communication (Fairclough 1992: 2). As such it is, like culture, a universal part of human experience. At a more specific level, it is possible to identify at least two meanings of discourse. First, *a* discourse most often refers to a particular mode of communication; a field characterized by its own linguistic conventions, which both draws on and generates a distinctive way of understanding the world. Thus, what counts as knowledge in scientific discourse is different from what counts as knowledge in, say, religious discourse, in that it is based on specific kinds of observation and subjected to particular forms of testing. Because they generate diverse ways of understanding the world, discourses can be said to 'compete' in given social contexts. For instance, in his analysis of environmental protest in rural Ireland, Peace showed how, in the context of a public hearing, a populist, oppositional discourse was dominated by a scientific discourse, as the latter was treated by the planning authorities as the appropriate idiom for discussing the merits and shortcomings of a particular development proposal (Peace 1993).

The second specific meaning of discourse is less complex. A discourse is an area of communication defined purely by its subject matter. In this sense, environmental discourse is communication about the environment, and environmentalist discourse is communication about the protection of the environment. There is no implication here that a particular mode of communication is being used, or that a particular way of understanding is being generated.

Discourses of this kind do not compete in social contexts; rather, they merge and separate as participants define and redefine their subject matter. For instance, James showed how, within a broad discourse on food, other discourses, on lifestyle, environment and health, were invoked as various marketing strategies were adopted (James 1993).

The two senses in which a discourse is used in analysis are easily confused. For instance, one of the most enduring debates in conservation concerns the relationship between science, represented by the perceived need to manage wildlife to ensure the survival of rare species, and morality, represented by concerns for the rights and welfare of animals (see Yearley 1993). In this context, science and morality can be seen as discourses in both the senses outlined above. The scientific discourse can be seen both as a mode of communication governed by certain principles, and as an area of communication about biological diversity. The moral discourse, similarly, can be seen as a way of understanding and talking about animals, and as communication about their welfare. Both of the more specific concepts of discourse are useful in

167

analysis and it is not always necessary, or possible, to distinguish them. However, I suggest that the second, less complex concept of a discourse, as an area of communication defined by its subject matter, is potentially more useful in cross-cultural analysis. The reason for this lies in the similarities and differences between discourses and cultures.

Cultures, discourses and transcultural discourses

Anthropologists have argued that the study of what happens to *culture* (in its general sense) in the global arena becomes easier if we cease to think of *cultures* as bounded units (see above). Degree of boundedness is thus considered important when formulating frameworks for analysing globalization. I suggest that the degree of boundedness associated with the first definition of a discourse outlined above is greater than that associated with the second definition. When a discourse is seen as a mode of communication, it carries conventions which constrain its participants. Because of these constraints, it is impossible to study discourses in this sense without paying attention to their boundaries. A discourse seen as an area of communication, on the other hand, is identified primarily by its centre, by the subject matter on which its participants focus. A discourse in this sense can still be said to have boundaries, defined by the limits of its subject matter, but these limits are often not important for analysis. Provided the participants in a discourse are generally agreed on what is being discussed, its boundaries need not come into play. For this reason, discourses as areas of communication can be treated, more or less, as unbounded. It is in this sense that the term is used in the analysis in Chapter 6.

It will not always be the case, however, that the boundaries of a discourse can be ignored in analysis. Quite often, the participants in a discourse will be trying to change its parameters, and the focus will be on the edges rather than the centre. For instance, in the example mentioned above, animal rights campaigners may try to redefine the boundaries of the discourse on conservation to include moral as well as (or even in precedence to) scientific issues. Cases such as this raise a question that is all too familiar to anthropologists: how can the object of analysis be defined without privileging particular cultural perspectives on it? For instance, in the following chapter, the object of analysis is environmentalist discourse (discourse about the protection of the environment) in the global arena. If I were to define 'the environment' as, say, the non-human part of the natural world, I would effectively exclude from the discourse to be analysed the views of those who wish to discuss human cultural diversity as an environmental issue, and those who regard at least some environmental forces as supernatural rather than natural. The way to avoid this kind of partiality is to set very wide parameters for the discourse, allowing the broadest possible range of definitions of its subject matter to enter. In other words, it is important that the participants in a discourse, and not the analyst, define its limits. This approach was used in Chapter 4, where the only analytical definition of the environment was simply 'that which surrounds' (Ingold 1993: 31). Similarly, in Chapter 6, I make no attempt to prejudge what the participants in environmentalist discourse take to be the object of their concern; the discourse is shaped by their understandings of the environment and of what constitutes its protection.

By defining a discourse as an area of communication identified by its subject matter we describe an object for analysis which can, in most contexts, be treated as more or less unbounded. This gives the concept of discourse a distinct advantage over the more established anthropological concept of culture, when it comes to analysing global processes. Unlike cultures, discourses have never been associated with territories; it would not be possible to draw the map of discourses as a mosaic. Instead, I suggest, it is in the character of discourse to flow across cultural boundaries. It goes wherever the channels of communication take it.

Hannerz distinguished between 'territorial' and 'transnational' cultures in order to separate those modes of understanding which remain more or less tied to their locations of origin from those that are transported through inter-societal space by cosmopolitans (see above). I think a more appropriate distinction is that between 'cultures', as ways of knowing that are associated with specific groups or categories of people (Cree Indians, Americans, engineers, cosmopolitans, locals), and 'transcultural discourses', as areas of communication that cross cultural boundaries. The concept of a transcultural discourse is an improvement on Hannerz's concept of a transnational culture for two reasons. First, it removes any need that might be felt to find a new way of thinking about cultures, and second, it removes the implication that 'nations' are the significant units being transcended in global communications.

169

As I pointed out in Chapter 3, the assumption that nations are necessarily the significant social units is alien to anthropologists, who more often ground their studies in cultures, societies and communities. The concept of a transcultural discourse defines a mechanism through which specific cultural phenomena are communicated beyond their locations of origin.

Environmentalism as a transcultural discourse

In Chapter 1, I defined environmentalism as a concern to protect the environment through human effort and responsibility, and argued that, as such, it might be seen as characterizing a particular kind of cultural perspective that might be found in both industrial and non-industrial societies. This idea was developed, in Chapter 4, through the comparison of several perspectives from diverse cultural contexts. Now I want to suggest that environmentalism also characterizes a particular discourse. Environmentalist discourse is discourse about the protection of the environment through human effort. I also want to suggest that it is a transcultural discourse in the sense outlined above, one that is not tied to any particular group or location, but which flows across cultural boundaries (however they might be defined) within a global network of communication.

The transcultural nature of environmentalist discourse is so obvious that it seems almost unnecessary to offer substantiating evidence. It is transcultural, rather than transnational or international in character, because the parties involved in the discourse do not all identify themselves in national terms. A great deal of communication about environmentalist concerns does takes place among governments (for instance at the Rio Earth Summit in 1992 and within international organizations such as the UN and the European Union). But far more takes place among NGOs (for instance at the Global Forum that accompanied the Earth Summit), between NGOs and governments (as when environmental groups lobby governments in their own and other countries in an attempt to influence policy), between NGOs and commercial companies (as when environmental groups lobby companies to reduce the environmental impacts of their operations), and between all these agencies (NGOs, governments, companies) and the public. Environmentalist messages are communicated through television programmes, books and magazines that are made available

throughout the world. In addition, individuals and groups concerned about environmental issues keep in touch with one another
by mail, phone and electronic communications.

As a transcultural discourse, environmentalism plays its own
role in the process of globalization. By linking individuals, communities, NGOs, companies and governments throughout the
world, it becomes a factor in the intensification of social relations
over long distances, it contributes to what Robertson called 'the
compression of the world'. I would also suggest, in accordance
with Robertson's model, that environmentalism is a particularly
effective globalizing discourse because it employs a well-developed
sense of the global. Environmentalists have come to define the
environment that forms the object of their concern as the entire
planet. Their particular understanding of the planet as 'one place'
has fuelled the development of environmentalist discourse as a
global phenomenon. The cultural content of global environmentalist discourse forms the subject of the next chapter.

6

THE CULTURE OF GLOBAL ENVIRONMENTALIST DISCOURSE

Visions of Utopia still jostle one another in the tainted air, and every fresh disaster is met with fresh plans of power and still more power.

(Ehrenfeld 1978: 12)

What can you do? First, I think that if you want to live in a world with a healthy environment you should learn to respect cultural diversity. The cultural diversity of the world of two hundred years ago, before we created this multinational culture that is more dangerous than a multinational enterprise, has gone ... we will have to develop a very profound respect for other cultures if we want to live in a sustainable world.

(Anil Agarwal, quoted in De La Court 1990: 26)

Once upon a time, the totality of human culture could be described as consisting of many individual cultures. This is no longer an appropriate image; contemporary human culture consists of many discourses. In some ways, this makes it much harder to analyse, for our vocabulary is plagued with boundedness – we speak of units, fields, sectors and distinctions – and discourses, as we have seen, often appear unbounded. But it can also be liberating, for it reduces the need for analysts to delineate their objects of analysis, and enables them instead to study how cultural things (perceptions, assumptions, values, perspectives) cluster around focal issues. In this chapter, I make no attempt to consider the full range of cultural things that might be said to 'belong', in some sense, to environmentalist discourse. I focus mainly on a prominent feature of that discourse, the global debate in which the environment is treated as a resource. The relationship of this debate to the wider environmentalist discourse is considered at the end of the chapter.

The discussion at the end of Chapter 3 suggested that anthropology provides a framework for interpreting environmentalism as a cultural perspective. Traditionally, within the discipline, long periods of residential fieldwork have enabled anthropologists to make detailed observations of people's activities, and one of the main ways of understanding cultural things has been to show how they are generated and sustained through those activities (see, for instance, Leach 1961, Holy 1986). In Chapter 5, I pointed out that this approach is difficult to use in the global arena. A great deal of communicative activity takes place where it cannot be observed by analysts, and residential fieldwork is of little use if cultural things are not tied to particular locations. On the other hand, contemporary communication yields a huge number of tangible products, in the form of written statements and opinions, laws, policies and manifestos, reports and recordings, which are available for analysis. Thus, while it may be difficult to reconstruct in detail the social processes that sustain contemporary perspectives, it is relatively easy to examine the content of those perspectives, and to show how their components – assumptions, values, norms, goals – relate to one another. This is the approach adopted in this chapter.

The discussion in the early chapters also indicated that anthropology's main tool for understanding cultural things is comparison across cultural boundaries. This approach was used in Chapter 4 to identify the essential features of an environmentalist perspective. In this chapter, the approach is also comparative, but there are significant differences. First, the perspectives compared here are identified as environmentalist, not by using external criteria, but through claims made by those who hold them. Second, following the discussion in Chapter 5, I no longer assume the existence of cultural boundaries. The perspectives compared here, like the discourse in which they are engaged, are transcultural, in that they are shared by people from diverse locations and social backgrounds and are communicated in the global arena. Third, unlike the perspectives discussed in Chapter 4, those compared here are interdependent. Because those who hold them are engaged in a debate, they are defined and developed in relation to one another.

The debate can be seen as a 'site of struggle' (Seidel 1985, 1989), in which the meanings of key concepts, 'development', 'sustainability', 'democracy', as well as versions of the past and visions of the future, are fiercely contested. The oppositional character of debate has an important consequence for the relationship between analysis and advocacy. An analyst seeking to understand a particular cultural perspective will examine closely the interests, goals and strategies of those who hold and express it. This is also the approach taken by protagonists in a debate who are concerned to expose the weaknesses in their opponents' arguments. This makes it very difficult to draw a line between analysis and advocacy. Studies which show, for instance, how particular ways of defining environmental problems and identifying solutions are tied to vested interests (Redclift 1984, Weale 1992, Sachs 1993, Chatterjee and Finger 1994) are, intentionally or otherwise, helping to articulate a perspective which opposes those interests. Thus analysts of contemporary discourse often participate in the object of their analysis to a much greater extent than those studying other aspects of social life, for participation in discourse is itself an analytical process (see Chapter 3, above). Later in this chapter, I shall consider whether the analysis presented here leads us to favour any particular stance in the debate.

The observation that analysis and participation are indistinguishable accords closely with Robertson's comment that, 'sociologists and others who are seeking to analyze and comprehend contemporary global complexity are participants in projects of globalization, reglobalization and, even, deglobalization' (1992: 10). I suggest that the global environmental debate encapsulates the tension between 'globalizing' and 'deglobalizing' tendencies identified by Robertson. One perspective holds that more globalization is the best way of protecting the environment as a resource for human use. Its supporters advocate the integration of all human societies into the global economy, the adoption, by all governments, communities and individuals, of common goals and standards, and the co-ordination of resource management on a worldwide scale. The opposing perspective holds that globalization is a major part of the problem, and that the only way of living sustainably is to dismantle the global economy and allow local communities more control over their own resources. Thus, in Robertson's words, the globalist view favours greater 'compression' of the world, while the opposing view seeks to 'undo' that compression.

In identifying these perspectives as the major components in the global environmental debate, I am not intending to deny the presence of diverse views within them, nor of other views which cannot be accommodated by them; there is, as I have indicated, a wider environmentalist discourse of which the debate is a part. Nor am I suggesting that there is no common ground between the two perspectives. The debate exists because its participants share an underlying 'sense of the global', an understanding of the whole planet as the human environment. The following analysis, in which the two main perspectives are described in turn, begins with this shared understanding.

A SENSE OF THE GLOBAL

One of the most enduring memories of my undergraduate anthropology course is Burridge's reproduction of a map drawn in the sand by a Manam Islander. At the centre was God's birthplace, surrounded by night, day and snow. The east was the land of black men, where Manam Island itself lay. The west was the land of white men, where Germany, England and North and South America were located. All these places were surrounded by Green Sea. Far to the west, beyond the White Sea and the Blue Sea, lay an unknown land whose name no one knew (Burridge 1960: 10). Most, if not all, societies hold an idea of the world as a place that extends beyond their immediate and familiar surroundings. Some, like the maps produced using modern technology, are complete in every minute detail. Others contain large areas of uncharted territory. But they all represent different understandings of what Robertson called 'the world as a whole' (1992: 8).

In recent decades, environmentalists have come to identify the world as a whole as our environment. The entire planet has become the object of environmental concern: 'Today's ecology', Sachs observed, 'is about saving nothing less than the planet' (1993: 17). Given the complexities of modern communications, it would be difficult to pinpoint the origins of this idea. Many authors have pointed to space travel as a significant factor in its development (Robertson 1992: 59; Sachs 1993: 18); the image of the Earth seen from space, first photographed in 1966, is frequently invoked as one of the most powerful in environmentalist discourse (see Dobson 1990: 1; WCED 1987: 308). Certainly, by the late 1960s and early 1970s, global models were an established part of environmental analysis (Meadows *et al.* 1972, Goldsmith *et al.* 1972), and two major international conferences – the Biosphere Conference,[1] in Paris in 1968, and the UN Conference on the Human Environment, in Stockholm in 1972 – unambiguously defined the environment in global terms (see McCormick 1989: 74ff.). Whatever the details of its history, the identification of the human environment with the entire globe can be seen as a combination of two emerging lines of thought: the idea that the Earth is a single ecosystem and the idea that humanity is a single moral community.

Global ecology

Giddens' understanding of globalization, as the intensification of relations linking distant localities, so that 'local happenings are shaped by events occurring many miles away and vice versa' (Giddens 1990: 64), might also apply to the way in which the Earth is understood to be a single ecosystem. Forests and buildings are damaged by acid rain sent on the prevailing winds by distant power stations. Industrial pollutants are found in the bodies of Arctic mammals living many miles from the source of pollution. The populations of island states, such as the Maldives, feel threatened by rising sea levels brought by changes in climate, which are seen as a consequence of industrial development and intensive agriculture elsewhere. But the concept of a global ecosystem does not just imply that locations many miles apart can affect one another; it also implies the linking of processes which were once thought of as unconnected. What is done on land affects the quality of water and air, so industry and agriculture affect marine life and, therefore, the quality and quantity of fish stocks for consumption by human beings and other species. Global ecology also implies that the whole system is affected by processes going on in specific locations. Industrial development in Europe and America, the destruction of forests in Brazil, are seen as having consequences for the climate of the entire world (cf. Yearley 1995b).

Understanding the whole Earth as a single ecosystem is a recent development in scientific thought: 'ecological research, after having for years focused on single and isolated ecosystems like deserts, marshes and rainforests . . . shifted its attention to the study of the biosphere' (Sachs 1993: 18). Global ecology takes an holistic view, not only of human–environment relations, but of all the biosphere's component processes and relationships. It is as important to understand the impact of an increasing number of termites on the Earth's climate as it is to understand the impact of increasing rice cultivation (McKibben 1990: 14–15). The shift in interest towards global ecology was made possible by the same technology that brought us the first evocative photographs of the Earth seen from space. By viewing the planet's surface from afar, scientists can monitor the rates of deforestation and desertification, the spread of intensive monoculture farming, changes in wind speed and direction, cloud patterns and temperatures; 'the technology available in the 1990s permits the biosphere to be surveyed and modelled' (Sachs 1993: 18). These methods generate a 'global' view that is held to be qualitatively different from local perspectives (Ingold 1993: 35; see below, p. 192). It may take days or weeks to walk through a rainforest, but satellite pictures reveal how quickly it is diminishing.

A single human community

Tension between the rights and interests of individuals and those of the community has always been an important factor in human interactions. 'The community', however, is not a constant unit; it might be defined as a kin group, a village, a nation, an ethnic group, a category identified by gender or sexuality. Increasingly, in recent decades, 'the community' has been defined as the whole of humanity. Robertson (1992) identified this trend as an important cultural component of globalization. This is not to suggest that 'individualism' has declined; personal profit continues to override the common good in a depressingly high proportion of decisions. Many would argue that individualism received a considerable boost in the industrial world during the 1980s. Communist regimes collapsed and the market ideologies of Thatcher in Britain, Reagan in America and 'neoconservatism' in Canada (Paehlke 1989) fostered an entrepreneurial ethos. Nor is the observation that the sense of a common humanity has grown intended to imply that other criteria for defining identity have not. The study of world systems and other perspectives on globalization has emphasized the increasing significance of the nation-state as a component of the 'global ecumene' (Hannerz 1992). Similar observations could be made about ethnicity, religion and gender. But, notwithstanding these other (and to some extent, counter-) trends, the idea of a common humanity has become a widely used and accepted

177

justification for a very wide range of actions and policies, and the ideal that it should take precedence over narrower interests is well established in political discourse.

Many specific events and developments have contributed to the increasing recognition of a common human identity (see Robertson 1992: 58–9). In particular, the sense of global insecurity following the two World Wars, heightened by the devastating impacts of the Holocaust and the atom bomb, considerably strengthened the idea that human beings have common interests over and above those of nation-states and resulted in the creation of the League of Nations, and later the United Nations, and other international alliances. This idea was given further impetus by the persistence of the Cold War until the late 1980s. The Holocaust, in particular, exposed the capacity of national governments to abuse their own populations, and generated a perceived need to separate the issue of human rights from the rights and interests of states. Expressions of this perceived need included the UN's Universal Declaration on Human Rights and the formation of NGOs such as Amnesty International, Human Rights Watch and Survival International. At the same time, the development of a global communications network, which facilitated relationships across national and cultural boundaries, helped to strengthen the sense of common human identity.

The consequences of thinking globally

The idea that the Earth is a single ecosystem and the idea that humanity is a single community, in which all individuals are entitled to the same rights and hold the same responsibilities, come together in the concept of a global human environment. The global environment is held to be both a common resource to which all, ideally, should have equal access, and an object of common responsibility for which all should care. Finger coined the term 'same boat ideology' to describe this global model:

> The 'same boat' ideology says that environmental degradation – like nuclear weapons before – is a threat to all inhabitants of planet Earth alike. We are, therefore, all in the same boat, with no choice but to dialogue and co-operate: we will either win or lose together.
>
> (Finger 1993: 42; see also Chatterjee and Finger 1994)

178

The model of a global environment has had a significant impact on the way individual environmentalists perceive their own roles and responsibilities. The definition of environmental problems as global problems makes them appear impossibly complex and difficult to solve (cf. Gott 1992), and places them outside what most individuals would regard as their own capacity to comprehend and act effectively. At the same time, the understanding that the global environment is everyone's responsibility places on individuals an obligation to contribute to the communal effort. The resulting combined sense of helplessness and obligation has created a demand for mechanisms, policies and programmes for action which make individuals feel involved in the effort to save the planet. This demand has been fed by advice from governments, NGOs and individuals on how to adopt more environmentally sensitive ways of living (see, for instance, Elkington and Hailes 1988, Seymour 1991, Friends of the Earth 1992). In 1992, the Tree of Life initiative, organized by a number of NGOs, enabled individuals to feel personally involved in the Rio Earth Summit.[2] One exhortation to take part read, 'The real question is not what other people are planning – it's what are you going to do?' (United Nations Association 1992: 4).

Defining environmental problems in global terms has also had the effect of legitimizing claims of competence made by organizations that operate at a global level (see Chatterjee and Finger 1994). These organizations include alliances of nation-states (such as the UN), international financial institutions (the World Bank, the International Monetary Fund), transnational corporations, development agencies and the larger environmental NGOs (such as WWF, the IUCN, Friends of the Earth and Greenpeace). People can be led to believe that something effective is being done about environmental problems when the global organizations are seen to be taking action (by holding international conferences, for example). It has also effectively marginalized, within the global environmental debate, those who are already disadvantaged by the existing power structure (cf. Chatterjee and Finger 1994: 104). It is difficult for groups whose views are ignored by their own national authorities, for instance, to make their voices heard in an arena in which they are assumed by others to be represented by those authorities. It is also difficult for those whose understanding of the environment differs fundamentally from the global model to influence a debate which takes that model as its starting point.

These issues are central to the tension between the main competing perspectives in environmentalist discourse, and will be discussed in more detail below.

Finally, the understanding that humankind shares a single environment for which all are jointly responsible provides the justification for assessing and sanctioning the activities of others. This function is fulfilled partly by the environmental NGOs, who habitually monitor the environmental impacts of the actions of governments, corporations and other organizations. National environmental laws constitute the main mechanism through which sanctions are brought to bear. In the United States, particularly, environmental activism frequently takes the form of litigation. There are, at present, few formal mechanisms through which environmentally unsound activities can be sanctioned across national boundaries. Most of the many international conventions on environmental matters depend, for their effectiveness, on informal pressures, though some are policed by the United Nations. Probably the strongest degree of international enforcement is achieved within the European Union (EU), whose laws are enforced through the European Court. Although the primary justification for environmental laws within the EU was to create a level playing field for economic competition (Yearley *et al.* 1994), they have sometimes been found effective in limiting environmental damage.

THE GLOBALIST PERSPECTIVE

In the terminology employed by Douglas and Wildavsky (1982), the globalist perspective on environmental conservation is a 'centre' position. It has been established through the words and actions of central and centralizing institutions, agencies that operate at a global level: the United Nations, national governments, transnational corporations and the larger NGOs representing sectoral interests (including environmental interests) in the international arena. The United Nations, in particular, has taken the lead in generating international discourse on environmental issues, by organizing conferences, commissioning reports and setting up research and development programmes. The most significant of these initiatives, for the emergence of a globalist view on environmental issues, have been the UN Conference on the Human Environment, held at Stockholm in 1972; the UN Environment

Programme initiated by that conference; the World Commission on Environment and Development (WCED), which published its report ('The Brundtland Report') in 1987; and the UN Conference on Environment and Development (UNCED, the 'Earth Summit') in Rio de Janeiro in 1992. The products of these initiatives, in the form of reports, published proceedings, declarations and agreements, constitute a major source of information on the globalist model.

In the following description, the globalist perspective is presented in terms of what I consider to be its three main components: the premium placed on 'development' as an essential human activity and as the solution to environmental problems, the idea that development can and must be made sustainable, and the understanding that sustainability must be managed at a global level.

The primacy of development

The United Nations Conference on the Human Environment has been described as 'such a watershed that global environmentalism can be divided into two phases – before and after Stockholm' (McCormick 1989: xi). Probably the most significant consequence of the Stockholm Conference was in establishing international recognition for the link between environment and development. In recognizing the link, the Stockholm Conference also established the primacy of development over the environment. Part of Paragraph 5 of the Stockholm Declaration on the Human Environment reads:

> Of all things in the world, people are the most precious. It is the people that propel social progress, create social wealth, develop science and technology and, through their hard work, continuously transform the human environment. Along with social progress and the advance of production, science and technology, the capability of man to improve the environment increases with each passing day.
>
> (United Nations 1973: 3)

Leave aside, for the moment, the unconcealed hubris of the final sentence, which is fundamental to the concept of global management and which will be considered later. The most striking thing about the above statement is the way in which development, in the form of 'social' progress, 'social' wealth, science, technology

181

and the transformation of the 'human environment', is presented almost as a legitimation of the value accorded to human beings. It is possible that this impression was not fully intended. It is easy to imagine the dilemma facing the authors of the document as they struggled to find an appropriate gloss for the statement that people are the most precious things in the world. Where this is held to be true, it is usually for religious reasons, because human beings are, so to speak, 'God's' chosen species. But religious references can be divisive and United Nations documents need to steer a harmonious course. Perhaps the reference to development was considered the least contentious way of legitimating the supremacy of humanity. Whatever the reasons, the implication is clear and was, we can assume, accepted by the assembled representatives of 113 countries in Stockholm. People are precious, it seems, *because* they 'propel' development.

The understanding that human value depends on development is expressed in two main ways in the environmental debate. First, development is presented as a natural and distinctively human imperative:

> Man is both creator and moulder of his environment, which gives him physical sustenance and affords him the opportunity for intellectual, moral, social and spiritual growth . . . .
> Man has constantly to sum up experience and go on discovering, inventing, creating and advancing.
>
> (United Nations 1973: 3)

This view is reinforced by the assumption that there is an evolutionary process of development, and that different societies are at different stages in that process (WCED 1987: ix). The effect is to devalue any societies that are seen not to be developing, or any communities that wish to opt out of the development process. Abstention from development is seen as unnatural and less than human; it is a failure to fulfil natural human potential.

Second, because development is natural, it is also a right. This view was enshrined in Principle 3 of the *Declaration on Environment and Development* produced at the Rio Earth Summit: 'The right to development must be fulfilled so as to equitably meet developmental and environmental needs of present and future generations' (United Nations 1993a: 3). Defining development as a right provides it with a moral imperative. It makes it wrong to deny development to anyone, and it might be taken to impose an obligation on the powerful to deliver development to the power-less. This implication has, not surprisingly, made some of the more powerful states uneasy. At Rio, the US government issued its own interpretation of Principle 3, indicating that it did not accept a 'right to development' (United Nations 1993b: 17).

It is unclear whether Principle 3 was intended to establish a legal right to development. Grubb *et al.* observed that 'Most see the "right" to development as rhetorical rather than legal' (1993: 91). But this is probably the case for most internationally recog-nized rights, given the difficulties of enforcement at international level. Establishing a right to development was a significant step for developing countries. It provided them with an agreed moral basis for any pressure they might wish to exert on the North, either actively to assist their development, or at least not to obstruct it.

Within environmentalist discourse, the primacy of development is legitimized by the argument that development is the solution to environmental problems. This argument depends on the assump-tion that poverty, resulting from a lack of development, is a major cause of environmental degradation (WCED 1987: 364). Indira Gandhi, in her address to the Stockholm Conference in 1972, stated that 'Poverty is the greatest polluter' (quoted in Strong 1994). *Caring for the Earth*, a UN and NGO publication on 'sustainable living', declared that poverty can force people to live in unsustainable ways (IUCN *et al.* 1991: 52). The need to eradi-cate poverty has been a central concern for the United Nations Environment Programme, for the World Commission on Environ-ment and Development (see WCED 1987) and for the Rio Earth Summit. It was also the theme of the United Nations Conference on Social Development, held in Copenhagen in March 1995, which was one of several follow-up conferences to the Rio Earth Summit. In these contexts, development was consistently presented as the means to alleviate poverty: 'the poor need economic and social development as the only means of relieving the vicious circle of poverty in which they are caught up' (Strong 1992b: 46). The possibility that the solution might lie elsewhere was not con-sidered. As the only accepted way of alleviating poverty, develop-ment also becomes the solution to environmental problems, by virtue of the understanding that poverty is a major cause of environmental degradation.

Making development sustainable

Essential though development is, in the terms of the globalist perspective, as a means of eradicating poverty and conserving the environment, it is not seen as trouble-free. On the contrary, it is acknowledged that development is responsible for many current and serious environmental problems. Global warming is seen as being 'caused by the gases which constitute the very underpinnings of industrialized societies' (Boutros-Ghali 1992: 35), and particularly by carbon emissions produced by transport and power generation. The depletion of ozone in the upper atmosphere is attributed to the release of CFCs (chlorofluorocarbons), used in aerosol sprays, refrigeration and other industrial processes.[3] It is also acknowledged that the consumption by the developed countries (the North) of raw materials and cash crops produced in the developing countries (the South), has undermined the capacity of those developing countries to meet the basic needs of their own populations. These problems have been exacerbated by the unfavourable conditions under which developing countries are forced to participate in the global economy: a heavy burden of financial debt owed by the South to the North, unfavourable prices for exports from the South and protectionist policies imposed by Northern nations (see WCED 1987: 67ff.).

Thus it is admitted that development, as we have known it in the past, has been responsible for environmental degradation both directly, through the impact of industrial processes on the environment, and indirectly, by creating poverty which itself is seen as causing environmental damage. Because it has had these consequences, development as we have known it is not considered sustainable (Boutros-Ghali 1992: 35; Strong 1992b: 45); it threatens to destroy the physical and social conditions on which it depends. The overriding conviction in the globalist perspective is that development can be *made* sustainable.[4] Indeed, it *must* be made sustainable if disaster is to be averted, for it is the only way of alleviating poverty, which is in turn essential to environmental protection.

Sustainable development is expected to be achieved through three main routes. First, 'patterns of production and consumption' (Strong 1992b: 45; Brundtland 1992: 56), especially in the developed North, need to change. The affluent need to 'adopt lifestyles within the planet's ecological means' (WCED 1987: 9). This means stabilizing and, in some cases, reducing their consumption of resources, particularly their use of energy. This, it is claimed, is possible without reducing the 'real' quality of life (IUCN *et al.* 1991: 5): 'On the contrary, it can lead to a richer life of expanded opportunities for self-realization and fulfilment. More satisfying and secure because it is sustainable, and more sustainable because its opportunities and benefits are more universally shared' (Strong 1992b: 46). Thus the North is being asked to look beyond the pursuit of short-term material profit for itself, which is assumed to have driven its development in the past, and aim instead to secure benefits for future generations throughout the world. It has often been observed that this is incompatible with what national governments perceive as their own interests. For instance, the failure of the United States to commit itself wholeheartedly to the Rio agreements is attributed to the concern of President Bush not to displease the American public in the run-up to the presidential election (Holmberg *et al.* 1993: 8).

Second, the international economy needs to be organized on more equitable lines. International trade needs to be freed from the constraints that disadvantage the Southern nations (Brundtland 1992: 56; United Nations 1993a: 413) and the debt burden of the developing countries needs to be reduced (IUCN *et al.* 1991: 82; United Nations 1993a: 416). In particular, funding needs to be made available for the implementation of *Agenda 21* in developing countries. In her opening statement to the Rio Earth Summit, Gro Harlem Brundtland presented an estimated figure of US$625 billion needed for this project. Eighty per cent of this ($500 billion), it was suggested, should come from the developing nations themselves, and the remainder ($125 billion) from the industrial countries (Brundtland 1992: 57). One of the most widespread criticisms of the post-Rio process is that, while the industrial nations appeared to accept this commitment, many have since reduced their financial contributions to overseas development.

Third, environmentally sound technologies need to be developed and made widely available. Environmentally sound technology is the principal means advocated, in the globalist perspective, for making economic growth sustainable. The expressed need to change production and consumption patterns in the North is not intended to imply that less wealth should be created, since more wealth, overall (albeit more evenly distributed), is needed to eradicate poverty (WCED 1987: 49–52). Thus growth itself is still a principal aim; economies that are 'on the move again' after a long period of stagnation or decline, are praised (Strong 1994). The key to achieving sustainable growth is to 'produce more with less' (WCED 1987: 206). We need to use less energy, produce less waste and less pollution, to create more material wealth, which means making industrial processes cleaner and more efficient. Since the greatest need for economic growth is assumed to lie in developing countries, some emphasis is placed on making environmentally sound technologies available to them. Chapter 34 of *Agenda 21* includes among its objectives, 'To promote, facilitate, and finance, as appropriate, the access to and the transfer of environmentally sound technologies and corresponding know-how, in particular to developing countries' (United Nations 1993a: 420).

Global management

'Thinking globally and acting locally is not enough. We must act globally as well' (IUCN *et al.* 1991: 77). The understanding that the use of the Earth's resources needs to be managed through international co-ordination has been an important component of environmentalist discourse since before the Stockholm Conference, and was heavily reinforced by the Brundtland Report (WCED 1987). It is no longer considered acceptable for nations to pursue their own independent environmental policies. The interdependence created by the global economy, plus the understanding of the earth as a single ecosystem, has set 'new imperatives for international co-operation' (WCED 1987: 312).

It is the perceived need for global management that has given rise to some of the most high-profile events and mechanisms in the environmental debate. The most conspicuous of these have been the intergovernmental conferences organized by the United Nations, of which the Stockholm Conference and the Rio Earth Summit have been the most comprehensive. In addition to the agreements and initiatives that have emerged from these and other conferences, there is a wide range of international mechanisms intended to co-ordinate the management of the Earth's resources. The better-known include the International Whaling Commission (IWC), the Montreal Protocol on the production of CFCs, the Intergovernmental Panel on Climate Change (IPCC) and the Convention on International Trade in Endangered Species (CITES).[5]

Global management is the logical outcome of the perceived need to assess and sanction the environmental activities of others. If, as is understood in global ecology, processes taking place in one location can affect the environment many miles away or the general state of the global ecosystem, then it makes sense to aim for the widest possible agreement on appropriate action. Agreements tend to be *international* because it is the nation-states that are seen as the principal regulators of human activity. Thus, through the objective of global management, the understanding of environmental problems in global terms has elevated the role of nation-states, just as it has elevated the roles of the international and transnational organizations, including the larger NGOs (see Chatterjee and Finger 1994).

The marshalling of concerted effort in the project of global management can be seen as an expression of what Ehrenfeld called 'the arrogance of humanism', a supreme faith in the ability of human reason to overcome all difficulties and solve all problems (Ehrenfeld 1978: 12). This confidence can be detected in many of the statements produced through international negotiation, particularly in the Stockholm Declaration quoted above. It has also been suggested that the drive for global management represents a shift in the meaning of the Earth as an environmentalist icon. The image of the Earth seen from space was initially used by environmentalists to evoke a sense of humility; to promote an understanding of the finite nature of our world and our total dependence on its sustainability as a bounded, inescapable system. For advocates of global management, this image has acquired a different meaning: 'That suggestive globe, suspended in the dark universe . . . has become the object of science, planning and politics' (Sachs 1993: 17–18).

OPPOSING GLOBALISM

The perspective described above amounts to an understanding that the environment can best be protected through more globalization: by increasing the participation of communities and nations in the global economy and through co-ordinated management of the Earth's resources. The opposing perspective seeks to reverse these processes, to give communities the choice to opt out of the global economy and to place the management of resources in local hands. The anti-globalist perspective is a product of the 'border' (in the terminology employed by Douglas and Wildavsky 1982) or the 'periphery' (in the terminology of world systems theory). It represents local rather than global interests and is therefore expressed through the words and actions of local community groups and the more localized environmental NGOs.

It is difficult for a perspective that supports local interests to find expression in a global arena, for local interests, by definition, are not organized at this level, and any attempt to co-ordinate their efforts may simply produce more structures of the kind to which they are opposed. Lohmann expressed this dilemma as follows:

> Are there any prospects for an alliance among globalism's opponents which is not itself another globalism? Can different groups join with others in furthering the interests of each without positing once again an oppressive common project or privileged common language?
>
> (1993: 165)

Because of these problems, and because it has emerged largely in response to, and therefore later than, the globalist model, the anti-globalist perspective is not as well established in the environmental debate. Perhaps not surprisingly, it has been left to individual analysts, both academics and environmental campaigners, to provide the clearest articulation of this view. The work of writers such as Shiva (1993a, 1993b), Sachs (1993), Chatterjee and Finger (1994) and others amounts to a coherent critique of globalism from which the essence of an opposing perspective can be distilled.

In the following description, the opposition to globalism is presented in terms of what I take to be its three principal arguments: that development is damaging to the environment; that the whole globalist project which promotes development is a conspiracy of the wealthy North, and their allies in the South, to further their own interests; and that the replacement of local cultural perspectives by western science, which is both a product of and a stimulus for development, is replacing sustainable ways of using the environment with destructive regimes.

Against 'development'

Sachs suggested that the task of global ecology can be understood in two ways: 'it is either a technocratic effort to keep development afloat against the drift of plunder and pollution; or it is a cultural effort to shake off the hegemony of ageing Western values and gradually retire from the development race' (Sachs 1993: 11). The image of development implied here is very different from that presented in the global arenas of Stockholm and Rio. There it was seen as a natural right and a definitive human characteristic. For Sachs it is a product of western culture; one which has had its day and has been rendered unsustainable by conditions of its own making. This critique hinges on an ambiguity in the meaning of 'development' in the globalist model. There it is understood both in a broad sense, as an improvement in the quality of human life, and in a narrow sense, as economic growth through participation in the global economy. It would be difficult for the critics of globalism to disagree that an improvement in the quality of human life is desirable. What they take issue with is the implication that this depends on expansion of the global economy. It is development of this kind which the globalist model is seen as consistently and relentlessly promoting, and from which Sachs suggested that we might consider retiring.

Opponents of globalism have been concerned to show that incorporation into the global economy causes poverty by depriving local communities of the ability to meet their basic needs, replacing sustainable ways of using the environment with far more destructive regimes. Shiva, in particular, has argued that local, traditional economic systems adequately meet people's needs and sustain the environment, while the global economy forces them to meet industry's needs instead of their own. For example, in parts of India, peasant farmers traditionally practised a form of 'decentred agroforestry', using multiple species: 'The honge, tamarind, jackfruit and mango, the jola, gobli, kagli and bamboo traditionally provided food and fodder, fertilizer and pesticide, fuel and small timber. The backyard of each rural home was a nursery, and each peasant a silviculturalist' (Shiva 1993a: 29). In contrast, the 'social forestry' sponsored by the World Bank replaced this local, diverse economy with monoculture plantations of eucalyptus, destroying local sustainability:

> Trees as a living resource ... were replaced by trees whose dead wood went straight to a pulp factory hundreds of miles away. The smallest farmer became a supplier of raw material to industry and ceased to be a supplier of food to local people.
>
> (Shiva 1993a: 29–30)

Lohmann, in a similar vein, argued that colonialism and development have consistently aimed to incorporate formerly autonomous communities into a global system, by destroying their local means of subsistence. In this process, outsiders have often had the assistance of local leaders, for whom the creation of state structures in colonized regions provided an external source of power (Lohmann 1993: 157). This observation points to a complicating factor in the opposition between the developed 'North' and the less developed 'South'. The changes that followed colonization created political and economic elites in the South whose interests are closer to those of their Northern counterparts than to the interests of the majority of their own populations. When the representatives of Southern governments argue, in arenas such as Stockholm and Rio, that development in the South should not be jeopardized by environmental considerations, they are arguing for the increasing participation of their nations in the global economy. Opponents of globalism thus support the interests of local communities against the forms of development promoted by those communities' own governments. Shiva criticized the *Convention on Biological Diversity*, signed at the Rio Earth Summit, for having promoted the rights of states to exploit their resources, not the rights of local communities (Shiva 1993a: 152). In the *International Treaty between NGOs and Indigenous Peoples*, produced by the Global Forum at Rio, NGOs pledged to avoid imposing, through their own projects, 'Western economic systems and values based on the market economy' (see Sutherland 1992).

A Northern conspiracy

'Development' is thus seen by opponents of globalism as a process through which the wealthier sectors of the world's population ('the North') have extended and established their power over the poorer sectors, by making them serve the needs of the global economy. Only the wealthy – the developed North and the political and economic elite in the South – are seen as benefiting from this economy. It is a short step from this view to the understanding that any attempt to extend the process of globalization into the future will also serve the interests of the North. The globalist approach to environmental problems is interpreted by its opponents as a Northern conspiracy. Northern interests are seen as having employed several strategies to 'capture' the environmental debate and turn it to their own ends (Hildyard 1993: 29).

For instance, it was noted above that one of the consequences of thinking globally about the environment is that it lends credence to claims that only agencies that operate on a global level are in a position to tackle environmental problems. Opponents of globalism therefore see the definition of environmental problems in global terms as a deliberate move by Northern interests to ensure that only global agencies will be considered competent to deal with them. Thus the Rio Earth Summit, 'by portraying environmental degradation as a global problem requiring global solutions ... gave added impetus to those multinational interests who would extend their global reach. By definition, only international institutions and national governments were up to the task in hand' (Hildyard 1993: 31; cf. Shiva 1993b).

Similarly, by defining the solutions to environmental problems in terms of more development, in the form of a revival of economic growth (WCED 1987: 49), Northern interests are seen by globalism's opponents as seeking to ensure that the needs of the global economy, and therefore their own needs, will continue to be met. As growth is enhanced, ostensibly in order to eradicate poverty, more communities will be made to feed their local resources into the global economy on terms dictated by the North, thus extending the pattern of dependence established as a consequence of colonial expansion.

By defining the solutions to environmental problems as technological, Northern interests are again seen as seeking to ensure the continuation of their power over the South. The globalist answer to the environmental crisis is sustainable development, development which, by using the appropriate technologies, enables industry to make more while reducing its impact on the environment (WCED 1987). These technologies are assumed, in the globalist model, to be produced by the developed world and transferred to the developing world (United Nations 1993a: 420). Opponents of globalism point out that this extends the dependence of the South by implying that they cannot solve their environmental problems without technology and expertise produced by the North.

Against scientific imperialism

The advance of globalism is seen not only as a process through which the control of local resources is increasingly centralized; it also destroys the ways in which local communities understand their environments, by devaluing them and replacing them with a western model. Shiva described this in terms of the destruction of local perspectives by western science:

> The first level of violence unleashed on local systems of knowledge is not to see them as knowledge. This invisibility is the first reason why local systems collapse without trial and test when confronted with the knowledge of the dominant west .... When local knowledge does appear in the field of the globalizing vision, it is made to disappear by denying it the status of a systematic knowledge, and assigning it the adjectives 'primitive' and 'unscientific'.
>
> (Shiva 1993a: 10; see also Shiva 1987, 1990)

In a distinctive attack on globalism, Ingold argued that western science is different from most local perspectives in assuming that true knowledge of our environment comes from detached observation (Ingold 1993: 35). This assumption, he suggested, has generated the distinctively western scientific model of the environment as a 'globe', an impenetrable object that can only be viewed from without. Local communities, in contrast, derive their knowledge of the environment by experiencing it from within. Western science privileges the knowledge gained from looking at the environment over knowledge gained from living in it. This argument echoes Marglin's distinction between two types of knowledge which he referred to as 'episteme' and 'techne'. 'Episteme' is the knowledge system of scientific management, characterized by 'its emphasis on analysis, its claim that knowledge must be articulate in order to exist, its pretence to universality, its cerebral nature, its orientation to theory and empirical verification of theory'. 'Techne' is knowledge derived from use; 'it is often implicit rather than articulate ... it makes no claim to universality; it is tactile and emotional where episteme is cerebral; it is practical rather than theoretical, and geared towards discovery rather than to verification' (Marglin 1990: 58; quoted in Saurin 1993: 56).[6]

Opponents of globalism argue that the imperialism of western science has replaced sustainable ways of using the environment based on practical experience with unsustainable managerial regimes based on scientific theory. They also argue that the dominance of western science continues in the debate about how to conserve the environment. Knowledge derived from scientific surveillance and monitoring of the Earth is seen as a more reliable basis for environmental management than knowledge derived from local experience.

CONTESTING THE PAST, CONTESTING THE FUTURE

The global environmental debate is about understanding the past and planning the future. It addresses the questions of how humanity created the current environmental crisis and how we might move out of it into a more sustainable future relationship with the environment. In the two competing perspectives, these questions are interpreted in different ways, given different degrees of emphasis and different answers. The globalist view, grounded as it is in western science, gives some prominence to the physical causes of environmental degradation. The emphasis is on understanding the processes of global warming, ozone depletion, species extinction, pollution, and so on, in order to devise the appropriate technological and managerial solutions to these problems (see, for instance, IUCN *et al.* 1991). Responsibility is impersonalized, in order to avoid any divisiveness that might threaten the proposed global alliance. Environmental damage is blamed, not on people, but on poor management practices, inadequate technology, insufficient knowledge. The opponents of globalism are concerned more with understanding the economic and political causes of environmental degradation, in order to identify the appropriate social arrangements for generating sustainable use. Responsibility is more personalized: environmental damage is blamed on the North, on transnational corporations, on governments and anyone seen as pursuing personal profit at the expense of the environment and of less powerful interests. These different interpretations of the past can be illustrated with reference to the issue of debt. The divergent visions of the future are encapsulated in the way democracy is understood.

The nature of the debt

In the globalist perspective, debt is presented as a financial problem experienced by low- and middle-income countries, which inhibits their development and directly causes poverty and environmental degradation. In the 1970s, economic development in the South, particularly in Africa and Latin America, was fuelled by loans from Northern countries. In attempting to repay these loans, a task made far more difficult by the worldwide recession of the 1980s, debtor nations have been obliged to produce exports instead of meeting the basic needs of their own populations (WCED 1987: 73–4). Proposals for making development sustainable usually include some measures for tackling the problem of debt. IUCN *et al.* recommend that the governments of high-income countries write off the debts owed to them by low-income countries, and that measures be taken to reduce the debts owed to commercial banks (IUCN *et al.* 1991: 82). *Agenda 21* stresses the importance of achieving 'durable solutions' to debt problems and encourages prompt action to provide debt relief 'for the poorest heavily indebted countries pursuing structural adjustment' (United Nations 1993a: 416).

The opponents of globalism also point to the difficulties caused by financial debt, but regard them as part of a much wider debt crisis. In their view, a far greater debt is owed to the South by the North, as a result of the unfair and unsustainable exploitation of the South's resources over many generations. The South may owe the North money, but the North owes the South its ecological sustainability, stolen from it in the drive to harness local resources for the global economy. The *NGO Debt Treaty*, agreed at the Global Forum in Rio, includes a commitment to 'Work for the recognition and compensation of planetary debt of the North with respect to the South', and a proposal to

> Put pressure on international organizations for the establish-
> ment of a system of accounting of planet Earth ... in order
> to quantify the cumulative debt of the Northern countries
> which results from the resources they have levied and the
> destruction and waste produced in the course of the last 500
> years.
>
> (See Sutherland 1992)

It is worth noting that the argument about ecological debt is also used by the Southern elites, who generally subscribe to the globalist view. Like the opponents of globalism, they are concerned to relieve the economic pressure on the South, but for a very different reason: to leave the Southern nations more able to participate in the global economy.

The nature of democracy

In the broadest sense, the two competing perspectives hold similar objectives for the future of the planet: they aim to create a world in which people are able to meet their needs without damaging the environmental resources on which they depend. Both perspectives also state that this should be achieved through democratic means, but there are crucial differences in the understanding of what democracy entails. In the globalist model, democracy means participation; in the anti-globalist perspective it means self-determination.

The globalist future is a 'common' future (WCED 1987), one in which all people and organizations unite in the common purpose of sustainable development. In this project, the 'Full and informed participation of people through democratic processes at every level, accompanied by openness and transparency', is seen as essential (Strong 1992b: 50). Accordingly, *Agenda 21* devotes nine chapters to the roles of 'major groups', including women, children and youth, indigenous peoples, NGOs, workers and trade unions, farmers and scientists. The 'commitment and genuine involvement of all social groups' is described as 'critical'; 'broad public participation in decision-making' is seen as one of the 'fundamental prerequisites for the achievement of sustainable development' (United Nations 1993a: 373). The project must not fail, for 'human survival and well-being could depend on success in elevating sustainable development to a global ethic' (WCED 1987: 308). What is advocated in the globalist perspective is total participation in an agenda that has already been set by the global agencies (cf. Chatterjee and Finger 1994: 53–4). Participation in decision-making 'at every level' does not provide the opportunity to opt out of the project, or to change its direction, it provides little more than the chance to decide how to move towards objectives set by the centre, under conditions fixed by the centre.

The opponents of globalism contend that democracy does not exist without self-determination. This argument was made most forcefully in the *International Treaty between NGOs and Indigenous Peoples*, agreed at the Global Forum in Rio: 'Self-determination of Indigenous Peoples is one of the essential bases for liberty, justice and peace, in each country as well as internationally. Without recognition of this right, democracy cannot be claimed' (see Sutherland 1992). Accordingly, the NGOs committed themselves to supporting the demarcation of indigenous territories and recognizing 'rights to autonomy and self-government'. The *NGO Debt Treaty* states that local communities must take greater control of their local development.

Neither interpretation of democracy is, of course, a specifically environmentalist commitment. Concepts of democracy are incorporated into the two environmentalist perspectives through their relationships with other ideas. As we have seen, in the globalist view, the overall objective of sustainable development defines the context within which democracy is allowed to operate. The anti-globalist understanding of democracy precludes this kind of constraint. Self-determination implies the choice of opting out of sustainable development. It also implies the option of acting in ways that damage the environment. The value attached to self-determination thus creates serious logical difficulties for the anti-globalist model, as the following discussion indicates.

CASTING A VOTE?

In a formal debate, those who have listened to the arguments assess them by casting votes in favour of one side or the other, or by abstaining. In view of the close relationship, noted above, between analysis and advocacy, it is appropriate to ask whether the analysis presented here leads us to favour one or other of the two perspectives. A much broader expertise than that provided by anthropology would be required to state whether the globalist or anti-globalist approach is the more likely to deliver effective environmental protection, and is therefore the better form of environmentalism. But like each of the other disciplines engaged in environmental discourse, anthropology offers specialist knowledge on whose basis a qualified assessment can be made. In particular, as Chapter 4 demonstrated, anthropology offers an understanding of cultural diversity which can be used to test environmentalist ideas.

Cultural diversity has been identified by both environmentalists and anthropologists as important for the long-term survival of humanity. This argument implicitly acknowledges the degree of difficulty involved in identifying sustainable cultures. If we knew which particular ways of understanding the world were going to 'work' in the future, we could set about trying to persuade people to adopt them. But because we cannot tell, the best option is to conserve the greatest possible diversity of cultural perspectives, in the hope that some will ultimately prove sustainable. Of the two environmentalist models that oppose each other in the global debate, globalism would appear, by its very nature, to be destined to destroy diversity. I think this a correct impression, but we need to understand why it is correct, for advocates of globalism would deny that this is their purpose. Opponents of globalism, on the other hand, celebrate and promote cultural diversity as the basis of sustainability, but this conflicts with the priority given, in their model, to self-determination.

Globalism and cultural diversity

In the globalist perspective, it is considered important not to lose anything that might contribute to the quest for sustainable development. It is for this reason that the cultures of indigenous and traditional peoples are seen as potentially important sources of knowledge. The Brundtland Report acknowledged that the advance of 'organized development' has led to the exploitation of local communities and the disappearance of their traditional practices, making them victims of 'what could be described as cultural extinction'. This is considered a loss for 'the larger society',[7] which could learn from their traditional skills in ecological management (WCED 1987: 114–15). Globalism therefore encourages a general respect for cultural diversity (IUCN *et al.* 1991: 53), insofar as it can serve the needs of sustainable development.

But a close examination of globalist ideas leads us to wonder what a respect for cultural diversity is taken to mean. The quality of human life is measured largely in terms of criteria that are considered important in industrial societies. The Human Development Index, adopted by the United Nations Development Programme as a measure of the quality of life, has three components: longevity; knowledge or educational attainment, 'measured by adult literacy and mean years of schooling'; and income, 'measured by per capita Gross Domestic Product' (IUCN *et al.* 1991: 198).

The Brundtland Report also treated education as a 'key dimension of "population quality"' (WCED 1987: 105). What is meant here is the kind of education generally provided by state systems, and not the training received traditionally by children in non-industrial societies through their participation in subsistence economies. Anti-globalists would argue that state education has been one of the principal mechanisms through which 'scientific imperialism' has advanced, through which 'techne' is replaced by 'episteme' (Marglin 1990).

Perhaps the most telling remark made from a globalist viewpoint on the subject of cultural diversity was Maurice Strong's comment on the impact of modern society on people's ability to comprehend and manage the processes in which they are involved: 'Caught up in the dynamics of universalization, it is no wonder that people react with anxiety and rejection, seeking refuge and identity in their own traditions and values' (Strong 1994). Thus, cultural traditions are not something to be respected and followed in their own right, but something to which people turn when they feel overwhelmed by modernism.

I suggest that the globalist image of cultural diversity is based on a fundamental misunderstanding of culture itself. What the globalist perspective understands by culture is not what anthropologists understand by it. In addressing the use of culture in the quest for sustainability, IUCN *et al.* suggest that 'Every society is likely to have special symbols, stories, sacred places, and other cultural features that can support the world ethic for living sustainably' (1991: 53).[8] If these things are seen as exemplifying 'cultural' features, then the globalist view of culture appears to be similar to that employed by some social scientists, who treat it as a residual category incorporating whatever is left once political and economic features have been identified (see Chapter 5).

This in itself is not a problem; there is no reason to expect the advocates of globalism to define culture as anthropologists do. But what is worrying is the implied assumption that cultural diversity can somehow be conserved within a single political and economic ethic devoted to global management for sustainable development. The fact that the globalist perspective supports *both* this single global ethic *and* cultural diversity suggests that globalists are confused about the nature of culture. They see it as separable from, and presumably unaffected by, the assumptions and values that drive development. It is this apparent lack of understanding of the

198

way in which the features *they* define as 'cultural' are related to other elements in people's understanding of the world, that represents a serious flaw in the globalists' argument. They fail to understand the extent to which the components of a culture or cultural perspective are related to one another.

As an illustration of this point, consider again the Dogon's respect for their trees (van Beek and Banga 1992), described in Chapter 4. This might appear to be precisely what is meant, in the globalist perspective, by a cultural feature that might be used to support the sustainability ethic. If the Dogon traditionally treat their trees with respect, only taking from them what they need and never felling a whole tree without serious and reverential consideration, then surely they can be recruited into the campaign for sustainable development through their own cultural values. But, as van Beek and Banga indicate, the Dogon respect for trees is based on an understanding that the environment has power beyond that of human beings. It would be inappropriate for people to try to manage or replenish the bush, for the bush itself is the source of all power and life. The sustainable development ethic, on the other hand, is based on an understanding that people have the power to manage their environment through the application of scientific knowledge. Would it be possible for the Dogon to become convinced that this is an appropriate way of interacting with their environment, without losing their traditional respect for it? Perhaps, given that inter-cultural exchanges have often produced new ways of understanding the world (see Chapter 5, above), but such outcomes are difficult both to predict and to control, and the experience of many non-industrial societies gives little cause for optimism.

Cultural diversity and the opposition to globalism

A concern to protect cultural diversity is central to the anti-globalist environmentalist perspective. The *Earth Charter*,[9] prepared by the NGOs gathered at the Global Forum in Rio, established this concern in its first two principles:

1 We agree to respect, encourage, protect and restore Earth's ecosystems to ensure biological and cultural diversity.
2 We recognize our diversity and our common partnership.

We respect all cultures and affirm the rights of all people to basic environmental needs.

The *Citizens' Commitment on Biodiversity*, also agreed at the Global Forum, defined biodiversity in such a way that it includes cultural diversity (see Chapter 4, note 13). 'Culture' is conceptualized in broader terms than in the globalist perspective, more in line with the older, broader anthropological sense of the term. In the *International Treaty between NGOs and Indigenous Peoples*, the NGOs committed themselves to respecting the indigenous peoples' 'systems of self-government' and their 'economic and development systems ... including their traditional technologies'. In other words, there is a concern to protect indigenous cultures in their entirety, not to select bits and pieces from them that might be considered useful in a wider context.

One of the main arguments against globalism is that, through its pursuit of 'development', it destroys cultural diversity by causing local cultures to be swallowed up in the expansion of the global economy. Shiva (1993a) and Sachs (1993) in particular have articulated this argument:

> Turning the South's societies into economic competitors ... required ... a cultural transformation, for many 'old ways' of living turned out to be 'obstacles to development'.... In the attempt to overcome these barriers to growth, the traditional social fabric was often dissected and reassembled according to the textbook models of macro-economics. To be sure, 'development' had many effects, but one of its most insidious was the dissolution of cultures which were not built around a frenzy of accumulation.
>
> (Sachs 1993: 4–5)

The concern to protect cultural diversity is part of the wider commitment to localism, and is supported by the same rationale: that local cultures are better guardians of the environment than globalism can be, and particularly of biodiversity, which is seen as the basis of evolution. Shiva, who pointed out that globalism is itself nothing more than a local cultural perspective that has colonized the world (1993a: 10), argued that cultural diversity goes hand in hand with biodiversity. Local cultures that depend on their local environments need to keep those environments diverse in order to fulfil all their needs. In the example cited earlier in this chapter, the Indian forests were able to provide 'food and fodder, fertilizer and pesticide, fuel and small timber' because they held a variety of species (Shiva 1993a: 29). When they were replaced by monocultures to supply the global economy, their capacity to meet local needs disappeared.

The argument that a large number of local cultures, each depending on its own immediate ecosystem, offers a good chance of conserving biodiversity, may sound reasonable, but it is difficult to reconcile with the anti-globalist emphasis on self-determination as a central ideal. Just as self-determination implies the choice to opt out of the quest for sustainable development (see above), it also implies a whole range of other options: to participate in the global economy, to exploit the environments of neighbouring or more distant communities, to emulate a western pattern of development. In other words, if local communities are to control their own destinies, then nothing can be guaranteed: neither the conservation of cultural diversity, nor protection of the environment. The argument, central to the anti-globalist view, that self-determination can deliver these things, depends on the assumption that people will not act in destructive ways – it depends on the myth of primitive ecological wisdom being true.

Swallowing the myth

Some of the documents which express broadly anti-globalist ideas display a remarkable faith in the myth of primitive ecological wisdom. The *International Treaty between NGOs and Indigenous Peoples* states, 'For centuries the Indigenous Peoples have had an intimate relationship with nature, passing along respect, interdependence and equilibrium. For this reason, these peoples have developed economic, social and cultural models that respect nature without destroying it.' The *NGO Forest Treaty* even defined indigenous and traditional peoples in terms of their harmonious relationship with their environment: 'Native, indigenous, and aboriginal people are those who have lived in relative harmony with their environment for many generations . . . . Traditional peoples are non native populations who have established non destructive relationships with their environment' (*NGO Forest Treaty*, see Sutherland 1992). It is not difficult to show that this faith is unfounded. There are known examples of non-industrial societies having destroyed their forests, for instance. In addition to the case

201

of Easter Island cited in Chapter 2, the Hopi Indians in North America were only saved from ecological crisis by the discovery of coal, having already cut down all their woodland.[10] In the 1980s, as part of a resettlement programme, the government of Indonesia recognized the ownership rights of the Nuaulu over a large area in central South Seram. This was followed by commercial logging and land sales on an unprecedented scale (Ellen 1993).

But in the global environmental debate, the myth of primitive ecological wisdom is not simply a notion imposed by romantic environmentalists on a sector of the world's population, it is an image which indigenous peoples accept and promote for themselves. During the run-up to the Rio Earth Summit, the representatives of indigenous peoples, like other interest groups, held meetings to discuss their role and reinforce their concerted position. The *Earth Charter of the Indigenous Peoples*, produced at a meeting in Kari-Oca in 1992, declares, 'We, the indigenous peoples of the world since the time of our ancestors, have constructed a culture, a civilization, a history and a vision of the world that has allowed us to coexist in a harmonious way with nature.'[11]

In the face of anthropological knowledge, this image is no more convincing when promoted by indigenous peoples themselves than it is when promoted by environmentalists. It might even be argued that it is less convincing, for it can be seen as having a clear political purpose. By presenting themselves as responsible guardians of the Earth's resources, indigenous people, many of whom are disadvantaged by the political systems of their own countries, can enlist the support of environmentalists worldwide in their efforts to assert their traditional rights. The fact that, in some contexts, members of non-industrial societies reject the romantic portrayal of their cultures by environmentalists (see Harries-Jones 1993: 49) lends weight to this interpretation. This particular myth, like many others, is asserted or rejected according to political expediency.

Ironically, the globalist environmentalist perspective also endorses the image of indigenous and traditional peoples as ecologically wise. The Brundtland Report treated indigenous peoples as a source of knowledge on environmental management, and referred to the 'harmony with nature and the environmental awareness characteristic of the traditional way of life' (WCED 1987: 115). Maurice Strong, in his opening statement at the Rio Earth Summit, described indigenous peoples as 'repositories of much of the traditional knowledge and wisdom from which modernization has separated most of us', and said that 'We must reinstate in our lives the ethic of love and respect for the Earth which traditional peoples have retained as central to their value systems' (Strong 1992b: 50). IUCN *et al.* state that traditional subsistence activities 'reinforce spiritual values, an ethic of sharing, and a commitment to stewardship of the land' (1991: 61). However, unlike the anti-globalist perspective, the globalist model does not depend on the myth being true. It is assumed that the overarching hegemony of global management will guarantee environmental protection by recruiting all peoples, regardless of their degree of ecological wisdom, to the quest for sustainable development. No one is offered the option of taking a different path.

We can now see how an anthropological understanding of culture, and a knowledge of cultural diversity, can expose inconsistencies and contradictions in environmentalist perspectives. The anti-globalist vision is based on unrealistic assumptions about the way people interact with their environments, while the globalist vision is based on a misunderstanding about the nature of culture. In addition, both perspectives are inconsistent in their understanding of cultural diversity. Both claim to value diversity as a principal mechanism through which sustainability might be achieved, but both impose limits which reveal a failure to grasp the full implications of cultural diversity. For the globalists, diverse cultures are acceptable only if they can contribute to the quest for sustainable development. For the anti-globalists, a diversity of cultures is the essence of sustainability, but only if those cultures conform to certain ideals; there is no room, in the anti-globalist world, for acquisitive, exploitative, imperialistic cultures. It would seem, then, that the analysis presented in this chapter leaves us with little option but to abstain from casting a vote in the global environmental debate, for both sides have built their arguments on foundations which, from an anthropological viewpoint, look rather shaky.

One further point is worth making, however. If we accept the shared premise from which the debate starts – that the environment is to be seen primarily as a resource for human use and that the main issue is one of human survival – and if we accept the argument that cultural diversity is itself an important resource for human survival, then we would have to cast our vote in favour of the anti-globalists. Although the anti-globalists, if they take seriously their ideal of self-determination for local communities, cannot guarantee that cultural diversity will be conserved, they are at least seeking to create conditions in which it can survive. The globalists, on the other hand, are putting all their cultural eggs in one basket. They are seeking to impose a global hegemony which, if successful, cannot help but destroy cultural diversity. Of course, both the assumption that the environment is primarily a human resource, and the understanding that human survival is the central environmental issue, are themselves questioned by participants in an environmentalist discourse which extends beyond the global environmental debate.

THE DISCOURSE BEYOND THE DEBATE

During the months preceding the Rio Earth Summit, the United Nations Association in Britain held conferences throughout the country to enable NGOs and members of the public to express their views on the main issues to be discussed in Rio. One of the topics for discussion at the conference held in Belfast was forestry. We were given a two-page briefing of background information and asked to consider a list of questions, one of which was, 'Who has the right to the forests and their management – indigenous peoples, the governments, the United Nations, the transnational corporations?' The group took the anti-globalist position and argued that indigenous peoples should have control over their own forest resources. One participant tried to widen the discussion by pointing out that the alternatives provided were all anthropo-centric, and suggested that the forests themselves, and the plants and animals that inhabit them, might be accorded the right to live without human interference. Although this suggestion met with murmurs of agreement, it was quickly dismissed as unrealistic, in the context of the Earth Summit, and the discussion reverted to matters of resource management.

The debate analysed in this chapter is about conserving the environment as a resource for human use. The two competing perspectives share this understanding of the environment; it is the starting point from which they diverge. But environmentalist discourse is wider than this debate, and involves perspectives in which the environment is not seen as a resource. In particular, it includes what are usually referred to as 'biocentric' or 'ecocentric' perspectives.[12] In this final section, I shall consider briefly how these perspectives are related to those engaged in the global environmental debate.

Two environmentalisms?

In Chapter 3, I discussed at some length the pervasive distinction, in social scientific analyses, between two kinds of environmentalism, one conservative in its attitude to industrial society, and one radical. I also raised the question of whether this distinction might present a rather narrow characterization of environmentalism. In the context of global environmental discourse, I would argue that it is not only narrow, but also misleading.

In some ways, the two perspectives described in this chapter fit quite closely some of the earlier analytical models of environmentalism. In terms of Milbrath's formulation (1984: 72), globalism can be accommodated within the structures of industrial society – indeed, it seeks to perpetuate them – while anti-globalism demands a fundamental change to those structures. In terms of Cotgrove's distinction (1976: 24), globalism offers no challenge to the 'dominant economic value system', since its goal is to enhance economic growth, whereas anti-globalism appears to place more value on welfare issues, on the fulfilment of basic needs, than on the pursuit of purely economic ends. Globalists advocate a 'piece-meal tinkering' with industrial processes, in terms of new technology, to bring about environmental improvements, while their opponents take an holistic view, based on ecological principles (Cotgrove 1976: 25).

Globalists also seem similar to O'Riordan's 'technocentrists', who wish to make industrial society more environmentally benign without questioning its goals or values, and anti-globalists appear similar to his 'ecocentrists', who preach humility for the processes and products of nature and advocate low-impact technology and self-reliance (O'Riordan 1981 [1976]). But the two perspectives can only be described as 'conservative' (globalism) and 'radical' (anti-globalism) in the context of industrial society. This was appropriate enough for the analysis of a social movement taking place largely within industrial societies, but it is not appropriate for analysing a global debate in which many different societies are involved.

From the standpoint of industrial society, globalism appears conservative because it advocates, more or less, business as usual: continued economic growth, continued pursuit of managerial control over the environment, continued and increasing centralization of that control. Anti-globalism appears radical because it seeks to reverse these processes, to decentralize control, to replace the pursuit of growth with security of subsistence for the greatest number of people. From the standpoint of, say, subsistence farmers, globalism is by far the more radical alternative, seeking to replace traditional structures with modern ones, to make local, relatively autonomous economies dependent on external relationships and subject to state control. It might be argued that it is incorporation into the global economy that has this effect, rather than globalist *environmentalism*, but the two are inseparable, because globalist environmentalists advocate the continued expansion of the global economy in order to involve all communities in the quest for sustainable development.

But even within the context of industrial society, the anti-globalist perspective does not amount to what more recent analyses have identified as radical environmentalism. For both Dobson (1990) and Eckersley (1992), the more radical form of environmentalism (to which they refer, respectively, as 'ecologism' and 'ecocentrism') is based on the understanding that the environment has a value independent of its use to human beings and that our proper treatment of it requires us to see ourselves as just one element in an ecological system rather than as the centre of the universe. In relation to this view, neither perspective engaged in the debate analysed above can properly be seen as radical, for they are competing models of resource use. The debate is defined in terms which do not admit any other understanding of human–environment relations.

'Radical' environmentalism

Radical environmentalism of the kind identified by Dobson and Eckersley is thus characterized by an opposition to the use of the environment solely as a resource for human benefit. But this opposition is shared by a number of perspectives, some of which, it has been argued, are fundamentally incompatible with 'ecocentrism'. In trying to identify the essential character of radical environmentalism, we are faced, as is to be expected given the nature of contemporary human culture, with a complex of seamlessly merging discourses and overlapping perspectives. For instance, within industrial societies, opposition to the view that the environment is a resource for purely human benefit has tended to be expressed most often through a concern for the rights of non-human animals. But such rights can include anything from the right to be treated without cruelty to the right to live their lives entirely without human interference. While the former can be accommodated within an understanding of the environment as a resource, the latter comes closer to the views expressed by radical environmentalists; but the fact that animal rights as such form the focus of a discourse tends to confuse the issue.

Several writers (Foreman 1986, Manes 1990, Eckersley 1992) have gone to some lengths to identify a boundary between radical environmentalism and the animal rights movement. Foreman pointed out that support for animal rights is concern for the well-being of individuals, whereas 'deep ecology' is based on respect for 'the life community': 'Animal Rights is compassionate, desiring to eliminate suffering and pain', while 'Deep Ecology is ecological, recognizing that life depends on life, that some suffering and pain is inherent in nature, that death is not evil', in short, 'that nature knows best' (Foreman 1986: 21, quoted in Manes 1990: 146). Eckersley pointed out that the animal rights perspective is essentially a concern for sentient beings (Eckersley 1992: 43–4; see also Manes 1990: 146), and therefore excludes many of the entities considered by radical environmentalists to be worthy of moral consideration. It could be argued that the concern for sentient beings is essentially anthropocentric, since it is based on the understanding that non-human animals are worthy of consideration insofar as they are *like us*.[13] In contrast, an ecocentric perspective recognizes the intrinsic value of all natural entities, human and non-human animals, plants, landscapes, ecosystems, the planet as a whole, and argues that, within practical limits, all such entities should be free to 'unfold in their own way unhindered by the various forms of human domination' (Fox 1989: 6, quoted in Eckersley 1992: 53). Thus, the true ancestors of the ecocentrists, in ideological terms, are those 'preservationists' who, at the beginning of the twentieth century, followed Muir in seeking to protect the environment from development rather than to conserve it for development (see Eckersley 1992: 42).

Just as the global environmental debate is about control over the distribution of resources, so too is most traditional politics, in both industrial and non-industrial societies. As Paehlke noted (1989: 188), the opposition between left and right within industrial states has centred on distributive issues (see Chapter 3, above). Thus ecocentric views are difficult to accommodate with established political alignments, and there tend to be no official mechanisms through which they can be expressed. Consequently, radical environmentalists seek to redefine political discourse, to redraw the boundaries of politics to include ecocentric goals. This usually means taking direct action against practices they see as contravening ecocentric principles, such as commercial logging and road building, and since many such practices are part of the accepted and routine functioning of industrial economies, opposing them often means acting outside the law.

Greenpeace is widely recognized as the organization that pioneered direct action for environmentalist purposes, having begun as a small group of determined individuals prepared to interfere, at considerable personal risk, with nuclear tests, whale hunts and seal hunts.[14] Direct action remains the hallmark of Greenpeace, but the organization is now more hierarchical than sectarian in character, to use the terminology of Douglas and Wildavsky (see Chapter 3), and is seen by some environmentalists as one of the established groups out of which a more radical approach has emerged.[15] In a move which echoed David Brower's departure from the Sierra Club to found Friends of the Earth a decade before, Paul Watson, one of the creators of Greenpeace, left the organization to found the Sea Shepherd Conservation Society in 1979 (see Manes 1990: 108ff.). Shortly afterwards, a group of American environmentalists, dissatisfied with the apparent inability of the mainstream organizations to have any impact on the rate of environmental damage, founded the group Earth First! (Manes 1990: 66ff.), which has become famous for interfering directly with destructive practices by, for instance, immobilizing machinery. A significant proportion of the direct actions in defence of the environment during the 1980s and early 1990s, not only in America, but also in Australia and Europe, have been taken in the name of Earth First!

Globalism, anti-globalism and ecocentrism

Perhaps surprisingly, given the parameters of the debate over control of the environment as a resource, both globalists and their opponents give an occasional nod in the direction of ecocentrism. Probably the most ecocentric statement published by a global organization was the *World Charter for Nature*, produced by the UN General Assembly in 1982. It expressed the conviction that 'Every form of life is unique, warranting respect regardless of its worth to man, and, to accord other organisms such recognition, man must be guided by a moral code of action'. The first of its General Principles was, 'Nature shall be respected and its essential processes shall not be impaired' (UN GA RES 37/7). IUCN *et al.* proposed that 'an ethic for living sustainably' should express 'the respect and care we owe each other and the Earth' and recognize 'that nature has to be cared for in its own right, not just as a means of satisfying human needs' (IUCN *et al.* 1991: 13). Even the Brundtland Report, which is thoroughly resource-orientated, acknowledged that there are moral and ethical (as well as utilitarian, aesthetic, cultural and purely scientific) reasons for conserving 'wild beings' (WCED 1987: 13).

. For the anti-globalists, the NGOs' *Earth Charter* began by claiming to speak for the whole planet and its inhabitants: 'We are the Earth, the people, plants and animals, rains and oceans, breath of the forest and flow of the sea.' The *Citizens' Commitment on Biodiversity* expressed the view that 'sustainable use means that [which] does not interfere with the ecological integrity of any living things or their ecosystems'. Shiva argued that the overriding reason for not allowing species to become extinct should be that 'All life forms have an inherent right to life', and used the term 'biodemocracy' to denote the recognition of this right (Shiva 1993a: 88, 92). She referred to other life-forms as 'our partners in co-evolution, not merely mines of genes to be exploited at will for profit and control' and wrote of the 'sovereignty' of biodiversity itself (1993a: 91). But like the conference discussion in Belfast, these publications, globalist and anti-globalist alike, quickly revert to their main purpose, that of establishing a case for a particular distribution of control over the environment as a resource for human use.

Nevertheless, the appearance of ecocentric values in the literature of the global environmental debate raises questions about how perspectives relate to one another in discourse. A closer examination of ecocentric ideas reveals further points of convergence. For instance, ecocentrists, at least as much as any other environmentalists, have accepted the myth of primitive ecological wisdom. To support this observation, it is worth quoting Manes at length:

> The argument that the environmental crisis is just another curlicue in the history of life on Earth is contradicted by the existence of numerous cultures that have developed a sustainable and harmonious relationship with their surroundings

because they neither industrialized nor turned to monoculture nor presumed to take upon themselves the megalomaniacal task 'to govern evolution': the Mbuti, the Penan, the !Kung, to name but a few. Out of some hidden source of wisdom these societies *chose* not to dominate nature. In the larger history of humanity, they are the norm and we are the exception.

(Manes 1990: 28, emphasis given)

Ecocentrism, like the anti-globalist perspective, contains a radical critique of industrialism. Its legitimacy therefore depends, to some extent, on the myth of primitive ecological wisdom being true. Ecocentrists, like anti-globalists, look to non-industrial peoples as models for a sustainable existence (Manes 1990: 122–3). It is no surprise to find that the ecocentric vision of an ideal society can look very similar to that envisaged by the opposition to globalism, an ideal represented by the concept of 'bioregionalism', which 'envisions communities of creatures living harmoniously and simply within the boundaries of distinct ecosystems' (Taylor 1991: 260). One of the founders of Earth First! identified bioregionalism as an appropriate way of describing what the group was seeking (Foreman 1987, cited in Taylor 1991: 261). Thus, anti-globalists and radical environmentalists share one of their main objectives, to transform biosphere people into ecosystem peoples, to recreate 'the future primitive' (Foreman 1987, Dasmann 1976).

A different kind of convergence is implied in the observation that, within industrial societies, conservative and radical environmentalists operate in a kind of alliance. Radical groups make demands which they know will be seen by the authorities as unreasonable. They do this through high-profile campaigns which grab media attention and win public support, thus making it difficult for the authorities to ignore them. In the early 1990s, for instance, activists opposing the British government's road building programme, some acting in the name of Earth First! and some on behalf of local groups, have made temporary homes in trees threatened by road developments. The developers' efforts to remove them have been reported widely in the media. Such activities make the more moderate environmental groups seem all the more reasonable, and create a better chance of negotiating some kind of advance for environmental protection. Indeed, the British Government has recently modified its policy on road-building, and the public perception is that radical protest is having some impact. Most of the time the alliance between radical and conservative environmentalists works informally and without being explicitly acknowledged. But Manes points out that Earth First! was originally set up at least partly for the purpose of making more established groups look moderate (Manes 1990: 70). More recently in Britain, some of the long-established NGOs, including WWF, Friends of the Earth and the Wildlife Trusts[16] have formed an alliance with Earth First! activists and local groups to oppose environmentally damaging development projects (Brown and Vidal 1995).

The shape of the discourse

While discourses often appear to merge seamlessly in contemporary human culture, perspectives can be said to have distinguishable boundaries. These boundaries are not necessarily agreed, for they might be drawn differently by any two individuals. Nor are they fixed; ideas that are taken to belong to a particular perspective in one context might be excluded from it in another. But the boundaries exist in the sense that it is possible to state, in any given context, what lies within a perspective and what does not. Thus, for instance, within the context of the global environmental debate, it is clear that the pursuit of economic growth belongs to the globalist perspective but not to the opposing model, while the understanding of democracy in terms of self-determination is a part of the anti-globalist perspective but not of globalism. Within the broader context of environmentalist discourse, we can say that the understanding of the environment as a resource for human use has no place in the ecocentric perspective.

However, because they have boundaries, perspectives can be said genuinely to overlap, in the sense that they can share assumptions, values, strategies and objectives, without becoming indistinguishable. The differences among the three perspectives discussed above can be identified quite clearly. And yet the myth of primitive ecological wisdom is shared by all three, the assumption that the environment is a resource for human use is shared by globalism and anti-globalism, and the ideal of locally autonomous communities living sustainably within ecosystems is shared by anti-globalists and ecocentrists.

The analysis of global environmentalist discourse makes it easy to agree with Norton, who argued that the differences between environmentalist ideologies, while undoubtedly important in the context of 'idealized argument', do not tend to divide environmentalists into exclusive camps (Norton 1991; see Chapter 3, above). A consideration of what environmentalists do and say in their engagement with each other and with the forces they oppose reveals a much more fluid and complex discourse than most social-scientific analyses have portrayed.

7

ANTHROPOLOGY, SOCIAL SCIENCE AND ENVIRONMENTALISM

> Cultural theory is a tool to dispel the fog of expressive propaganda. Cultural analysis is a practice that forces argument onto a franker plane.
>
> (Douglas 1992: 269)

Anthropology still has a long way to go in establishing its role in environmental discourse, and in convincing other participants of the value of that role. This book is intended as a step along the way, not as a definitive and final statement. What follows is a selective review of the ground covered on this exploratory journey, and a glance forward at where it might lead. The arguments presented in this book have implications for three main areas of interest. First, within anthropology, the exploration of ways in which the discipline might contribute to environmental discourse has generated ideas which have consequences both for cultural theory in general and for the analysis of contemporary human culture. Second, the identification of a role for anthropology brings into focus its relationship with the other social sciences and raises questions about the development of interdisciplinary approaches. Finally, there is the potential influence of cultural analysis on environmental discourse itself: the messages anthropology holds for environmentalism.

BACK TO CULTURE

In Chapter 1, I suggested that anthropology might contribute to environmental discourse in two main ways. In its guise as the study of human ecology, it can provide an understanding of how human beings interact with their environments, and by analysing

213

environmentalism as a cultural phenomenon it can throw light on the character and content of environmentalist thought. But the discussion in subsequent chapters (particularly Chapters 2 and 5) indicated that anthropology, as it has evolved over recent decades, is not as well equipped as it could be to tackle either of these tasks. Both require some revision of established analytical concepts and traditions. The task of analysing human–environment relations throws the spotlight on culture in its more general sense, as a universal component of human experience, and requires us to consider whether established anthropological models of culture are entirely appropriate for the study of human ecology. The task of analysing environmentalism throws the spotlight on the relationship between 'culture' in general and 'cultures', in the more specific sense of the term. It requires us to consider what happens to culture in a world in which the boundaries between cultures are easily crossed by people and their products.

Culture and human ecology

In Chapter 2, I argued that the constructivist view of culture, which has been the prevailing model in post-structuralist anthropology, is of limited value for studying the interaction between human beings and their environments (cf. Ingold 1992a). The assumption that reality is 'constructed' through social interaction, that meanings learned through participation in human society are imposed on an otherwise meaningless world, denies any role for the environment itself. It prevents us from studying the impact of the environment on human society and culture because the existence of a world outside cultural construction is not acknowledged. Ingold's solution to this problem was to invoke Gibson's concept of 'direct perception', according to which we discover reality through our active engagement with the world, rather than imposing meanings upon it (Ingold 1992a: 42ff.).

The constructivist perspective has enabled anthropologists to think of culture as being composed of 'models' (Caws 1974, Holy and Stuchlik 1981). But, as indicated in Chapter 2, this understanding of culture contains a contradiction. It is not possible to conceive of an entirely modelled reality, for it leaves no raw material out of which to construct the models. This argument can be made clearer by considering the role of metaphor in cultural analysis. Metaphors, or symbols, are often treated by anthropologists as the main mechanisms through which people build their cultural models (Gudeman 1986, Bird-David 1992a). The concept of metaphor depends on a distinction between spheres of reality which are assumed to be understood in different ways. In other words, something has to provide the metaphors through which something else is understood. For instance, in Bird-David's comparative analysis of the 'metaphorization of human–nature relatedness' (Bird-David 1993), interpersonal relationships are seen as providing metaphors for the interaction between selected hunter-gatherer societies and their environments. Thus, the relationship between Cree hunters and their quarry is expressed through a sexual metaphor – hunting is described as an act of sexual intercourse – while the Nayaka, Batek and Mbuti describe the forest as a parent (Bird-David 1993: 113, 120). In these cases, the human–environment relationships are presented as 'metaphorized' reality, and human social relationships are the 'unmetaphorized' reality from which appropriate metaphors are drawn.

The constructivist model has led anthropologists to focus heavily on metaphorized reality: the world as understood through models and symbols. What Ingold's (1992a) critique of constructivism does is remind us that there has to be an 'unmetaphorized' reality of which people are aware, otherwise they would have no source from which to draw their metaphors. If I have understood his argument correctly, 'direct perception' is the process through which people become aware of this 'unmetaphorized' or 'unconstructed' reality, and ecological anthropologists in particular should focus on it as the essence of human–environment relations. As it stands, however, Ingold's argument has little impact on cultural theory, for the meanings discovered through direct perception do not, for him, belong within culture (Ingold 1992a: 52–3). In his terms, anthropologists can go on regarding culture as consisting entirely of models.

In Chapter 2, I argued that this concept of culture, one that excludes perceptions, would be unworkable because of the difficulties involved in distinguishing empirically between perceptions and knowledge gained in other ways (cf. Bird-David 1992a: 45). Instead, I suggested that we see culture as consisting of everything we know, think and feel about the world, regardless of the processes through which it is acquired. By defining culture in this way, we can study the role of the environment in human affairs, as well as the impact of human activity on the environment, and still treat culture as a principal mechanism through which this relationship operates. The acknowledgement that culture consists of both constructed and unconstructed meanings, of both 'metaphorized' and 'unmetaphorized' reality, can, I suggest, shed light on a long-standing debate within anthropology: that concerning the relationship between nature and society in human thought.

Nature and society

In Chapter 3, I discussed Douglas' views on the relationship between social organization and people's understanding of the natural environment. While many anthropologists would not accept her assertion that forms of social organization cause people to think about nature in certain ways, the view that human society provides models for understanding the world beyond is quite widely held. It is expressed, for instance, in the work of Bird-David referred to above. Social relationships provide the framework through which selected hunter-gatherer communities describe their interaction with their environment. This kind of analysis has been seen as misrepresenting the cultures being described. Ingold argued that it reproduces a western dichotomy between society and nature which is denied by hunter-gatherer cultures (Ingold 1992b: 42). Richards (1993) argued that at least some of what people know about their environment comes from direct empirical observation.

The acknowledgement that culture consists of both constructed and unconstructed reality provides both a way of identifying this misrepresentation, if such it is, and the prospect of avoiding it. The type of analysis characterized by the work of Douglas and Bird-David appears to be based on the assumption that the unconstructed, 'unmetaphorized' sector of reality, the source of metaphors for describing other things, will be the same in every culture; it will always be human society. It is inevitable that any analysis based on this assumption will reproduce the dichotomy between society and nature, since this is its starting point. However, there is no reason to suppose that what is and what is not metaphorized will be any less culturally variable than anything else. While some societies may draw predominantly on social metaphors to describe 'nature', others may do the reverse, while others, like the hunter-gatherers to which Ingold referred, may not recognize the distinctions which generate these particular metaphors, but will have other ways of classifying their environments. It also seems likely that these kinds of variations will be found, not only between cultures, but also between groups and individuals within a community, and among different social contexts: domestic and public, religious and secular. I suggest that being aware of the possibility of such variations, rather than making prior assumptions about what will and will not be 'metaphorized' in any situation, is the key to making more 'culture-sensitive observations' (Bird-David 1992b).

Culture in a globalized world

The second task which I have suggested makes up anthropology's role in environmental discourse is the study of environmentalism as a cultural phenomenon. Again, the discipline's established analytical conventions are not entirely appropriate for this task, so some rethinking is necessary. In Chapter 1, I pointed out that anthropologists use the term 'culture' in both a general and a specific sense, but often fail to distinguish between them. In studying environmentalism, it has proved useful to make this distinction. Environmentalism is cultural in the general sense of the term, in that it belongs to people's understanding of the world, but unlike many of the things anthropologists study, it does not belong to a specific culture – a particular way of understanding the world that is associated with a distinct group or category of people. Instead, environmentalism is a perspective shared by people from a wide range of cultures. What happens to cultural things in a global arena is that they lose their ties to particular societies and groups, and what we need in order to analyse them in this context is a way of describing their free-moving character.

Hannerz and Appadurai have both suggested that the solution to this problem is to find new ways of thinking about cultures, in the specific sense of the term; to see them not as bounded and territorially based but as open and able to cross boundaries. I have argued against this (see Chapter 5, above), partly because I do not think it represents a genuinely new way of thinking about cultures, but mainly because I think it is unnecessary to adapt a well-established concept when more suitable ones are available. The movement of cultural things in the global arena is essentially a product of communication, and it seems appropriate to select ideas which reflect this condition. I therefore suggested that we use the concept of 'discourse' to describe the constituents of contemporary human culture. Discourses, defined as fields of communication identified by their subject matter, are not tied to territories or groups of people, but spread wherever the mechanisms of communication take them. Discourses cross the boundaries (such as they are) of what we normally think of as cultures, and so tend to generate perspectives, particular ways of understanding the world, which are also transcultural. In Chapter 6, I showed how environmentalist discourse – discourse about protection of the environment – encompasses a number of transcultural perspectives which both compete and overlap with one another. Although the framework suggested here was developed for the purpose of analysing environmentalism, it could obviously be used in the study of any contemporary discourse.

Studying culture in the global arena, as well as requiring anthropologists to adopt new analytical concepts, also leads us to think about our research methods and objectives. Traditionally, anthropologists have tended to select particular fieldwork locations or communities and to study the cultural processes operating within those contexts. But many cultural phenomena have no location within the global arena, and the products of contemporary discourse can be made available to anyone with access to the appropriate technology. I suggested in Chapter 6 that this makes it easier for anthropologists to analyse the content and composition of transcultural perspectives, but harder to understand how they are generated and sustained. We assume that, like the cultural traditions of a small community, transcultural perspectives are formulated, sustained and changed primarily through social activity, and that in order to study these processes we need to know who does and says what with whom. It is relatively easy for an anthropologist in a village to listen to conversations and record the composition of work parties, but it is very difficult, in a global context, to know who has read which books or pamphlets, who has said what to whom on the telephone or through electronic mail, who has consulted which files on the Internet. Thus contemporary culture presents anthropologists with the practical challenge of identifying and studying the activities that are made to count in the global arena. In meeting this challenge, our methods of data collection are more likely to resemble those of investigative journalists than those of the traditional anthropologist.

AN INTERDISCIPLINARY APPROACH?

This book was motivated partly by the call from social scientists for 'interdisciplinary approaches' to the study of environmental issues (Jamison *et al.* 1990: vii). An 'interdisciplinary approach' implies the pooling of knowledge and expertise, the creation of a joint enterprise to produce a deeper or more complete understanding. According to Benton and Redclift, such an enterprise is already under way. The breakdown of disciplinary boundaries is already 'well advanced': 'a growing body of knowledge and explanation is to be found within intellectual territory that can only be described as "common ground"' (Benton and Redclift 1994: 13). I suggest that we can only identify common ground if we know where the boundaries of other territories lie, that we can only effectively pool the expertise of diverse disciplines if we know what each has to offer. There was, it seemed to me, a need for anthropology to stake out its territory on 'the environment', to make its expertise in this field known to other specialists, if it was not to be excluded from any joint enterprise – hence this book. However, having gone some way down this path, I feel inclined to be rather cautious about the trend towards interdisciplinary approaches. If this process is not handled carefully, we could end up losing more than we gain.

Drawing the boundaries

The distinctiveness of anthropology's contribution to environmental discourse, and to any other field, rests on the discipline's particular way of defining and using the concept of culture. By defining culture, in general terms, as the totality of what people know, think and feel about the world, anthropologists are able to treat all differences in human action, whether they are observed within or between communities, as expressions of cultural diversity. This is not widely understood by specialists in other disciplines. If it were, then the recent interest in culture among sociologists and their discovery of its analytical potential would not have been seen as a new development in social science (Featherstone 1992: vii).

The important question here is, what are the implications of anthropology's distinctive characteristics for the pooling of expertise and the creation of an interdisciplinary approach? In other words, is an anthropological approach compatible with those of other disciplines?[1] The discussion on models of globalization, in Chapter 5, drew attention to the gulf between an anthropological understanding of culture and those employed in the other social sciences. Specialists in sociology and political science speak readily of politics, economics and culture as distinct spheres. Anthropologists cannot do this without denying the concept of culture that characterizes their discipline, in whose terms politics and economics must be seen, at least in part, as cultural phenomena. In anthropology, the central analytical distinctions have not been between different components of culture, but between culture itself, as something that exists in people's minds, and the phenomena with which culture is assumed to interact: activities, forms of social organization and social processes.

If the anthropological concept of culture is incompatible with the ways in which other disciplines have defined it, then any attempt to break down the boundary between them could have one of two consequences: either the distinctive anthropological understanding of culture will be lost, or else other social scientists will have to start thinking like anthropologists. There are signs that the latter process is starting to happen. Wallerstein, as we saw in Chapter 5, has declared an interest in unthinking the 'unholy trinity' of politics, economics and culture (Wallerstein 1990b: 65). One ready-made way of doing this would be to adopt an anthropological understanding of culture (see Chapter 5, note 4). And if, as Featherstone observed, social scientists are becoming interested in defining culture in such a way that it can 'challenge the viability of our existing modes of conceptualization' (Featherstone 1992: vii), they might move closer to an anthropological way of thinking. There are also indications that anthropologists are prepared to adopt the 'unholy trinity' when they engage in discourse about globalization (for instance, Hannerz 1992: 219), despite the fact that, in doing so, they implicitly contradict their own concept of culture.

Different paths across common ground

Whether or not we should be concerned about either of these developments depends on the value we place on intellectual diversity. It is widely assumed that, by looking at something in a number of different ways, we increase our understanding of it.

This is not an uncontentious assumption, but it drives a great deal of intellectual activity. If we accept this, then there is a strong case for protecting a range of different approaches, since the loss of any one of them might reduce our overall capacity to understand. Protecting a diversity of approaches does not necessarily mean retaining the existing disciplinary boundaries, since these do not always coincide with differences in approach. The boundary between anthropology and 'cultural studies', for instance, might be something of an illusion (see Chapter 1, note 5), and it could be argued that the boundary between sociology and anthropology is largely a product of the historical interest of the two disciplines in different kinds of human society (industrial states in the case of sociology and small, non-industrial communities in the case of anthropology) and that similar theoretical perspectives have evolved, in parallel, in both disciplines. But, equally, we should not rush to dismantle the boundaries between disciplines in case they do represent significant differences in approach. Not surprisingly, I consider the anthropological understanding of culture to be a valuable analytical tool, and would not wish to see it sacrificed. I assume that the practitioners of other disciplines feel the same way about some of their cherished concepts.

None of this is to deny that there is 'common ground' among the social sciences. There have always been shared areas of interest, the most obvious of which include economics, politics, kinship, religion, sexuality and gender. The environment and globalization are relatively recent additions to this list. But there is a significant difference between a shared area of interest, which might be viewed from several different perspectives, and a shared *approach*, which implies a common perspective. I suggest that the study of environmental issues, globalization and other areas of common ground should be multidisciplinary rather than interdisciplinary. We should continually make each other aware of what our diverse approaches have to offer, without striving for a single framework. In this process, we might well find some of the traditional disciplinary boundaries dissolving away. We might also find that some are reinforced, and that new ones are created, but these changes lie beyond my vision, and beyond the scope of this book.

CULTURAL THEORY AND ENVIRONMENTALISM

The prime motivation for this book was the conviction that anthropology can benefit the environmentalist cause; that it can help us to identify our responsibilities for protecting the environment and work towards their fulfilment. Environmentalists have operated largely in ignorance of what anthropology has to offer. In particular, their understanding of the human–environment relationship has not been informed by a knowledge of how culture mediates this relationship, and the absence of this knowledge has seriously undermined the arguments presented in the global environmental debate. It is appropriate to end this exploration by considering how the study of culture can help environmentalists to a better understanding of human ecology and a more informed discourse on the search for sustainable ways of living.

Dispelling the myths

One of the clearest messages that anthropologists can give to environmentalists is that human beings have no 'natural' propensity for living sustainably with their environment. Primitive ecological wisdom is a myth, not only in the anthropological sense, as something whose truth is treated as a dogma, but also in the popular sense, as something that is untrue, a fantasy. The reasons why the myth persists have been discussed in Chapters 4 and 6 and are easy to understand. In some contexts it provides support for political arguments, against industrialism and its associated developments, and in favour of autonomy for indigenous and traditional communities. But perhaps the main reason for its persistence is that it gives environmentalists hope that there is a ready-made solution to environmental problems, albeit one that is very difficult to achieve. The myth implies that if industrial societies could 'get back' to a more 'natural' existence, by emulating the practices and cultural perspectives of non-industrial peoples, then our difficulties would be solved. The knowledge generated by the comparative analysis of human cultures indicates that this is not so.

Does this mean that the message anthropology brings to environmentalism is essentially pessimistic? Not necessarily, for the message is not that environmentally benign cultures do not or cannot exist, but that identifying them is not as easy as pointing to non-industrial peoples. An understanding of cultural diversity can be a source of ecological wisdom, but nowhere is this wisdom ready-made. It has to come from a knowledge of the range of possibilities, and an understanding of how human cultures and the environments in which they develop impact upon each other. It may be possible to manufacture sustainable ways of living out of bits and pieces selected from diverse cultures, but it would be unwise to attempt this without first understanding them in their original contexts, and appreciating the consequences of taking them out of those contexts. The discussion in this book does not point to a clear way forward. Anthropology could not, in any case, do this on its own; hence the need for 'multidisciplinary' approaches that include the physical as well as the social sciences. But the arguments and evidence presented here do indicate ways in which anthropological knowledge might inform environmental discourse.

First, and most important, the assumption that some cultures are more natural than others is a damaging distraction and should be abandoned. It fuels established prejudices, reinforcing the divisions that sustain discrimination and conflict. It also creates the misleading impression that creating a sustainable way of life is a matter of 'going back', and this makes it harder to persuade many people of its value, particularly those who, in the minds of many environmentalists, most need to be persuaded: those who pursue the equally distracting ideal of 'progress', in the form of economic growth. The alternative is to adopt the view expressed in Chapter 4: to see nature as the all-encompassing scheme of things to which all human cultures and practices, as well as non-human species and physical processes, belong. In this view, a dam built by people is as natural as one built by beavers, computer technology is as natural as collecting fruit from the rainforest. There is no other nature to get back to. This is it – we are already there. This frees us to examine all human practices and cultural phenomena without prejudice. It enables us to consider their ecological value without assuming from the outset that some are 'naturally' better than others.

Second, we need to be aware of the fundamental character of culture and therefore of cultural variation. It is not just a matter of different symbols with similar meanings, different ways of expressing the same things. Cultures can differ radically in the way they allocate power within the universe, the way they perceive or conceptualize time, the way they define humanity and the relationship between life and death. The acceptability of environmentalist arguments can depend on these variations. The concept of extinction is likely to be very differently received by those for whom cross-species reincarnation is an indisputable fact, than it is by western scientists. As we saw in Chapter 4, the idea of protecting the environment makes little sense to people who see it as their protector.

Third, and following from the previous point, we need to appreciate the way in which the different components of cultural perspectives are related to one another: how fundamental assumptions about the world relate to values, goals, norms and so on. These relationships again affect the extent to which environmentalist arguments can be accommodated. The analysis in Chapter 4 showed how people's receptiveness to the idea of environmental protection depends on the relationship between their understanding of power, the way they allocate responsibility, both within human society and between human and non-human forces, the way they think about time and the extent to which they envisage and plan for the future. These relationships also affect the extent to which cultural phenomena can be imported from one context into another. It might seem like a good idea for industrial societies to emulate the Dogon respect for trees, for instance. But this is not an isolated phenomenon; it is part of a cultural complex whose other components do not fit easily into an industrial context.

A great deal of knowledge which could provide environmentalists with a better understanding of human ecology is already present in the anthropological literature, though not always in a form that is accessible to non-anthropologists. One way of making this knowledge more available is for anthropologists to participate more fully in environmental discourse (cf. Rayner 1989). But moves can also be made by environmentalists. Efforts to introduce new conservation measures, to formulate new environmental policies and to change damaging practices are usually preceded by research to determine the nature of the problems and identify possible solutions. The arguments presented in this book are intended to communicate the message that problems and solutions are as much cultural as they are physical or biological, and that cultural research should be a part of the package.

Cultural analysis and global discourse

The same principles and methods that are used to compare cultures and cultural perspectives, and to reveal their underlying assumptions and fundamental commitments, are also relevant for understanding what I have called 'transcultural' discourses and perspectives, those generated by communication across cultural boundaries. Environmentalist discourse is clearly transcultural in this sense, as are the dominant perspectives that compete and overlap within it. The analysis presented in Chapter 6 is inconclusive on the question of which transcultural perspective, globalist or anti-globalist, anthropocentric or ecocentric, holds out the best prospect for an environmentally sustainable future. This is inevitable, since this kind of judgement depends on knowing what such a future might be, and this knowledge cannot come from anthropology alone. Again, this is why we need a mixture of disciplines. But cultural analysis reveals other things that have implications for global environmental discourse.

It reveals, for instance, that the diverse perspectives share a certain amount of common ground, that there is potential for agreement among globalists, anti-globalists and ecocentrists on some practical environmental measures, despite their fundamental disagreements on other things. It reveals that, while both globalists and anti-globalists claim to respect the cultures of non-industrial peoples, they differ in their commitment to this claim. The anti-globalists see this respect as central to the creation of a sustainable future, but in doing so they tie their arguments to a faith in the myth of primitive ecological wisdom, which anthropological knowledge exposes as untenable. The globalists, on the other hand, seek to impose an overarching hegemony which renders more or less worthless their claim to respect cultural diversity, and which reveals their understanding of culture to be particularly naïve and uninformed. It also calls into question their commitment to democratic principles.

Cultural diversity becomes particularly important when viewed in the context of observations made above. If no human culture holds the key to ecological wisdom, then it is essential to conserve the greatest possible number of ways of interacting with the environment if we are to maximize the chances of survival, both of our own species and of those with which we share the planet. To this extent, I agree with the anti-globalist view that protecting

225

cultural diversity might offer the best chance of conserving biodiversity, though I would not accept the argument presented by some anti-globalists, that cultural diversity can guarantee the protection of biodiversity. What the analysis in Chapter 6 indicates is that neither the anti-globalist nor the globalist perspective has identified the political circumstances in which cultural diversity can be effectively conserved.

That environmentalist arguments can be ill-founded and inconsistent is not itself a surprising revelation. Environmental discourse is essentially political, shaped by vested interests struggling to control the future, and shrouded, therefore, in a great deal of 'expressive propaganda'. In such contests, it matters more to be convincing than to conform to standards of truth and logic. But cultural analysis can demonstrate in what ways arguments are ill-founded and inconsistent. It can, in Douglas' words, 'dispel the fog', by replacing a general cynicism towards, and suspicion of, political debate with a more precise understanding of why we should be unconvinced by some arguments and, perhaps, cautiously receptive to others. If participants in the discourse are willing to listen, then such understanding can only force environmentalist argument on to a franker plane.

NOTES

INTRODUCTION: SOCIAL SCIENCE AND ENVIRONMEN-TAL DISCOURSE

1 It is reasonable to question whether we need to take up a position of detachment in order to observe (see Ingold 1993). This issue is touched on, though not fully addressed, in later chapters.
2 Anthropology is a very broad discipline. This book is concerned only with what would be called 'social anthropology' in Britain and (perhaps more appropriately) 'cultural anthropology' in America. (The differences between these fields, which are significant in some contexts, are of little importance here.) I accept that some might be offended by the use of the label 'anthropology' to refer to just a part of the discipline; I can only ask their forgiveness in the interests of brevity (cf. Carrithers 1992: 5-6).
3 It is widely understood that research undertaken from a moral stand-point is devalued because it cannot claim to be impartial. But partiality is only a problem if it is not transparent. If the analyst's values and assumptions are exposed through the application of 'systematic doubt' the analysis can be judged accordingly.
4 See, for instance, Douglas (1972), Douglas and Wildavksy (1982) and Redclift (1984, 1987).
5 The terms 'industrial' and 'non-industrial' are not entirely satisfactory, since they imply a rather narrow understanding of industry, but they are more accurate and less objectionable than 'western' and 'non-western', 'developed' and 'less-developed' and 'complex' and 'simple'. They also reflect the importance attached by environmentalists to industrial development as marking a new kind of relationship between human beings and their environments.

1 ANTHROPOLOGY, CULTURE AND ENVIRONMENTALISM

1 The terms 'indigenous' and 'traditional' are now used widely in inter-national discourse on human rights and environmental issues, to

227

describe societies whose economies have never been industrial in character. The labels are difficult to define in precise terms, but are probably the more useful for that. For instance, Chapter 26 of *Agenda 21*, the most comprehensive of the agreements to have emerged from the United Nations Conference on Environment and Development (UNCED, the Rio Earth Summit), states, 'Indigenous people and their communities have an historical relationship with their lands and are generally descendants of the original inhabitants of such lands' (United Nations 1993a: 385). Needless to say, it is often impossible to establish who were the 'original' inhabitants of a region.

2 For instance Hannerz (1980, 1992) and Miller (1991).

3 For instance, nationalism (Gellner 1983, 1994), violence (Riches 1986), famine (Richards 1986 and 1992b) and, most relevant for the purposes of this book, risk and the understanding of environmental threats (Douglas and Wildavsky 1982, Douglas 1972, 1985, 1992; see Chapter 3 for a more detailed discussion of this work).

4 For instance, Strathern (1992) on new reproductive technologies, and Komito (1994) on information technology.

5 The boundary between anthropology and cultural studies is one of the least well-defined in social science, and may be a product more of mutual ignorance sustained by separate development than of genuine theoretical divergence. The way in which the theoretical concerns of cultural studies are sometimes defined (for instance, Blundell *et al.* 1993) is indistinguishable from the way in which many anthropologists would define their own concerns.

6 I am grateful to Nigel Rapport for this phrase, which he used as the title for a session of the Association of Social Anthropologists' 4th Decennial Conference at Oxford in 1993.

7 At the same time, Cohen described the global entity which she designated the 'Total Culture System', as 'open, indeterminate and highly unstable' (1988: 21), and Barth characterized societies as disordered systems (1992).

8 The leading theorists in the shift away from structuralist anthropology towards a more interpretative approach (and, with it, a narrower understanding of culture) were Barth (1959, 1966), Keesing (1971), Scheffler (1965, 1966), Geertz (1965, 1966, 1973) and Goodenough (1981 [1971]). This development is comprehensively discussed in the work of Stuchlik (1976, 1977) and Holy (1974, 1976). There is a common perception that the older, broad concept of culture is associated with the American tradition in anthropology while the later, narrow concept is more associated with the European (and particularly the British) tradition. But this is misleading, since many of the theorists who led the shift are American scholars. It would be more accurate to say that in America the broad and narrow definitions of culture continued to be used in parallel, while in Britain the narrower concept more or less replaced the broader one.

9 The 'observability' of actions is problematic, and has been discussed in some detail by Holy and Stuchlik (1981: 2–3). I feel it is beyond the scope of this book to enter this discussion, though it is important

to be aware of it since it reminds us that, like many analytical devices, the distinction between what people know, think and feel and what they do does not always sit easily on reality as we experience it.

10 There are several notable discussions in the literature of how this process works, though more by sociologists than by anthropologists (see, for instance, Berger and Luckmann 1966, Giddens 1976).

11 This gap in the literature is quite rapidly being filled; see, for instance, Croll and Parkin (1992), Einarsson (1993), Harries-Jones (1993), Ingold (1993) and Kumar (1993).

12 For instance, Tylor's classic definition of religion as 'a belief in spiritual beings' (see Keesing 1981: 330) effectively excludes Buddhism, and Horton's adaptation of it, 'an extension of the field of social relationships beyond the confines of purely human society' (Horton 1960), would seem to include people's relationships with pets and livestock.

13 Nevertheless, it is surprising how many social scientists become involved in debating the 'true' nature of social phenomena. A case in point is the debate about social movements, which is referred to in Chapter 3.

14 The label 'primitive' is often interpreted in a derogatory sense. Its use throughout this book is intended to have no such connotations. Here the term describes, not a particular type of culture or society, but the ecological wisdom that human beings as a species are assumed by many (but not by anthropologists) to possess. The assumption is that the ability of human beings to live in harmony with their environment is somehow 'natural' or innate, and that those communities who live closest to what is taken to be a 'natural' way of life possess more ecological wisdom than those who, through economic development, have become alienated from 'nature'.

15 Both the definition of culture and the concept of a 'cultural perspective' will be discussed more fully in Chapter 2.

2 CULTURE AND ECOLOGY

1 For this reason, the discussion of ecological anthropology presented here is highly selective and much of the literature that has made significant contributions to the field is omitted. Several excellent reviews of the development of ecological anthropology are available. For detailed and critical appraisals see Bennett (1976), Hardesty (1977) and, in particular, Ellen (1982). For a review of more recent developments see Moran (1990).

2 It has been argued that there is no significant difference, in this context, between cause and limitation, that by setting limits on what *can* be done, environmental factors exercise a determining influence on what *is* done: 'So possibilism is logically an inverted determinism in which phrases such as "the environment limits but does not determine" are nonsense. In any empirical analysis the one must *functionally* dissolve into the other' (Ellen 1982: 50, emphasis given).

3 For a more detailed criticism of this viewpoint, see Shiva (1993a: 10ff.; see also Chapter 6 below).

4 Turnbull's account of Ik society has been the object of much criticism and debate in anthropology. For a concise review of this debate, see Knight (1994).

5 For a concise account of the development of the ecosystem concept in biology, see Moran (1990: 3–8).

6 I am not qualified to speak for psychologists on this point.

7 This is not intended to imply that each individual holds a single perspective, nor that the perspectives held by one individual will necessarily be consistent with one another.

3 ENVIRONMENTALISM IN SOCIAL SCIENCE

1 The Natural History Book Society's *Ecology and Environment* catalogue for Spring/Summer 1994 claims to contain over 6,000 titles. An early example of the 'green' novel is Edward Abbey's *The Monkey Wrench Gang* (1975), about a group of environmentalist saboteurs, which inspired the founders of Earth First!. Recent examples include Ben Elton's *Stark* (1989) and *Gridlock* (1991).

2 Sometimes the best indication of whether a piece of work was produced for academic purposes is the length and style of its bibliography!

3 This is not the place for a full discussion of environmental economics. Useful summaries can be found in O'Riordan (1981 [1976]: ch. 5) and Jacobs (1994). For a more thorough analysis see Jacobs (1991), and for a clear defence of the neoclassical approach see Pearce *et al.* (1989) and Pearce, D. (1991, 1994).

4 While recognizing that the roots of environmentalist thought have been growing over centuries, most commentators attribute the rise of popular contemporary environmentalism to the publication of key texts during the 1960s (Carson 1962, Commoner 1963, Hardin 1968) and 1970s (Ehrlich 1970, Meadows *et al.* 1972, Goldsmith *et al.* 1972). Comprehensive accounts of the history of environmentalism can be found in O'Riordan (1981 [1976]), Nicholson (1987), McCormick (1989), Paehlke (1989) and Norton (1991).

5 Ecology's involvement in environmental discourse has been shaped considerably by political and economic circumstances (the need for policy makers and activists to substantiate their arguments, the availability of funding for ecological research, the creation of employment opportunities for ecologists), and the personal strategies of scientists responding to those circumstances (see Yearley 1995a).

6 Connoisseurs of *The Hitch-hiker's Guide to the Galaxy* will recall that the Total Perspective Vortex destroyed the egos of its victims by giving them a true sense of proportion (see Adams 1980: 58-65). The image of the Earth seen from space has been the object of similarly contradictory interpretations; see Sachs (1993) and Chapter 6 below.

7 Here again, the terminology might tend to confuse. The ecocentrism identified by Eckersley is not that of which O'Riordan wrote some

NOTES

fifteen years earlier. For O'Riordan, all our conscious actions are, by definition, anthropocentric (O'Riordan 1981 [1976]: 11). It would therefore be impossible to adopt an ecocentric perspective that is, in any sense, opposed to an anthropocentric one. Instead, the anthropocentric subsumes the ecocentric; nature may be valued 'for its own sake', but the valuer is still human (cf. Dobson 1990: 51). A discussion of the nature of 'intrinsic' value is beyond the scope of this book, but for a useful summary see O'Neill (1993: 8–25).

8 See, for instance, Kimber and Richardson (1974), Cotgrove and Duff (1980), Van Liere and Dunlap (1980), Lowe and Goyder (1983), Baker (1990), Yearley and Milton (1990), Peace (1993), Prato (1993), and many, many more.

9 See Scott (1990) for a discussion of the European tradition in social movement theory.

10 Despite Goodin's observation that 'linking the green case to spiritual values ... seems to borrow an awful lot of trouble' (1992: 40), his analysis does seem to imply a comparison between environmentalism and religion which, it could be argued, seems to fulfil the same psychological need.

11 Other analysts have also used Douglas' grid–group model to identify diverse sectors of a culturally complex society (James et al. 1987) and diverse levels within single organizations (Thompson and Wildavsky 1986).

12 Many examples exist in the ethnographic literature. Most famously, the Nuer (Evans-Pritchard 1951) and the Trobriand Islanders (Malinowski 1929) both believed that incest kills. In the Kenyan community where I conducted fieldwork, there lived a man whose chronic and apparently incurable illness was said to have been caused by incest with his daughter, and parents regularly expressed the fear that adultery by their partner threatened the health of their children.

13 It is worth noting that similar factors were identified by Wallis as important in generating a demand for new religions in America at this time (Wallis 1984), fostering the development of sects with a different orientation but, Douglas would no doubt argue, similar organizational problems.

14 The assertion characteristic of functionalist and structuralist approaches, that change occurs as a result of factors external to the society in question, was seen as inadequate by post-structuralist anthropologists, on the grounds that change only takes place if members of that society respond to – in other words, choose to act upon – such external factors.

4 ENVIRONMENTALISM AND CULTURAL DIVERSITY

1 The film From the Heart of the World: the Elder Brothers' Warning, was made by BBC Television and the Goldsmith Foundation.

2 The film may have given an exaggerated impression of the Kogi's isolation (for instance, film taken some years before had shown that,

231

like many of the indigenous societies, the Kogi had suffered from the effects of easily available western-imported alcohol), but there is no reason to suppose that its portrayal of the way they understand their environment was inaccurate.

3 *The Rainbow Warrior* was Greenpeace's most famous ship, acquired in 1978 for an anti-whaling mission and sunk by French military personnel in New Zealand in 1985 (see Brown and May 1989, Pearce, F. 1991). The name 'Rainbow Warrior' was taken from a prophecy made by a Cree woman 200 years ago, that a band of warriors, under the symbol of the rainbow, would fight against the destruction of the Earth (Hunter 1979: 28).

4 For instance, protesters against the motorway extension at Twyford Down, in southern England, sought to protect the Celtic field systems, burial sites and prehistoric tracks on the site.

5 'Hunter-gatherers' is the term normally used, though it is occasionally reversed to 'gatherer-hunters' (for instance, Bird-David 1990) to reflect the fact that gathering is often a more important source of food than hunting.

6 Bird-David's principal sources of information on the Mbuti are Turnbull (1961), Hart (1978), Hart and Hart (1986), and on the Batek, Endicott (1979, 1984).

7 For instance, secondary school pupils took the British General Certificate of Education (GCE), Ordinary and Advanced levels, which was known locally as 'taking Cambridge'. The syllabus was very similar to that which I had studied ten years earlier in England!

8 In Britain, the Royal Society for the Protection of Birds (RSPB) has been in existence since 1889, and the Royal Society for Nature Conservation (RSNC) since 1912. Yearley (1992a: 54–67) described the history of these groups, and the RSPB published an account of its own development to celebrate its centenary (Samstag 1988). In America, the Audubon Society was founded in 1905, the National Conservation Association in 1909 and the National Wildlife Federation in 1936. Descriptions of the early development of conservation interest in America can be found in McCormick (1989) and Paehlke (1989).

9 For instance, they set aside areas of habitat as nature reserves and manage them for the benefit of wildlife, and they establish captive breeding programmes to replenish the populations of endangered species. The most famous of these include the efforts to conserve the Californian Condor, and the release in Brazil of Golden Lion Tamarins bred in the Channel Islands by the Jersey Wildlife Preservation Trust. When such programmes are successful, they serve to reinforce the assumption that nature cannot do without our help.

10 Many authors have continued to refer to Gaia as a hypothesis (Yearley 1992a: 145; Simmons 1993: 31-3; Ehrlich 1993; Shearer 1993). However, in his second Gaia book, Lovelock documented its transformation from a hypothesis into a theory:

In science, a hypothesis is really no more than a 'let's suppose'. The

first Gaia book was hypothetical . . . a rough pencil sketch that tried
to catch a view of the Earth seen from a different perspective . . . .
Much new evidence has accumulated, and I have made new theoretical models. We can now fill in some of the finer details, though
fortunately there seems little need to erase the original lines. As a
consequence this second book is a statement of Gaia theory.

(Lovelock 1988: 11)

11 When the environment is viewed ecocentrically, seen as having intrinsic
value, independent of its use to human beings, then the degree of
importance attributed to it is not affected by people's needs (see Eckersley 1992).

12 For instance, the location of chemical factories in rural Ireland and
India, with damaging and (in the case of Bhopal) catastrophic consequences (see Baker 1990, Khare 1987). It is worth pointing out that
this trend results from the desire not only of industrial nations to
export their pollution, but also of the recipient nations to import
industrial development (see Yearley 1992a: 157-8; Allen and Jones
1990).

13 Some environmentalists have tried to link cultural diversity with biological diversity ('biodiversity'). The *Convention on Biological Diversity* was one of the agreements produced at the Rio Earth Summit in
1992. In an alternative document, produced by the Global Forum, the
gathering of NGOs which accompanied the Earth Summit, the concept
of biodiversity was defined in the following way: 'an expression of
life which includes variability of all life forms and their organizations
and interrelationships from the molecular to biosphere level, *which
includes cultural diversity*' (*Citizens Commitment on Biodiversity*,
emphasis added; see Sutherland 1992).

5 GLOBALIZATION, CULTURE AND DISCOURSE

1 I wish I could use a less ugly word. Alas, 'globalization' is the term
social scientists appear to have settled on.

2 See the discussion in Chapter 1, on cultures as systems.

3 There are many descriptions, analyses and critiques of Wallerstein's
model. One of the most useful summaries is given by Chirot and Hall
(1982).

4 It is not my intention to argue that anthropology can be the saviour
of social science, but it is worth mentioning that if Wallerstein is
seeking to unthink the unholy trinity of politics, economics and culture, he might do worse than turn to anthropology, where the trinity
has never existed. I suspect that one unfortunate consequence of the
trinity's pervasiveness in sociology and political science is that the practitioners of these disciplines tend to misjudge anthropology. They
assume (correctly) that anthropologists study culture, but because they
are trapped within the politics-economics-culture perspective, they
tend not to understand what anthropologists mean by culture. If the
concept of culture employed in anthropology was more widely under-

stood, then the breadth and radical nature of the discipline might be better appreciated. This point will be discussed further in the final chapter.

5 In Wallerstein's model, the international division of labour is central to the development of the global economy; capitalism and industrialism, which Giddens treated as separate dimensions, are inseparable in world systems theory.

6 Appadurai, like Wallerstein, sees contemporary conditions as having developed over several centuries, and the process of development as having speeded up significantly over the past hundred years (Appadurai 1990: 1-2).

6 THE CULTURE OF GLOBAL ENVIRONMENTALIST DISCOURSE

1 The full title of the Biosphere Conference was the 'Intergovernmental Conference of Experts on the Scientific Basis for Rational Use and Conservation of the Resources of the Biosphere'.

2 The 'Tree of Life' was a tree-shaped structure with paper leaves on which individuals expressed their personal 'pledges for the planet'. The project was organized by Christian Aid, the World Wide Fund for Nature (WWF), Friends of the Earth, the International Institute for Environment and Development (IIED), the World Development Movement, and other NGOs. The 'tree' formed 'the symbolic heart of the Global Forum', the gathering of NGOs which paralleled the UN Conference on Environment and Development at Rio (Holmberg *et al.* 1993). Maurice Strong, Secretary-General of the Conference, expressed the view that public participation, or 'people power', was the key to its success (Strong 1992a).

3 These issues are extensively covered in the literature. For a useful summary see Yearley (1992a: 11-46).

4 For a statement of the general principles of sustainable development, see the Tokyo Declaration (WCED 1987: 363-6).

5 There is no need for me to comment in detail on these mechanisms, which have been thoroughly analysed in the literature (see, for instance, Lyster 1985, McCormick 1989, Leggett 1990).

6 See also Giddens' observation that modern society removes knowledge from the context of its use through the creation of 'expert systems' (Giddens 1990; see Chapter 5 above).

7 This an interestingly ambiguous choice of words. 'The larger society' was presumably intended to refer to humanity in general, but it could also be taken to mean a larger and external society intent on harnessing the knowledge of traditional communities for its own use. The opponents of globalism would no doubt favour this interpretation.

8 WWF's campaign to promote environmental awareness through religious teachings can be seen as an attempt to make use of such cultural features (see Chapter 2).

9 It had been Maurice Strong's intention that the *Rio Declaration on*

NOTES

Environment and Development (see United Nations 1993a: 3-8) should take the form of an 'Earth Charter'. At the end of the Earth Summit he expressed the wish that the Declaration might continue to evolve towards an Earth Charter that could be sanctioned on the fiftieth anniversary of the UN in 1995 (Strong 1992c: 70). Meanwhile, the NGOs produced their own version of an Earth Charter at the Global Forum.

10 A statement to this effect was made in the film *In Search of the Noble Savage*, shown in BBC Television's *Horizon* series on 27 January 1992.
11 This declaration is quoted at the beginning of the *International Treaty between NGOs and Indigenous Peoples*.
12 These two terms are often used interchangeably, but 'biocentrism', according to Manes, is a 'misnomer which stuck': 'Deep ecologists were placing not life, bios, at the centre of this new ethic, but the entire community of living and non-living entities that make up an ecosystem' (1990: 144).
13 In this respect, I suggest that the project to extend the moral community to include the great apes, far from opposing anthropocentrism, actually strengthens it, since it implies that the degree of moral consideration due to an animal depends on the extent to which it resembles human beings (Cavalieri and Singer 1993). Arguments which support the conservation of whales on the grounds that they share human characteristics (intelligence, family groups, and so on) have the same effect (see Einarsson 1993).
14 For a detailed description of the early Greenpeace campaigns, see Hunter (1979).
15 Such splits are often engendered by the fear (which, for the Sierra Club, became a reality; see Chapter 3) that the organization might lose its tax-exempt status if its members take overt political action, as well as by the dissatisfaction of the more radical members with established ways of operating.
16 Formerly the Royal Society for Nature Conservation.

7 ANTHROPOLOGY, SOCIAL SCIENCE AND ENVIRONMENTALISM

1 Of course, this question could be asked of any discipline. I do not assume, in my concern with anthropology, that all other disciplines are compatible with one another.

235

BIBLIOGRAPHY

Abbey, E. (1975) *The Monkey Wrench Gang*, New York: J. B. Lippincott.

Adams, D. (1980) *The Restaurant at the End of the Universe*, London and Sydney: Pan Books.

Agar, M. H. and Hobbs, J. R. (1985) 'How to grow schemata out of interviews', in J. W. D. Dougherty (ed.) *Directions in Cognitive Anthropology*, Urbana: University of Illinois Press.

Ahmed, A. S. and Donnan, H. (1994) 'Chapter 1: Islam in the age of postmodernity', in A. S. Ahmed and H. Donnan (eds) *Islam, Globalization and Postmodernity*, London: Routledge.

Allen, R. and Jones, T. (1990) *Guests of the Nation: People of Ireland versus the Multinationals*, London: Earthscan.

Appadurai, A. (1989) 'Global ethnoscapes: notes and queries for a transnational anthropology', in R. Fox (ed.) *Interventions: Anthropology of the Present*, Commission of the European Communities.

——(1990) 'Disjuncture and difference in the global cultural economy', *Public Culture* 2, 2: 1–24.

Armen, J.-C. (1976) *Gazelle-Boy*, London: Picador.

Atkinson, A. (1992) 'Developing a green political theory', in W. Rüdig (ed.) *Green Politics Two*, Edinburgh: Edinburgh University Press.

Bahro, R. (1982) *Socialism and Survival*, London: Heretic Books.

Baker, S. (1990) 'The evolution of the Irish ecology movement', in W. Rüdig (ed.) *Green Politics One*, Edinburgh: Edinburgh University Press.

Banks, J. (1972) *The Sociology of Social Movements*, London: Macmillan.

Barber, K. (1987) 'Popular arts in Africa', *African Studies Review* 30, 3: 1–78.

Barth, F. (1959) *Political Leadership among the Swat Pathans*, London: Athlone.

—— (1966) *Models of Social Organization*, Royal Anthropological Institute Occasional Paper 23, London: RAI.

—— (ed.) (1969) *Ethnic Groups and Boundaries*, London: Allen & Unwin.

—— (1992) 'Towards greater naturalism in conceptualizing societies', in A. Kuper (ed.) *Conceptualizing Society*, London and New York: Routledge.

Bauman, Z. (1989) *Modernity and the Holocaust*, Oxford: Polity Press.

Bell, D. (1983) *Daughters of the Dreaming*, Sydney: George Allen & Unwin.
Bennett, J. (1976) *The Ecological Transition*, London: Pergamon.
—— (1990) 'Ecosystems, environmentalism, resource conservation and anthropological research', in E. F. Moran (ed.) *The Ecosystem Approach in Anthropology*, Ann Arbor: University of Michigan Press.
Benton, T. and Redclift, M. (1994) 'Introduction', in M. Redclift and T. Benton (eds) *Social Theory and the Global Environment*, London: Routledge.
Berger, P. (1963) *Invitation to Sociology*, Harmondsworth: Penguin Books.
Berger, P. and Luckmann, T. (1966) The Social Construction of Reality, Harmondsworth: Penguin Books.
Bergesen, A. (1990) 'Turning world-system theory on its head', in M. Featherstone (ed.) *Global Culture: Nationalism, Globalization and Modernity*, London: Sage.
Berlin, B., Breedlove, D. E. and Raven, P. H. (1974) *Principles of Tzeltal Plant Classification: An Introduction to the Botanical Ethnography of a Mayan-speaking People of Highland Chiapas*, New York: Academic Press.
Berreman, G. D. (1968) 'Is anthropology alive? Social responsibility in social anthropology', *Current Anthropology* 9, 5: 391–6.
Beyer, P. (1994) *Religion and Globalization*, London: Sage.
Bird-David, N. (1990) 'The giving environment: another perspective on the economic system of gatherer-hunters', *Current Anthropology* 31, 2: 189–96.
—— (1992a) 'Beyond "the original affluent society": a culturalist reformulation', *Current Anthropology* 33, 1: 25–47.
—— (1992b) 'Beyond "The hunting and gathering mode of subsistence": culture-sensitive observations on the Nayaka and other modern hunter-gatherers', *Man* (NS) 27: 19–44.
—— (1993) 'Tribal metaphorization of human-nature relatedness: a comparative analysis', in K. Milton (ed.) *Environmentalism: The View from Anthropology*, London and New York: Routledge.
Black, M. B. (1969) 'Eliciting folk taxonomy in Ojibwa', in S. Tyler (ed.) *Cognitive Anthropology*, New York: Holt, Rinehart & Winston.
Blundell, V., Shepherd, J. and Taylor, I. (1993) 'Editors' Introduction', in V. Blundell, J. Shepherd and I. Taylor (eds) *Relocating Cultural Studies*, London and New York: Routledge.
Bohannan, P. (1973) 'Rethinking culture: a project for current anthropologists', *Current Anthropology* 14, 4: 357–72.
Boutros-Ghali, B. (1992) Opening statement to the United Nations Conference on Environment and Development, in United Nations (1993b) *Report of the United Nations Conference on Environment and Development, Rio de Janeiro, 3–14 June 1992*, vol. II: *Proceedings of the Conference*, New York: United Nations.
Bowers, J. (1990) *Economics of the Environment: The Conservationists' Response to the Pearce Report*, Newbury: British Association of Nature Conservationists.

Bowman, J. S. (1975) 'The ecology movement', *Journal of Environmental Studies* 8: 91–7.

Brandt Commission (1983) *Common Crisis*, London: Pan Books.

Bright, J. O. and Bright, W. (1965) 'Semantic structures in Northwestern California and the Sapir-Whorf hypothesis', *American Anthropologist* 67, 5, ii (Special Publication): 249–58.

Brown, M. and May, J. (1989) *The Greenpeace Story*, London: Dorling Kindersley.

Brown, P. and Vidal, J. (1995) 'Eco soundings', *Guardian*, Society Supplement, 19 July.

Brundtland, G. H. (1992) Opening statement to the United Nations Conference on Environment and Development, in United Nations (1993b) *Report of the United Nations Conference on Environment and Development, Rio de Janeiro, 3-14 June 1992*, vol. II: *Proceedings of the Conference*, New York: United Nations.

Bulmer, R. (1957) 'A primitive ornithology', *Australian Museum Magazine* 12: 224–9.

—— (1967) 'Why is the cassowary not a bird? a problem of zoological taxonomy among the Karam of the New Guinea Highlands', *Man* (NS) 2: 5–25.

Burbridge, J. (1994) 'Radical action and the evolution of consistency', *Ecos* 15, 2: 7–11.

Burnham, P. C. (1973) 'The explanatory value of the concept of adaptation in studies of culture change', in C. Renfrew (ed.) *Explanation of Culture Change*, London: Duckworth.

Burnham, P. C. and Ellen, R. F. (eds) (1979) *Social and Ecological Systems*, London: Academic Press.

Burridge, K. O. L. (1960) *Mambu: A Melanesian Millennium*, London: Methuen.

Callicott, J. B. (1982) 'Traditional American Indian and Western European attitudes toward nature: an overview', *Environmental Ethics* 4: 293–318.

Cancian, F. (1975) *What are Norms?* Cambridge: Cambridge University Press.

Carneiro, R. (1968) 'Cultural adaptation', in D. Sells (ed.) *International Encyclopaedia of the Social Sciences* 3: 551–4.

Carrithers, M. (1992) *Why Humans have Cultures*, Oxford: Oxford University Press.

Carson, R. (1962) *Silent Spring*, Boston: Houghton Mifflin.

Cavalieri, P. and Singer, P. (eds) (1993) *The Great Ape Project: Equality beyond Humanity*, London: Fourth Estate.

Caws, P. (1974) 'Operational, representational and explanatory models', *American Anthropologist* 76: 1–10.

Chatterjee, P. and Finger, M. (1994) *The Earth Brokers: Power, Politics and World Development*, London and New York: Routledge.

Chirot, D. and Hall, T. D. (1982) 'World-system theory', *Annual Review of Sociology* 8: 81–106.

Clifford, J. (1986) 'Introduction: partial truths', in J. Clifford (ed.) *Writing Culture*, Berkeley and Los Angeles: University of California Press.

Clift, R. (1994) Review of D. Pearce (ed.) *Blueprint 3: Measuring Sustainable Development, The Chemical Engineer* 568: 28.

Codere, H. (1950) *Fighting with Property,* Seattle: University of Washington Press.

Cohen, B. (1988) *Global Perspectives: The Total Culture System in the Modern World,* London: Codek Publications.

Commoner, B. (1963) *Science and Survival,* New York: Viking Press.

Conklin, H. C. (1955) 'Hanunoo color categories', *Southwestern Journal of Anthropology* 11: 339–44.

—— (1967) 'Some aspects of ethnographic research in Ifugao', *New York Academy of Sciences Transactions* 30: 99–121.

Cotgrove, S. (1976) 'Environmentalism and Utopia', *Sociological Review* 24: 23–42.

—— (1982) *Catastrophe or Cornucopia: The Environment, Politics and the Future,* New York: John Wiley & Sons.

Cotgrove, S. and Duff, A. (1980) 'Environmentalism, middle-class radicalism and social change', *Sociological Review*: 333–51.

Cowell, A. (1990) *The Decade of Destruction,* Sevenoaks: Hodder & Stoughton.

Crick, M. (1982) 'Anthropological field research, meaning creation and meaning construction', in D. Parkin (ed.) *Semantic Anthropology,* London: Academic Press.

Croll, E. and Parkin, D. (1992) 'Anthropology, the environment and development', in E. Croll and D. Parkin (eds) *Bush Base: Forest Farm: Culture, Environment and Development,* London and New York: Routledge.

Cummings, B. J. (1990) *Dam the Rivers, Damn the People,* London: Earthscan.

Dalton, R. J. (1992) 'Alliance patterns of the European environmental movement', in W. Rüdig (ed.) *Green Politics Two,* Edinburgh: Edinburgh University Press.

D'Andrade, R. G. (1976) 'A propositional analysis of US American beliefs about illness', in K. H. Basso and H. A. Selby (eds) *Meaning in Anthropology,* Albuquerque: University of New Mexico Press.

Dasmann, R. (1976) 'Future primitive: ecosystem people versus biosphere people', *CoEvolution Quarterly* 11: 26–31.

Dawkins, R. (1986) *The Blind Watchmaker,* Harmondsworth: Penguin Books.

De La Court, T. (1990) *Beyond Brundtland: Green Development in the 1990s,* London and New Jersey: Zed Books.

Descola, P. (1992) 'Societies of nature and the nature of society', in A. Kuper (ed.) *Conceptualizing Society,* London and New York: Routledge.

Devall, W. B. (1970) 'Conservation: an upper-middle class social movement: a replication', *Journal of Leisure Research*: 123–6.

Diamond, A. W., Schreiber, R. L., Attenborough, D. and Prestt, I. (1987) *Save the Birds,* Cambridge: Cambridge University Press.

Diani, M. (1990) 'The Italian ecology movement: from radicalism to moderation', in W. Rüdig (ed.) *Green Politics One,* Edinburgh: Edinburgh University Press.

Diener, P., Nonini, D. and Robkin, E. E. (1980) 'Ecology and evolution in cultural anthropology', *Man* (NS) 15: 1–31.

Dobson, A. (1990) *Green Political Thought*, London: HarperCollins.

Donald, J. and Hall, S. (1986) *Politics and Ideology*, Milton Keynes: Open University Press.

Donnan, H. (1976) 'Inter-ethnic friendship, joking and rules of interaction in a London factory', in L. Holy (ed.) *Knowledge and Behaviour*, The Queen's University Papers in Social Anthropology 1, Belfast: The Queen's University of Belfast.

Dougherty, J. W. D. and Keller, C. M. (1985) 'Taskonomy: a practical approach to knowledge structures', in J. W. D. Dougherty (ed.) *Directions in Cognitive Anthropology*, Urbana: University of Illinois Press.

Douglas, M. (1957) 'Animals in Lele religious symbolism', *Africa* 27: 46–58.

—— (1966) *Purity and Danger: An Analysis of Concepts of Pollution and Taboo*, London: Routledge & Kegan Paul.

—— (1970) *Natural Symbols: Explorations in Cosmology*, London: Cresset.

—— (1972) 'Environments at risk', in J. Benthall (ed.) *Ecology, the Shaping Enquiry: A Course Given at the Institute of Contemporary Arts*, London: Longman.

—— (1978) *Implicit Meanings: Essays in Anthropology*, London: Routledge & Kegan Paul.

—— (1985) *Risk Acceptability According to the Social Sciences*, London: Routledge & Kegan Paul.

—— (1990) 'The pangolin revisited: a new approach to animal symbolism', in R. Willis (ed.) *Signifying Animals: Human Meaning in the Natural World*, London: Unwin Hyman.

—— (1992) *Risk and Blame: Essays in Cultural Theory*, London: Routledge.

Douglas, M. and Wildavsky, A. (1982) *Risk and Culture: An Essay on the Selection of Technical and Environmental Dangers*, Berkeley: University of California Press.

Durkheim, E. (1964 [1895]) *The Rules of Sociological Method*, London: Macmillan.

Durkheim, E. and Mauss, M. (1963) *Primitive Classification*, London: Cohen & West.

Eckersley, R. (1992) *Environmentalism and Political Theory: Towards an Ecocentric Approach*, London: University College London Press.

Ehrenfeld, D. (1978) *The Arrogance of Humanism*, New York: Oxford University Press.

Ehrlich, P. R. (1970) *The Population Bomb*, New York: Ballantine Books.

—— (1993) 'Coevolution and its applicability to the Gaia hypothesis', in S. H. Schneider and P. J. Boston (eds) *Scientists on Gaia*, Cambridge, MA: MIT Press.

Einarsson, N. (1993) 'All animals are equal but some are cetaceans: conservation and culture conflict', in K. Milton (ed.) *Environmentalism: The View from Anthropology*, London and New York: Routledge.

Elkington, J. and Hailes, J. (1988) *The Green Consumer Guide*, London: Victor Gollancz.

—— (1993) *The LCA Sourcebook: A European Business Guide to Life-cycle Assessment*, London: SustainAbility, SPOLD and Business in the Environment.

Ellen, R. F. (1982) *Environment, Subsistence and System: The Ecology of Small-scale Social Formations*, Cambridge: Cambridge University Press.

—— (1986) 'What Black Elk left unsaid: on the illusory images of Green primitivism', *Anthropology Today* 2, 6: 8–12.

—— (1990) 'Trade, environment, and the reproduction of local systems in the Moluccas', in E. F. Moran (ed.) *The Ecosystem Approach in Anthropology*, Ann Arbor: University of Michigan Press.

—— (1993) 'Rhetoric, practice and incentive in the face of the changing times: a case study in Nuaulu attitudes to conservation and deforestation', in K. Milton (ed.) *Environmentalism: The View from Anthropology*, London and New York: Routledge.

Elton, B. (1989) *Stark*, London: Warner Books.

—— (1991) *Gridlock*, London: Warner Books.

Endicott, K. (1979) *Batek Negrito Religion: The World View and Rituals of a Hunting and Gathering People of Peninsular Malaysia*, Oxford: Clarendon Press.

—— (1984) 'The economy of the Batek of Malaysia: annual and historical perspectives', *Research in Economic Anthropology* 6: 29–52.

Erdoes, R. (1976) *Lame Deer: Seeker of Visions*, New York: Simon & Schuster.

Ereira, A. (1990) *The Heart of the World*, London: Jonathan Cape.

Evans-Pritchard, E. E. (1951) *Kinship and Marriage among the Nuer*, Oxford: Clarendon.

—— (1940) *The Nuer: A Description of the Modes of Livelihood and Political Institutions of a Nilotic People*, Oxford: Clarendon.

Everett, M. J., Hepburn, I., Ntiamoa-Baidu, Y. and Thomas, G. J. (1987) 'Roseate terns in Britain and West Africa', *RSPB Conservation Review* 1, Sandy, Bedfordshire: Royal Society for the Protection of Birds.

Eyerman, R. and Jamison, A. (1991) *Social Movements: A Cognitive Approach*, Cambridge: Polity Press.

Fairclough, N. (1992) *Discourse and Social Change*, Cambridge: Polity Press.

Featherstone, M. (ed.) (1992) 'Cultural theory and cultural change: an introduction', in M. Featherstone (ed.) *Cultural Theory and Cultural Change*, London: Sage.

Feit, H. (1973) 'The ethno-ecology of the Waswanipi Cree: or how hunters can manage their resources', in B. Cox (ed.) *Cultural Ecology: Readings on Canadian Indians and Eskimos*, Toronto: McClelland & Stewart.

—— (1991) 'Metaphors of nature and the love of animals: animal rights supporters and James Bay Cree hunters', Paper presented at the Annual Conference of the American Anthropological Association, Chicago, November 1991.

Ferraro, G. (1992) *Cultural Anthropology: An Applied Perspective*, St Paul, MN: West Publishing Company.

241

Fewkes, J. W. (1896) 'The Tusayan ritual: a study of the influence of environment on aboriginal cults', *Annual Report of the Smithsonian Institution for 1895*: 683–700, Washington, DC.

Finger, M. (1993) 'Politics of the UNCED process', in W. Sachs (ed.) *Global Ecology: A New Arena of Political Conflict*, London: Zed Books.

Fitzgerald, E. (1947) *Rubáiyát of Omar Khayyám*, Glasgow and London: Collins.

Forde, C. D. (1949) *Habitat, Economy and Society*, London: Methuen.

Foreman, D. (1986) 'Cat tracks', *Earth First!*, 21 June: 21.

—— (1987) 'Reinhabitation, Biocentrism and self defense', *Earth First!*, 1 August.

Foucault, M. (1972) *The Archaeology of Knowledge*, London: Tavistock.

—— (1979) *Discipline and Punish: The Birth of the Prison*, Harmondsworth: Penguin Books.

Fouts, R. S., Fouts D. H., and van Cantfort, T.T. (1989) 'The infant Loulis learns signs from cross-fostered chimpanzees', in R. A. Gardner, B. T. Gardner and T. T. van Cantfort (eds) *Teaching Sign Language to Chimpanzees*, Albany: State University of New York Press.

Fowler, C. S. (1977) 'Ethnoecology', in D. L. Hardesty, *Ecological Anthropology*, New York: John Wiley & Sons.

Fox, W. (1989) 'The deep ecology–ecofeminism debate and its parallels', *Environmental Ethics* 11: 5–25.

Frake, C. O. (1962) 'Cultural ecology and ethnography', *American Anthropologist* 64: 53–9.

Frank, A. G. (1967) *Capitalism and Underdevelopment in Latin America*, New York: Monthly Review Press.

—— (1969) *Latin America: Underdevelopment or Revolution*, New York: Monthly Review Press.

Friedberg, C. (1979) 'Socially significant plant species and their taxonomic position among the Bunaq of Central Timor', in R. Ellen and D. Reason (eds) *Classifications in their Social Context*, London: Academic Press.

Friedman, J. (1990) 'Being in the world: globalization and localization', in M. Featherstone (ed.) *Global Culture*, London: Sage.

Friends of the Earth (1992) *Don't Throw It All Away: Friends of the Earth Guide to Waste Reduction and Recycling*, London: Friends of the Earth.

Gardner, R. A., Gardner, B. T. and van Cantfort, T. T. (eds) (1989) *Teaching Sign Language to Chimpanzees*, Albany: State University of New York Press.

Gatewood, J. B. (1985) 'Actions speak louder than words', in J. W. D. Dougherty (ed.) *Directions in Cognitive Anthropology*, Urbana: University of Illinois Press.

Geertz, C. (1963) *Agricultural Involution: The Process of Ecological Change in Indonesia*, Berkeley and Los Angeles: University of California Press.

—— (1965) 'Ideology as a cultural system', in D. Apter (ed.) *Ideology and Discontent*, Glencoe, IL: Free Press.

—— (1966) 'Religion as a cultural system', in M. Banton (ed.) *Anthropological Approaches to the Study of Religion*, London: Tavistock.

—— (1968) *Islam Observed: Religious Development in Morocco and Indonesia*, Chicago: University of Chicago Press.

—— (1973) *The Interpretation of Cultures*, New York: Basic Books.

—— (1976) '"From the native's point of view": on the nature of anthropological understanding', in K. H. Basso and H. A. Selby (eds) *Meaning in Anthropology*, Albuquerque: University of New Mexico Press.

Gellner, E. (1983) *Nations and Nationalism*, Oxford: Blackwell.

—— (1994) *Encounters with Nationalism*, Oxford: Blackwell.

Gibson, J. J. (1979) *The Ecological Approach to Visual Perception*, Boston: Houghton Mifflin.

—— (1982) *Reasons for Realism: Selected Essays of James J. Gibson*, ed. E. Reed and R. Jones, Hillsdale, NJ: Lawrence Erlbaum.

Giddens, A. (1976) *New Rules of Sociological Method*, London: Hutchinson.

—— (1979) *Central Problems in Social Theory*, London: Macmillan.

—— (1990) *The Consequences of Modernity*, Cambridge: Polity Press.

Glick, L. B. (1964) 'Categories and relations in Gimi natural science', in J. B. Watson (ed.) *New Guinea: The Central Highlands*, American Anthropologist Special Publication: 273–80.

Global 2000 (1982) *Report to the President*, Harmondsworth: Penguin Books.

Goldsmith, E., Allen, R., Allaby, M., Davoll, J. and Lawrence, S. (1972) 'A blueprint for survival', *The Ecologist* 2, 1: 1–43.

Goodenough, W. H. (1957) 'Cultural anthropology and linguistics', in P. Garvin (ed.) *Report of the Seventh Annual Round Table Meeting in Linguistics and Language Study*, Washington, DC: Georgetown University.

—— (1961) 'Comments on cultural evolution', *Daedalus* 90: 521–8.

—— (1981 [1971]) *Culture, Language and Society*, Menlo Park, CA: Benjamin/Cummings.

Goodin, R. E. (1992) *Green Political Theory*, Cambridge: Polity Press.

Goodman, D. and Redclift, M. (1991) *Refashioning Nature: Food, Ecology and Culture*, London and New York: Routledge.

Goody, J. (1961) 'Religion and ritual: the definition problem', *British Journal of Sociology* 12: 143–64.

Gott, R. (1992) 'Last word: comment', in J. Vidal (ed.) *Earth* (a *Guardian* publication in association with Oxfam to mark the Earth Summit in Rio, June 1992), London: *Guardian*.

Gough, K. (1959) 'The Nayars and the definition of marriage', *Journal of the Royal Anthropological Institute* 89: 23–34.

Grove-White, R. (1993) 'Environmentalism: a new moral discourse for technological society?', in K. Milton (ed.) *Environmentalism: The View from Anthropology*, London and New York: Routledge.

Grubb, M., Koch, M., Munson, A., Sullivan, F. and Thomson, K. (1993) *The Earth Summit Agreements: A Guide and Assessment*, London: Earthscan.

Gudeman, S. (1986) *Economics as Culture: Models and Metaphors of Livelihood*, London: Routledge & Kegan Paul.

Guha, R. (1993) 'The malign encounter: the Chipko Movement and competing visions of nature', in T. Banuri and F. A. Marglin (eds) *Who Will Save the Forests?*, London: Zed Books.

Hallowell, A. I. (1960) 'Ojibwa ontology, behaviour and world view', in S. Diamond (ed.) *Culture in History: Essays in Honour of Paul Radin*, New York: Columbia University Press.

Hannerz, U. (1980) *Exploring the City*, New York: Columbia University Press.

—— (1989) 'Culture between centre and periphery: toward a macroanthropology', *Ethnos* 54: 200–16.

—— (1990) 'Cosmopolitans and locals in world culture', in M. Featherstone (ed.) *Global Culture*, London: Sage.

—— (1992) *Cultural Complexity: Studies in the Social Organization of Meaning*, New York: Columbia University Press.

Hardesty, D. L. (1977) *Ecological Anthropology*, New York: John Wiley & Sons.

Hardin, G. (1968) 'The tragedy of the commons', *Science* 162: 1243–8.

Harpending, H. (1976) 'Regional variation in !Kung populations', in R. B. Lee and I. DeVore (eds) *Kalahari hunter-gatherers: studies of the !Kung San and their neighbours*, Cambridge, MA: Harvard University Press.

Harries-Jones, P. (1986) 'From cultural translator to advocate: changing circles of interpretation', in R. Paine (ed.) *Advocacy and Anthropology: First Encounters*, St John's, Newfoundland: Institute of Social and Economic Research, Memorial University.

—— (ed.) (1991) *Making Knowledge Count: Advocacy and Social science*, Montreal and Kingston: McGill-Queen's Press.

—— (1993) 'Between science and shamanism: the advocacy of environmentalism in Toronto', in K. Milton (ed.) *Environmentalism: The View from Anthropology*, London and New York: Routledge.

Harris, G. (1978) *Casting Out Anger*, Cambridge: Cambridge University Press.

Harris, M. (1968) *The Rise of Anthropological Theory: A History of Theories of Culture*, London: Routledge & Kegan Paul.

Harry, J., Gale, R. and Hendee, J. (1969) 'Conservation: an upper-middle class social movement', *Journal of Leisure Research*: 246–54.

Hart, J. A. (1978) 'From subsistence to market: a case study of the Mbuti net hunters', *Human Ecology* 6: 325-53.

Hart, T. B. and Hart, J. A. (1986) 'The ecological basis of hunter-gatherer subsistence in African rain forests: The Mbuti of western Zaire', *Human Ecology* 14: 29–55.

Hawley, A. H. (1944) 'Ecology and human ecology', *Social Forces* 22: 398–405.

—— (1950) *Human Ecology: A Theory of Community Structure*, New York: The Ronald Press.

Herskovits, M. J. (1949) *Man and his Works*, New York: Knopf.

Hicks, D. and Gwynne, M. A. (1994) *Cultural Anthropology*, New York: HarperCollins.

Hildyard, N. (1989) 'Adios Amazonia? A report from the Altimira gathering', *The Ecologist* 19, 2: 53–62.

—— (1993) 'Foxes in charge of the chickens', in W. Sachs (ed.) *Global Ecology: A New Arena of Political Conflict*, London: Zed Books.

Holmberg, J., Thomson, K. and Timberlake, L. (1993) *Facing the Future: Beyond the Earth Summit*, London: Earthscan.

Holmes, W. H. (1919) *Handbook of Aboriginal American Antiquities*, Bureau of American Ethnology, Bulletin 60, Part 1, Washington: Smithsonian Institution.

Holy, L. (1974) *Neighbours and Kinsmen: A Study of the Berti People of Darfur*, London: Hurst.

—— (1976) 'Knowledge and behaviour', in L. Holy (ed.) *Knowledge and Behaviour*, The Queen's University Papers in Social Anthropology 1, Belfast: The Queen's University of Belfast.

—— (1979) 'Nuer politics', in L. Holy (ed.) *Segmentary Lineage Systems Reconsidered*, The Queen's University Papers in Social Anthropology 4, Belfast: The Queen's University of Belfast.

—— (1986) *Strategies and Norms in a Changing Matrilineal Society: Descent, Succession and Inheritance among the Toka of Zambia*, Cambridge: Cambridge University Press.

Holy, L. and Stuchlik, M. (1981) 'The structure of folk models', in L. Holy and M. Stuchlik (eds) *The Structure of Folk Models*, London: Academic Press.

Horton, R. (1960) 'A definition of religion and its uses', *Journal of the Royal Anthropological Institute* 90: 201–26.

Howard, M. C. (1986) *Contemporary Cultural Anthropology*, Boston: Little, Brown & Co.

Hunn, E. (1985) 'The utilitarian factor in folk biological classification', in J. W. D. Dougherty (ed.) *Directions in Cognitive Anthropology*, Urbana, IL: University of Illinois Press.

Hunter, R. (1979) *Warriors of the Rainbow: A Chronicle of the Greenpeace Movement*, New York: Holt, Rinehart & Winston.

Huntington, E. (1924) *Civilization and Climate*, New Haven, CT: Yale University Press.

Icke, D. (1990) *It doesn't have to be like this: Green politics explained*, London: Green Print.

Ingold, T. (1986) *The Appropriation of Nature: Essays on Human Ecology and Social Relations*, Manchester: Manchester University Press.

—— (1991) 'The case against the motion', *Human worlds are culturally constructed*, University of Manchester: Group for Debates in Anthropological Theory.

—— (1992a) 'Culture and the perception of the environmment', in E. Croll and D. Parkin (eds) *Bush Base: Forest Farm*, London: Routledge.

—— (1992b) Response to Bird-David's 'Beyond the original affluent society', *Current Anthropology* 33, 1: 41–2.

—— (1993) 'Globes and spheres: the topology of environmentalism', in

BIBLIOGRAPHY

K. Milton (ed.) *Environmentalism: The View from Anthropology*, London and New York: Routledge.

—— (1996) 'Hunting and gathering as ways of perceiving the environment', in R. Ellen and K. Fukui (eds) *Redefining Nature: Ecology, Culture and Domestication*, London and New York: Berg.

IUCN, UNEP and WWF (1991) *Caring for the Earth: A Strategy for Sustainable Living*, Gland, Switzerland: The World Conservation Union.

Jacobs, M. (1991) *The Green Economy*, London: Pluto Press.

—— (1994) 'The limits to neoclassicism: towards an institutional environmental economics', in M. Redclift and T. Benton (eds) *Social Theory and the Global Environment*, London and New York: Routledge.

James, A. (1993) 'Eating green(s): discourses of organic food', in K. Milton (ed.) *Environmentalism: The View from Anthropology*, London and New York: Routledge.

James, P., Tayler, P. and Thompson, M. (1987) *Plural rationalities*, Warwick Papers in Management 9, Coventry: Institute for Management Research and Development, University of Warwick.

Jamison, A., Eyerman, R., Cramer, J. and Læssøe, J. (1990) *The Making of the New Environmental Consciousness*, Edinburgh: Edinburgh University Press.

Jarvie, I. C. (1964) *The Revolution in Anthropology*, London: Routledge & Kegan Paul.

Jenkins, R. (1981) 'Thinking and doing: towards a model of cognitive practice', in L. Holy and M. Stuchlik (eds) *The Structure of Folk Models*, London: Academic Press.

Jenness, D. (1935) *The Ojibwa Indians of Parry Island, Their Social and Religious Life*, Canadian Department of Mines Bulletin No. 78, Ottawa: Museum of Canada Anthropological Series No. 17.

Kay, P. (1965) 'Ethnography and the theory of culture', *Bucknell Review* 19: 106–13.

Keat, R. and Urry, J. (1982) *Social Theory as Science*, London: Routledge & Kegan Paul.

Keesing, R. (1970) 'Shrines, ancestors and cognatic descent: the Kwaio and Tallensi', *American Anthropologist* 72: 755–75.

—— (1971) 'Descent, residence and cultural codes', in L. R. Hiatt and C. Jaywardena (eds), *Anthropology in Oceania: Essays Presented to Ian Hogbin*, Sydney: Angus & Robertson.

—— (1974) 'Theories of culture', *Annual Review of Anthropology* 3: 73–97.

—— (1975) *Kin Groups and Social Structure*, New York: Holt, Rinehart & Winston.

—— (1981) *Cultural Anthropology: A Contemporary Perspective*, 2nd edn, New York: Holt, Rinehart & Winston.

Kesby, J.D. (1979) 'The Rangi classification of animals and plants', in R. Ellen and D. Reason (eds) *Classifications in their social context*, London: Academic Press.

Khare, R. S. (1987) 'The Bhopal industrial accident: anthropological and civic issues', *Anthropology Today* 3, 4: 4–6.

246

Kimber, R. and Richardson, J. J. (eds) (1974) *Campaigning for the Environment*, London: Routledge & Kegan Paul.

Kitsuse, J. I. and Spector, M. (1981) 'The labelling of social problems', in E. Rubington and M. S. Weinberg (eds) *The Study of Social Problems*, New York: Oxford University Press.

Knight, J. (1994) ' "The Mountain People" as tribal mirror', *Anthropology Today* 10, 6: 1–3.

Komito, L. (1994) 'Communities of practice and communities of trust: global culture and information technology', *Anthropology Ireland* 4, 1: 33–45.

Kroeber, A. L. (1939) *Cultural and Natural Areas of Native North America*, Berkeley: University of California Press.

Kroeber, A. L. and Parsons, T. (1958) 'The concept of culture and of social system', *American Sociological Review* 23: 582–3.

Kruse, H. (1974) 'Development and environment', *American Behavioural Science* 17, 5: 676–89.

Krutilla, J. V. and Cicchetti, C. J. (1972) 'Evaluating benefits of environmental resources with special application to Hells Canyon', *Natural Resources Journal* 12: 1–29.

Kumar, V. (1993) 'Ecology, industrialization and development planning: an Indian view on the problems of cultural survival', in G. Dahl (ed.) *Green Arguments and Local Subsistence*, Stockholm Studies in Social Anthropology 31, Stockholm: Stockholm University.

Leach, E. R. (1955) 'Polyandry, inheritance, and the definition of marriage, with particular reference to Sinhalese customary law', *Man* 55: 182–6.

—— (1960) 'The Sinhalese of the dry zone of northern Ceylon', in G. P. Murdock (ed.) *Social Structure in South-east Asia*, Viking Fund Publications in Social Anthropology 29: 116–26.

—— (1961) *Pul Eliya, a Village in Ceylon: A Study of Land Tenure and Kinship*, Cambridge: Cambridge University Press.

—— (1976) *Culture and Communication*, Cambridge: Cambridge University Press.

Leakey, R. and Lewin, R. (1992) *Origins Reconsidered: In Search of What Makes Us Human*, London: Little, Brown & Co.

Lee, R. B. (1969) '!Kung Bushman subsistence: an input-output analysis', in D. Damas (ed.) *Contributions to Anthropology: Ecological Essays*, National Museum of Canada Bulletin 230, Ottawa: Queen's Printers for Canada.

Leggett, J. (ed.) (1990) *Global Warming: The Greenpeace Report*, Oxford and New York: Oxford University Press.

Lohmann, L. (1993) 'Resisting green globalism', in W. Sachs (ed.) *Global Ecology: A New Arena of Political Conflict*, London: Zed Books.

Lovelock, J. E. (1979) *Gaia: A New Look at Life on Earth*, Oxford: Oxford University Press.

—— (1988) *The Ages of Gaia: A Biography of Our Living Earth*, Oxford: Oxford University Press.

Lowe, P. and Goyder, J. (1983) *Environmental Groups in Politics*, London: Allen & Unwin.

Lowe, P. and Rüdig, W. (1986) 'Review article: political ecology and the social sciences – the state of the art', *British Journal of Political Science* 16: 513–50.

Lyster, S. (1985) *International Wildlife Law*, Cambridge: Grotius Publications.

McCormick, J. (1989) *The Global Environmental Movement*, London: Belhaven.

McKibben, B. (1990) *The End of Nature*, New York: Viking.

Malinowski, B. (1929) *The Sexual Life of Savages in North-western Melanesia*, London: Routledge & Kegan Paul.

—— (1935) *Coral Gardens and their Magic*, 2 vols, London: George Allen & Unwin.

Manes, C. (1990) *Green Rage: Radical Environmentalism and the Unmaking of Civilization*, Boston: Little, Brown & Co.

Mannheim, K. (1966) *Ideology and Utopia*, London: Routledge & Kegan Paul.

Marglin, S. A. (1990) 'Towards a decolonization of the mind', in F. A. Marglin and S. A. Marglin (eds) *Dominating Knowledge: Development, Culture and Resistance*, Oxford: Clarendon Press.

Marwick, M. (1965) *Sorcery in its Social Setting: A Study of the Northern Rhodesian Cewa*, Manchester: Manchester University Press.

Mason, O. T. (1896) 'Influence of environment upon human industries or arts', *Annual Report of the Smithsonian Institution for 1895*: 639–65, Washington DC.

Meadows, D. H., Meadows, D. L., Randers, J. and Behrens, W. W., III (1972) *The Limits to Growth*, London and Sydney: Pan Books.

Meggers, B. J. (1954) 'Environmental limitation on the development of culture', *American Anthropologist* 56: 803–23.

Melucci, A. (1980) 'The new social movements: a theoretical approach', *Social Science Information* 19, 2: 199–226.

Merchant, C. (1992) *Radical Ecology*, London and New York: Routledge.

Milbrath, L. W. (1984) *Environmentalists: Vanguard for a New Society*, Albany: State University of New York Press.

Miller, D. (1991) *Material Culture and Mass Consumption*, Oxford: Blackwell.

Milton, K. (1977) 'The myth of King Dutthagamani and its social significance', in M. Stuchlik (ed.) *Goals and Behaviour*, The Queen's University Papers in Social Anthropology 2, Belfast: The Queen's University of Belfast.

—— (1981) 'On the inference of folk models: discussion and demonstration', in L. Holy and M. Stuchlik (eds) *The Structure of Folk Models*, London: Academic Press.

—— (1982) 'Meaning and context: the interpretation of greetings in Kasigau', in D. Parkin (ed.) *Semantic Anthropology*, London: Academic Press.

—— (1989) 'Anthropology: a conservationists' science', *Ecos* 10, 1: 29–33.

—— (1991) 'Interpreting environmental policy: a social-scientific approach', in R. Churchill, J. Gibson and L. Warren (eds) *Law, Policy and the Environment*, Oxford: Blackwell.

—— (1993) 'Introduction: environmentalism and anthropology', in K.

Milton (ed.) *Environmentalism: The View from Anthropology*, London and New York: Routledge.

Moran, E. F. (1990) 'Ecosystem ecology in biology and anthropology: a critical assessment', in E. F. Moran (ed.) *The Ecosystem Approach in Anthropology*, Ann Arbor: University of Michigan Press.

Morgan, G. (ed.) (1983) *Beyond Method: Strategies for Social Research*, Beverly Hills, CA: Sage.

—— (1991) 'Advocacy as a form of social science', in P. Harries-Jones (ed.) *Making Knowledge Count: Advocacy and Social Science*, Montreal and Kingston: McGill-Queen's Press.

Morphy, H. (1991) *Ancestral Connections: Art and an Aboriginal System of Knowledge*, Chicago: University of Chicago Press.

Munn, N. (1973) *Walbiri Iconography: Graphic Representation and Cultural Symbolism in a Central Australian Society*, Ithaca, NY: Cornell University Press.

Naess, A. (1989) *Ecology, Community and Lifestyle*, Cambridge: Cambridge University Press.

Nanda, S. (1987) *Cultural Anthropology*, Belmont, CA: Wadsworth.

Nash, J. (1981) 'Ethnographic aspects of the world capitalist system', *Annual Review of Anthropology* 10: 393–423.

Neihardt, J. G. (1972 [1932]) *Black Elk Speaks: Being the Life Story of a Holy Man of Oglala Sioux*, London: Barrie & Jenkins.

Netting, R. McC. (1969) 'Ecosystems in process: a comparative study of change in two West African societies', in D. Damas (ed.) *Contributions to Anthropology: Ecological Essays*, National Museum of Canada Bulletin 230, Ottawa: Queen's Printers for Canada.

Nicholson, M. (1987) *The New Environmental Age*, Cambridge: Cambridge University Press.

Norton, B. G. (1991) *Toward Unity among Environmentalists*, New York and Oxford: Oxford University Press.

Odum, E. (1953) *Fundamentals of Ecology*, Philadelphia: Saunders.

O'Neill, J. (1993) *Ecology, Policy and Politics*, London and New York: Routledge.

O'Riordan, T. (1981 [1976]) *Environmentalism*, London: Pion.

Paehlke, R. C. (1989) *Environmentalism and the Future of Progressive Politics*, New Haven, CT and London: Yale University Press.

Paine, R. (ed.) (1986) *Advocacy and Anthropology: First Encounters*, St John's, Newfoundland: Institute of Social and Economic Research, Memorial University.

Peace, A. (1993) 'Environmental protest, bureaucratic closure: the politics of discourse in rural Ireland', in K. Milton (ed.) *Environmentalism: The View from Anthropology*, London and New York: Routledge.

Pearce, D. (1972) 'The economic evaluation of noise-generating and noise abatement projects', in *Problems of Environmental Economics: Record of the Seminar held at the OECD in June 1971*, Paris: OECD.

—— (1974) 'Economic and ecological approaches to the optimal level of pollution', *International Journal of Social Economics* 1: 146–59.

—— (ed.) (1991) *Blueprint 2: Greening the World Economy*, London: Earthscan.

—— (ed.) (1994) *Blueprint 3: Measuring Sustainable Development,* London: Earthscan.

Pearce, D., Markandya, A. and Barbier, E.B. (1989) *Blueprint for a Green Economy,* London: Earthscan.

Pearce, F. (1991) *Green Warriors: The People and Politics Behind the Environmental Revolution,* London: The Bodley Head.

Peoples, J. and Bailey, G. (1988) *Humanity: An Introduction to Cultural Anthropology,* St Paul, MN: West Publishing Company.

Ponting, C. (1991) *A Green History of the World,* London: Sinclair-Stevenson.

Porritt, J. (1986) *Seeing Green,* Oxford: Blackwell.

Prato, G. B. (1993) 'Political decision-making: environmentalism, ethics and popular participation in Italy', in K. Milton (ed.) *Environmentalism: The View from Anthropology,* London and New York: Routledge.

Pridham, G. (1994) 'National environmental policy-making in the European framework: Spain, Greece and Italy in comparison', in S. Baker, K. Milton and S. Yearley (eds) *Protecting the Periphery: Environmental Policy in the Peripheral Regions of the European Union,* Ilford, Essex, and Portland, OR: Frank Cass.

Ranger, T. (1989) 'Whose heritage? The case of the Matopo National Park', *Journal of Southern African Studies* 15, 2 (Special Issue on the Politics of Conservation in Southern Africa): 217–49.

Rappaport, R. A. (1968) *Pigs for the Ancestors,* New Haven, CT: Yale University Press.

—— (1969) 'Some suggestions concerning concept and method in ecological anthropology', in D. Damas (ed.) *Contributions to Anthropology: Ecological Essays,* National Museum of Canada Bulletin 230, Ottowa: Queen's Printers for Canada.

—— (1971) 'Nature, culture and ecological anthropology', in H. L. Shapiro (ed.) *Man, Culture and Society,* Oxford: Oxford University Press.

Rasa, A. (1985) *Mongoose Watch: A Family Observed,* London: John Murray.

Ratzel, F. (1896) *The History of Mankind,* London: Macmillan.

Rayner, S. (1989) 'Fiddling while the globe warms?', *Anthropology Today* 5, 6: 1–2.

Redclift, M. (1984) *Development and the Environmental Crisis: Red or Green Alternatives?,* London and New York: Methuen.

—— (1987) *Sustainable Development: Exploring the Contradictions,* London and New York: Methuen.

—— (1992) 'At work in the greenhouse: ESRC's Global Environmental Change Programme', *Global Environmental Change,* December: 341–4.

Revkin, A. (1990) *The Burning Season: The Murder of Chico Mendes and the Fight for the Amazon Rain Forest,* London: Collins.

Richards, P. (1986) *Coping with Hunger: Hazard and Experiment in an African Rice-farming System,* London: Allen & Unwin.

—— (1992a) 'Saving the rain forest? Contested futures in conservation', in S. Wallman (ed.) *Contemporary Futures: Perspectives from Social Anthropology,* London and New York: Routledge.

—— (1992b) 'Famine (and war) in Africa: what do anthropologists have to say?', *Anthropology Today* 8, 6: 3–5.

—— (1993) 'Natural symbols and natural history: chimpanzees, elephants and experiments in Mende thought', in K. Milton (ed.) *Environmentalism: The View from Anthropology*, London and New York: Routledge.

Riches, D. (1977) 'Discerning the goal: some methodological problems exemplified in analyses of hunter-gatherer aggregation and migration', in M. Stuchlik (ed.) *Goals and Behaviour*, Belfast: The Queen's University of Belfast.

—— (ed.) (1979) *The conceptualisation and explanation of processes of social change*, The Queen's University Papers in Social Anthropology 3, Belfast: The Queen's University of Belfast.

—— (ed.) (1986) *The Anthropology of Violence*, Oxford: Blackwell.

Ritzer, G. (1992) *The McDonaldization of Society: An Investigation into the Changing Character of Contemporary Social Life*, Beverly Hills, CA: Sage.

Robertson, R. (1990) 'Mapping the global condition: globalization as the central concept', in M. Featherstone (ed.) *Global Culture: Nationalism, Globalization and Modernity*, London: Sage.

—— (1992) *Globalization: Social Theory and Global Culture*, London: Sage.

Robertson, R. and Lechner, F. (1985) 'Modernization, globalization and the problem of culture in world-systems theory', *Theory, Culture & Society* 2, 3: 103–18.

Robinson, M. (1968) ' "The House of the Mighty Hero" or "The House of Enough Paddy"? some implications of a Sinhalese myth', in E. R. Leach (ed.) *Dialectic in Practical Religion*, Cambridge: Cambridge University Press.

Ross, J.-K. (1975) 'Social borders: definitions of diversity', *Current Anthropology* 16: 53–72.

Rüdig, W., Mitchell, J., Chapman, J. and Lowe, P. (1990) 'Social movements and the social sciences in Britain', in D. Rucht (ed.) *Research on Social Movements: The State of the Art*, Boulder, CO: Westview.

Sachs, W. (1993) 'Global ecology and the shadow of "development" ', in W. Sachs (ed.) *Global Ecology: A New Arena of Political Conflict*, London: Zed Books.

Sahlins, M. (1961) 'The segmentary lineage: an organization of predatory expansion', *American Anthropologist* 63: 322–45.

—— (1968) 'Notes on the original affluent society', in R. B. Lee and I. DeVore (eds) *Man the Hunter*, Chicago: Aldine.

—— (1972) *Stone Age Economics*, Chicago: Aldine-Atherton.

Samstag, T. (1988) *For Love of Birds*, Sandy, Bedfordshire: Royal Society for the Protection of Birds.

Sandbach, F. (1980) *Environment, Ideology and Policy*, Oxford: Blackwell.

Sankhala, K. S. and Jackson, P. (1985) 'People, trees and antelopes in the Indian desert', in J. A. McNeely and D. Pitt (eds) *Culture and Conservation: The Human Dimension in Environmental Planning*, London: Croom Helm.

Sansom, B. (1980) *The Camp at Wallaby Cross*, Canberra: Australian Institute of Aboriginal Studies.

Sapir, E. (1961) *Culture, Language and Personality: Selected Essays*, ed. D. G. Mandelbaum, Berkeley: University of California Press.

Saurin, J. (1993) 'Global environmental degradation, modernity and environmental knowledge', *Environmental Politics* 2, 4: 46–64.

Scheffler, H. W. (1965) *Choiseul Island Social Structure*, Berkeley and Los Angeles: University of California Press.

—— (1966) 'Ancestor worship in anthropology: or observations on descent and descent groups', *Current Anthropology* 7: 541–51.

Schensul, S. L. and Schensul, J. J. (1978) 'Advocacy and applied anthropology', in G. H. Weber and G. J. McCall (eds) *Social Scientists as Advocates: Views from the Applied Disciplines*, Beverly Hills, CA: Sage.

Schneider, S. H. and Boston, P. J. (eds) (1993) *Scientists on Gaia*, Cambridge, MA: MIT Press.

Scott, A. (1990) *Ideology and the New Social Movements*, London: Unwin/Hyman.

Scott, C. (1989) 'Knowledge construction among Cree hunters: metaphors and literal understanding', *Journal de la Société des Americanistes* 75: 193–208.

Seidel, G. (1985) 'Political discourse analysis', in T. A. van Dijk (ed.) *Handbook of Discourse Analysis*, vol. 4, London: Academic Press.

—— (1989) 'We condemn apartheid, BUT . . . a discursive analysis of the European Parliamentary debate on sanctions', in R. Grillo (ed.) *Social Anthropology and the Politics of Language*, Sociological Review Monograph 36, London and New York: Routledge.

Seymour, J. (1991) *Changing Lifestyles: Living as though the World Mattered*, London: Victor Gollancz.

Shearer, W. (1993) 'A selection of biogenic influences relevant to the Gaia hypothesis', in S. H. Schneider and P. J. Boston (eds) *Scientists on Gaia*, Cambridge, MA: MIT Press.

Shiva, V. (1987) 'The violence of reductionist science', *Alternatives* 12: 243–4.

—— (1990) *The Violence of the Green Revolution*, London: Zed Books.

—— (1993a) *Monocultures of the Mind: Perspectives on Biodiversity and Biotechnology*, London: Zed Books.

—— (1993b) 'The greening of the global reach', in W. Sachs (ed.) *Global Ecology: A New Arena of Political Conflict*, London: Zed Books.

Sillitoe, P. (1993) 'Local awareness of the soil environment in the Papua New Guinea highlands', in K. Milton (ed.) *Environmentalism: The View from Anthropology*, London and New York: Routledge.

Simmons, I. G. (1993) *Interpreting Nature: Cultural Constructions of the Environment*, London and New York: Routledge.

Smith, A. D. (1990) 'Towards a global culture?', in M. Featherstone (ed.) *Global Culture*, London: Sage.

Smith, M. (1995) 'Slings and arrows', *Guardian* 'On Line', 23 February: 2.

Spencer, B. and Gillen, F. (1968 [1899]) *The Native Tribes of Central Australia*, London: Macmillan.

Spiro, M. E. (1966) 'Religion: problems of definition and explanation', in

M. Banton (ed.) *Anthropological Approaches to the Study of Religion*, London: Tavistock.

Spretnak, C. and Capra, F. (1985) *Green Politics: The Global Promise*, London: Paladin.

Stenning, D. J. (1957) 'Transhumance, migratory drift, migration', *Journal of the Royal Anthropological Institute* 87: 57–73.

Steward, J. (1955) *Theory of Culture Change*, Urbana, IL: University of Illinois Press.

Stowe, T. and Coulthard, N. (1990) 'The conservation of a Nigerian wetland: the Hadejia-Nguru Wetland Conservation Project', *RSPB Conservation Review* 4, Sandy, Bedfordshire: Royal Society for the Protection of Birds.

Strathern, M. (1992) *Reproducing the Future: Essays on Anthropology, Kinship and the New Reproductive Technologies*, Manchester: Manchester University Press.

Strehlow, T. G. H. (1965) 'Culture, social structure and environment in Aboriginal Central Australia', in R. M. Berndt and C. H. Berndt (eds) *Aboriginal Man in Australia*, Sydney: Angus & Robertson.

—— (1970) 'Geography and the totemic landscape in Central Australia: a functional study', in R. M. Berndt (ed.) *Australian Aboriginal Anthropology: Modern Studies in the Social Anthropology of the Australian Aborigines*, Nedlands: University of Western Australia Press.

Strong, M. (1992a) 'People power is the key to success for the Earth Summit', *Earth Summit News*, January, London: United Nations Association.

—— (1992b) Opening statement to the United Nations Conference on Environment and Development, in United Nations (1993b) *Report of the United Nations Conference on Environment and Development, Rio de Janeiro, 3–14 June 1992*, vol. II: *Proceedings of the Conference*, New York: United Nations.

—— (1992c) Closing statement to the United Nations Conference on Environment and Development, in United Nations (1993b) *Report of the United Nations Conference on Environment and Development, Rio de Janeiro, 3–14 June 1992*, vol. II: *Proceedings of the Conference*, New York: United Nations.

—— (1994) Indira Gandhi Memorial Lecture, Delhi, 18 November 1994, in *Earth Times*, 15 December.

Stuchlik, M. (1976) *Life on a Half-share: Mechanisms of Social Recruitment among the Mapuche of Southern Chile*, London: Hurst.

—— (1977) 'The emergence of a group: the case of a Mapuche sports club', in M. Stuchlik (ed.) *Goals and Behaviour*, The Queen's University Papers in Social Anthropology 2, Belfast: The Queen's University of Belfast.

Sutherland, W. (1992) *The Rio Treaties of the Global NGO Movement: A Documentary Sourcebook*, London: Adamantine Press.

Tambiah, S. J. (1969) 'Animals are good to think and good to prohibit', *Ethnology* 8: 423–59.

—— (1970) *Buddhism and the Spirit Cults in North-east Thailand*, Cambridge: Cambridge University Press.

Tanner, A. (1979) *Bringing Home Animals: Religious Ideology and Mode of Production of the Mistassini Cree Hunters*, St John's, Newfoundland: Institute of Social and Economic Research, Memorial University of Newfoundland.

Taylor, B. (1991) 'The religion and politics of Earth First!', *The Ecologist* 21, 6: 258–66.

Thomas, K. (1983) *Man and the Natural World: Changing attitudes in England 1500–1800*, Harmondsworth: Penguin Books.

Thompson, M. and Tayler, P. (1986) *The Surprise Game: An Exploration of Constrained Relativism*, Warwick Papers in Management 4, Coventry: Institute for Management Research and Development, University of Warwick.

Thompson, M. and Wildavsky, A. (1986) 'A cultural theory of information bias in organizations', *Journal of Management Studies* 23: 272–86.

Timmerman, P. (1986) 'Mythology and surprise in the sustainable development of the biosphere', in W. Clark and R. E. Munn (eds) *Sustainable Development of the Biosphere*, Cambridge: Cambridge University Press.

Touraine, A. (1981) *The Voice and the Eye*, Cambridge: Cambridge University Press.

Turnbull, C. (1961) *The Forest People: A Study of the Pygmies of the Congo*, New York: Simon & Schuster.

—— (1972) *The Mountain People*, New York: Simon & Schuster.

Turner, V. W. (1967) *The Forest of Symbols: Studies in Ndembu Ritual*, Ithaca, NY: Cornell University Press.

—— (1968) *The Drums of Affliction: A Study of Religious Processes among the Ndembu of Zambia*, Oxford: Clarendon Press.

—— (1969) *The Ritual Process: Structure and Anti-structure*, Chicago: Aldine Publishing Co.

—— (1974) *Dramas, Fields and Metaphors: Symbolic Action in Human Society*, Ithaca, NY: Cornell University Press.

Tyler, S. (1969) 'Introduction', in S. Tyler (ed.) *Cognitive Anthropology*, New York: Holt, Rinehart & Winston.

Tylor, E. B. (1871) *Primitive Culture: Researches into the Development of Mythology, Philosophy, Religion, Art and Custom*, London: John Murray (Publishers) Ltd.

Udall, S. (1972) 'First Americans, first ecologists', in *Look to the Mountain Top*, San José, CA: Gousha Publications.

United Nations (1973) *Report of the United Nations Conference on the Human Environment*, Stockholm, 5–16 June 1972 (A/CONF.48/14/Rev.1), New York: United Nations.

—— (1993a) *Report of the United Nations Conference on Environment and Development, Rio de Janeiro, 3-14 June 1992*, vol. I: *Resolutions Adopted by the Conference*, New York: United Nations.

—— (1993b) *Report of the United Nations Conference on Environment and Development, Rio de Janeiro, 3–14 June 1992*, vol. II: *Proceedings of the Conference*, New York: United Nations.

United Nations Association (1992) *Earth Summit News: UNCED Special Issue*, London: United Nations Association.

van Beek, W. E. A. and Banga, P. M. (1992) 'The Dogon and their trees', in E. Croll and D. Parkin (eds) *Bush Base: Forest Farm*, London: Routledge.

Van Liere, K. D. and Dunlap, R. E. (1980) 'The social bases of environmental concern: a review of hypotheses, explanations and empirical evidence', *Public Opinion Quarterly* 44: 181–97.

Vayda, A. P. and McCay, B. J. (1975) 'New directions in ecology and ecological anthropology', *Annual Review of Anthropology* 4, Palo Alto, CA: Annual Reviews Inc.

Vayda, A. P. and Rappaport, R. A. (1968) 'Ecology, cultural and noncultural', in J. Clifton (ed.) *Introduction to Cultural Anthropology: Essays in the Scope and Methods of the Science of Man*, Boston: Houghton Mifflin.

Wallerstein, I. (1974) *The Modern World-system: Capitalist Agriculture and the Origins of the European World Economy in the Sixteenth Century*, New York: Academic Press.

—— (1979) *The Capitalist World Economy*, Cambridge: Cambridge University Press.

—— (1980) *The Modern World-system II: Mercantilism and the Consolidation of the European World Economy, 1600-1750*, New York: Academic Press.

—— (1983) 'Crisis: the world-economy, the movements and the ideologies', in A. Bergesen (ed.) *Crisis in the World System*, Beverly Hills, CA: Sage.

—— (1990a) 'Culture as the ideological battleground of the modern world-system', *Theory, Culture and Society* 7: 31–55.

—— (1990b) 'Culture is the world-system: a reply to Boyne', in M. Featherstone (ed.) *Global Culture: Nationalism, Globalization and Modernity*, London: Sage.

Wallis, R. (1984) *The Elementary Forms of the New Religious Life*, London: Routledge & Kegan Paul.

Weale, A. (1992) *The New Politics of Pollution*, Manchester: Manchester University Press.

Weber, T. (1988) *Hugging the Trees: The Story of the Chipko Movement*, Harmondsworth: Penguin Books.

Wenzel, G. (1991) *Animal Rights, Human Rights: Ecology, Economy and Ideology in the Canadian Arctic*, London: Belhaven.

Wissler, C. (1926) *The Relation of Nature to Man in Aboriginal America*, New York: Oxford University Press.

Woodburn, J. (1980) 'Hunters and gatherers today and reconstruction of the past', in E. Gellner (ed.) *Soviet and Western Anthropology*, London: Duckworth.

—— (1982) 'Egalitarian societies', *Man* (NS) 17: 431–51.

World Commission on Environment and Development (1987) *Our Common Future* (The Brundtland Report), Oxford: Oxford University Press.

Worsley, P. (1957) *The Trumpet Shall Sound: A Study of 'Cargo' Cults in Melanesia*, London: MacGibbon & Kee.

Wright, G. (1984) *Sons and Seals: A Voyage to the Ice*, St John's, Newfoundland: Institute of Social and Economic Research, Memorial University.

Wuthnow, R. (1978) 'Religious movements and the transition in world order', in J. Needleman and G. Baker (eds) *Understanding the New Religions*, New York: Seabury.
—— (1980) 'World order and religious movements', in A. Bergesen (ed.) *Studies of the Modern World System*, New York: Academic Press.
—— (1983) 'Chapter 3: Cultural crises', in A. Bergesen (ed.) *Crisis in the World System*, Beverly Hills, CA: Sage.
Wuthnow, R., Hunter, J. D., Bergesen, A. and Kurzweil, E. (1984) *Cultural Analysis: The Work of Peter L. Berger, Mary Douglas, Michel Foucault and Jürgen Habermas*, London: Routledge & Kegan Paul.
WWF (1986) *The New Road: The Bulletin of the WWF Network on Conservation and Religion*, Issue No. 1, Gland, Switzerland: WWF International.
—— (1988) *The New Road: The Bulletin of the WWF Network on Conservation and Religion*, Issue No. 7, Gland, Switzerland: WWF International.
Yearley, S. (1992a) *The Green Case: A Sociology of Environmental Issues, Arguments and Politics*, London: Routledge.
—— (1992b) 'Chapter 3: Environmental challenges', in S. Hall, D. Held and A. McGrew (eds) *Modernity and its Futures*, Cambridge: Polity Press.
—— (1993) 'Standing in for nature: the practicalities of environental organizations' use of science', in K. Milton (ed.) *Environmentalism: The View from Anthropology*, London and New York: Routledge.
—— (1994) 'Social movements and environmental change', in M. Redclift and T. Benton (eds) *Social Theory and the Global Environment*, London and New York: Routledge.
—— (1995a) 'The environmental challenge to science studies', in S. Jasanoff, G. E. Markle, J. C. Petersen and T. Pinch (eds) *Handbook of Science and Technology Studies*, Beverly Hills, CA: Sage.
—— (1995b) 'Dirty connections: transnational pollution', in J. Allen and C. Hamnett (eds) *A Shrinking World? Global Unevenness and Inequality*, Milton Keynes: Open University in association with Oxford University Press.
Yearley, S., Baker, S. and Milton, K. (1994) 'Environmental policy and peripheral regions of the European Union: an introduction', in S. Baker, K. Milton and S. Yearley (eds) *Protecting the Periphery*, Ilford, Essex: Frank Cass.
Yearley, S. and Milton, K. (1990) 'Environmentalism and direct rule: the politics and ethos of conservation and environmental groups in Northern Ireland', *Built Environment* 16, 3: 192–202.

INDEX

Barth, F. 18, 156, 163, 228 nn.7, 8
Batek 117, 128, 215
Bauman, Z. 153
BBC 107, 235 n.10
bees 64
Belfast 204
Bell, D. 129
Bennett, J. 8, 37, 229 n.1
Benton, T. 1, 4, 219
Berger, P. 20, 39, 48, 229 n.10
Bergesen, A. 145–6
Berlin, B. 49
Berreman, G.D. 2
Beyer, P. 54
Biosphere Conference 176
Bird-David, N. 135, 216; (1990) 117, 126, 232 n.5; (1992a) 117, 215; (1992b) 117–18, 123, 217; (1993) 128–9, 215
Bishnoi 157
Black, M.B. 49
Blundell, V. 228 n.5
Boas, F. 41
Bohannan, P. 11, 14, 26, 79
Boston, P.J. 132
Boutros-Ghali, B. 184
Bowers, J. 71
Bowman, J.S. 73
Brandt Commission 148
Brazil, destruction of forests 151, 176
Brazzaville 158
Bright, J.O. 51
Bright, W. 51
Britain: anthropologists 41; environmental activists 111, 210–11; environmentalism 96; forestry 5; Green activists 84; Green Party 138; market ideology 177; road building 210–11
Brower, D. 94–5, 208
Brown, M. 232 n.3
Brown, P. 211
Brundtland, G.H. 181, 184–6, 197–8, 202, 209
Buddhism 54, 158
Bulmer, R. 49, 53
Burbridge, J. 111

Burnham, P.C. 23, 41, 55
Burridge, K.O.L. 175
Bush, G. 185

Callicott, J.B. 126–7
Canada: neoconservatism 177; seal campaigns 5, 151
Cancian, F. 49
Capra, F. 25, 85
Caring for the Earth 183
Carneiro, R. 39
Carrithers, M. 227 n.2
Carson, R. 230 n.4
Cartesian dualism 11, 22
cassowaries 53
causality 101–2
Cavalieri, P. 235 n.13
Caws, P. 214
Cewa 91
CFCs 184
Chatterjee, P. 144, 174, 178–9, 187–8, 195
chimpanzees 64
Chipko movement 28, 157
Chirot, D. 12, 144–5, 148, 233 n.3
Christianity 54, 111, 122
Cicchetti, C.J. 71
Citizens' Commitment on Biodiversity 200, 209, 233 n.13
Clifford, J. 22, 50, 142
Clift, R. 71
Coca-Cola 157
Codere, H. 139
Cohen, B. 228 n.7
Cold War 178
Colombia 107
Common Agricultural Policy 5
Commoner, B. 230 n.4
community, single human 177–8
Conklin, H.C. 49–50
conservationists 74, 124–5
constructivism 50–2, 54–5, 60, 103, 214
Convention on Biological Diversity 190, 233 n.13
Convention on International Trade in Endangered Species (CITES) 186
Cotgrove, S. 76; (1976) 74–5, 82,

INDEX

globalism: cultural diversity and
197–9; cultural diversity and
opposition to 199–201;
ecocentrism and anti-globalism
208–11; opposing 187–93;
perspective 180–7
globalization 142–71; as
consequence of modernity 150–4;
as dual process 164–6; concept in
social science 12–13, 141, 142–3;
cultural diversity and 154–9;
cultural perspectives 68, 141;
cultural theory and 159–64;
debate 15, 174–5, 187–8, 190;
models of 143–4, 220; study of
world systems 144–50, 177
Gola Forest 54, 125–6
Goldsmith, E. 175, 230 n.4
Goodenough, W.H.: (1957) 11, 61;
(1961) 18, 39; (1981) 11, 13,
228 n.8
Goodin, R.E. 25, 70, 83–4, 231 n.10
Goodman, D. 152
Goody, J. 26
Gott, R. 179
Gough, K. 26
Goyder, J. 231 n.8
Green Party 88, 138
Greenpeace 142, 151, 179, 208,
232 n.3
Gridlock 230 n.1
Grove-White, R. 12, 25
Grubb, M. 142, 183
Gudeman, S. 118, 215
Guha, R. 28
Gwynne, M.A. 17

Habermas, J. 81
Hailes, J. 152, 179
Hall, S. 82–3, 95
Hall, T.D. 12, 144–5, 148, 233 n.3
Hallowell, A.I. 127
Hannerz, U. 161, 169, 217; (1980)
228 n.2; (1989) 149, 156–7,
159–60, 162; (1990) 156, 159–60,
163; (1992) 155, 158–60, 177,
220, 228 n.2
Hardesty, D.L. 42, 52, 55–6, 229
n.1

Hardin, G. 230 n.4
Harpending, H. 117
Harries-Jones, P. 21–2, 113, 202,
229 n.11
Harris, G. 121
Harris, M. 45
Harry, J. 79
Hart, J.A. 117, 232 n.6
Hart, T.B. 232 n.6
Hawley, A.H. 39, 48
Herskovits, M.J. 19
Hicks, D. 17
Hildyard, N. 112, 191
Hinduism 54
Hitch-hiker's Guide to the Galaxy,
The 230 n.6
Hobbs, J.R. 50
Holland 81
Holmberg, J. 110, 185, 234 n.2
Holmes, W.H. 41
Holocaust 178
Holy, L.: (1974) 228 n.8; (1976) 18,
228 n.8; (1979) 62; (1986) 19, 21,
173; and Stuchlik (1981) 15,
18–19, 26–7, 48, 214, 228 n.9
homeostasis 56
Hopi Indians 202
Horizon 235 n.10
Horton, R. 26, 229 n.12
Howard, M.C. 14, 17, 139
Human Development Index 197
Human Rights Watch 178
Hunn, E. 50
Hunter, R. 232 n.3, 235 n.14
hunter-gatherers: idealized image
109–10; relationship with
environment 116–19, 123, 125,
131, 135, 215
Huntington, E. 41

Icke, D. 85
Ik people 53
In Search of the Noble Savage 235
n.10
India: Chipko movement 28, 157;
food, 157; forestry 189, 201;
Nayaka people 117
Indonesia, forestry 202
industrial societies: belief in